DAME DAPHNE SHELDRICK is a Kenyan author, conservationist, and expert in animal husbandry, particularly the raising and reintegrating of orphaned elephants into the wild. From 1955 to 1976, Sheldrick worked alongside her husband, David Sheldrick, the founding warden of Tsavo National Park. She lives in Kenya.

LOVE, LIFE,

✦ AND ✦

ELEPHANTS

AN AFRICAN LOVE STORY

DAME DAPHNE
SHELDRICK

PICADOR

FARRAR, STRAUS AND GIROUX
NEW YORK
✦

www.picadorusa.com
www.twitter.com/picadorusa • www.facebook.com/picadorusa
picadorbookroom.tumblr.com

Picador® is a U.S. registered trademark and is used by Farrar, Straus and Giroux
under license from Pan Books Limited.

For book club information, please visit www.facebook.com/picadorbookclub
or e-mail marketing@picadorusa.com.

Maps by Dr Ian Games

The Library of Congress has cataloged the Farrar, Straus and Giroux edition as follows:

Sheldrick, Daphne Jenkins, 1934–
    Love, life, and elephants : an African love story / Dame Daphne Sheldrick. —
1st American ed.
        p.   cm.
    "Originally published in 2012 by Viking, an imprint of Penguin Books, Great Britain,
as *An African Love Story: Love, Life and Elephants*."
    Includes index.
    ISBN 978-0-374-10457-3
    1. Sheldrick, Daphne Jenkins, 1934–   2. Women conservationists—Kenya—Tsavo
National Park—Biography.   3. Wildlife conservationists—Kenya—Tsavo National
Park—Biography.   4. Elephants—Conservation—Kenya—Tsavo National Park.
I. Title.

SD411.52.S44 A3 2012
639.97'967092—dc23
[B]

                                                                        2011052457

Picador ISBN 978-1-250-03337-6

Picador books may be purchased for educational, business, or promotional use. For information
on bulk purchases, please contact Macmillan Corporate and Premium Sales Department at
1-800-221-7945, extension 5442, or write specialmarkets@macmillan.com.

Originally published in Great Britain as *An African Love Story: Love, Life and Elephants*
by Viking, an imprint of Penguin Books

First published in the United States by Farrar, Straus and Giroux

First Picador Edition: July 2013

10   9   8   7   6   5   4   3   2   1

I dedicate this book to Wilderness and all that it embraces, to the memory of David and the pioneer wardens of Kenya's National Parks, and to my family and grandchildren so that they may know how it was once upon a time.

Contents

List of Illustrations

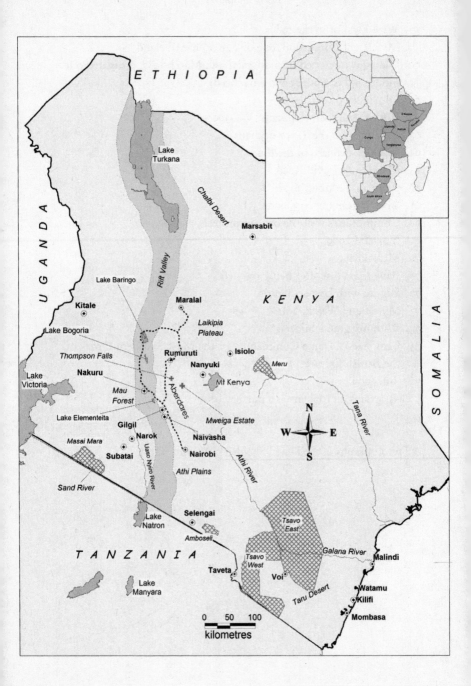

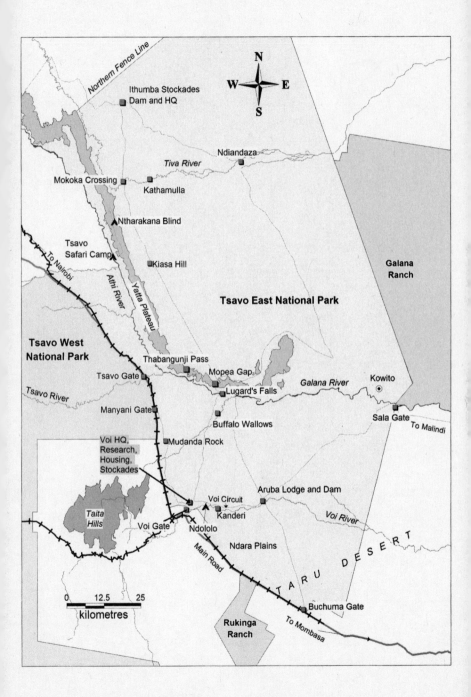

Prologue

The day had begun well. My friend and I were in Tsavo National Park, among the tangled vegetation and wild herds, searching for Eleanor. I was eager to find my most treasured orphaned elephant. Over my many years of involvement with elephants, there was no doubt about it: Eleanor had taught me the most about her kind. We had been through many ups and downs together. She was my old friend.

Finding her was not an easy task. Tsavo spreads over 8,000 square miles. We were looking now in the place where I had heard she had been just the day before. There had been many occasions in the past when, suspecting that Eleanor might be among a wild herd, I had simply called her name and she had turned quietly from her group and come to me. We had shared many tender moments, her massive trunk prickly as she wrapped it gently around my neck, one huge foot raised in greeting for me to hug with both my arms.

I had known Eleanor since she had become an orphan at two – now she was in her forties, almost the same age as Jill, my elder daughter – and there existed between us an amazing bond of friendship and trust that had persisted beyond her return to the wild.

At last – in the right area – we spotted a wild herd. From a distance it was never easy to identify Eleanor among a milling crowd of her fellow adults, and I had never felt the need to do so, certain that she would always know me. Unlike the other wild elephants of Tsavo, who had no reason to either like or trust humans, Eleanor would always want to come when called, to greet me, simply for old times' sake. I have come to know a lot about elephant memory and how very similar to ourselves elephants are in terms of emotion – after all, greeting an old friend makes you feel good, remembered, wanted.

There stood a large cow elephant drinking at a muddy pool, her family already moving off among the bushes. From this distance, it didn't look much like Eleanor, for although as large, this elephant was stockier. I told my friend as much.

'How disappointing,' he said. 'I was so hoping to meet her.'

'I'll call her,' I replied, 'and if this is Eleanor, she will respond.'

She did. The elephant looked up at me, her ears slightly raised, curious. She left the pool and walked straight up to us.

'Hello, Eleanor,' I said. 'You've put on weight.'

I looked into her eyes, which curiously were pale amber. I had a fleeting thought that Eleanor's eyes were darker, but I dismissed this instantly. This must be Eleanor. Wild elephants in Tsavo simply did not behave in this way, approaching humans so trustingly. The Tsavo herds were now innately suspicious of our kind, having been relentlessly persecuted in the poaching holocaust of the 70s, 80s and early 90s.

'Yes,' I said to my friend. 'This is Eleanor.'

Reaching up, I touched her cheeks and felt the cool ivory of her tusks, caressing her below the chin in greeting. Her eyes were gentle and friendly, fringed with long dark lashes; her manner was welcoming.

'She's beautiful,' murmured my friend. 'Stand next to her so that I can take a photo.'

I positioned myself beside one massive foreleg, reaching up my hand to stroke her behind the ear, something that I loved doing with Eleanor. The hind side of an elephant's ear is as soft and smooth to the touch as silk and always deliciously cool.

I was totally unprepared for what happened next.

The elephant took a pace backwards, swung her giant head and, using her trunk to lift my body, threw me like a piece of weightless flotsam high through the air with such force that I smashed down onto a giant clump of boulders some twenty paces away. I knew at once that the impact had shattered my right leg, for I could hear and feel the bones crunch as I struggled to sit up. I could see too that I was already bleeding copiously from an open wound in my thigh. Astonishingly, there was no pain – not yet, anyway.

My friend screamed. The elephant – I knew for certain now that this was not Eleanor – rushed at me, towering above my broken body as I braced myself for the end. I closed my eyes and began to pray. I had a lot to be thankful for, but I did not want to leave this world quite yet. Inside I began to panic, jumbled thoughts crowding my mind. But suddenly there was a moment of pure stillness – as if the world had simply stopped turning – and as I opened my eyes I could feel the elephant gently insert her tusks between my body and the rocks. Rather than a desire to kill, I realized that the elephant was actually trying to help me by lifting me to my feet, encouraging me to stand. I thought: this is how they respond to their young.

But lifting me now could be catastrophic for my broken body.

'No!' I shouted, as I smacked the tip of the wet trunk that reached down to touch my face.

She gazed down at me, her ears splayed open in the shape of Africa, her eyes kind and concerned. Then, lifting one huge foot, she began to feel me gently all over, barely touching me. Her great ears stood out at right angles to her huge head as she contemplated me lying helpless, merely inches from the tip of two long, sharp tusks. I knew then that she did not intend to kill me – elephants are careful where they tread and do not stamp on their victims. If they do intend to kill, they kneel down and use the top of the trunk and forehead.

And it was at this moment – with an astonishing clarity of thought that I can still feel within me to this day – I realized that if I were to live, I needed to fulfil the debt I owed to Nature and all the animals that had so enriched my life. For even as I could feel the broken bones within my crumpled body, feel the fire of pain now engulfing me, and even though it was one of my beloved creatures that had caused me this distress, I knew then and there that I had an absolute duty to pass on my intimate knowledge and understanding of Africa's wild animals and my belonging to Kenya.

I thought: if I survive this, I will write. This will be my legacy. I will set down everything I have learned in my efforts to contribute to the conservation, preservation and protection of wildlife in this magical land.

It was as if the elephant had heard my thoughts. There was a tense silence as she took one more look at me and moved slowly off. I would live on. In a state of some distress, my friend managed to find his way back to our driver to fetch help.

After many hours of lying beneath that boulder, experiencing agonizing pain such as never before, I was rescued by the Flying Doctors. My ordeal was far from over. I was to endure endless operations, raging infections, bone grafts and a lengthy convalescence in which it took me months of learning to walk again. But I was alive, still here in Africa. I had survived because of elephants' extraordinary ability to communicate very sophisticated messages to each other, messages that often go against all their natural instinct. For we discovered that Eleanor knew Catherine – as we subsequently named my wild attacker – and had somehow told her that I was a friend.

As for my epiphany – the certainty that I had to write about my life and my work – here it is, some years down the line. This is the story of my settler ancestors; of growing up on my parents' farm; of safaris and nights under the stars; of my soulmate David, my daughters Jill and Angela, the birth of our elephant orphanage, my life lived – all interwoven with spellbinding stories of the many different animals that have immeasurably enriched my life, animals I have reared and loved and come to know as a surrogate mother.

Set against the majestic land of Africa, the birthplace of mankind, my story begins.

1 Settlers

'What we are is God's gift to us; what we become is our gift to God.'

– Anon

It was quite by chance that my ancestors came to settle in Kenya.

In the early 1900s my Great-Uncle Will was living a relatively prosperous life in the Eastern Cape of South Africa. His family – my great-grandmother was Will's sister – had left rural Scotland for Africa in the mid 1820s. A truly capable and resourceful man, Will had worked hard in difficult conditions, farming the land, raising a family and helping others around him to survive the effects of the Boer Wars. He was garrulous and charismatic, a twinkle in his eye, passionate about big game hunting, and from time to time could afford a ticket to Kenya on one of the early steamships to satiate his lust for the land and the animals. The great profusion of wildlife, the rolling grass plains – the storehouse of life itself – Kenya was where his heart seemed to soar, where he was transformed from the inside out.

It was during one of these hunting expeditions, in the spring of 1907, that Will befriended Sir Charles Eliot, Governor of the fledgling British colony of Kenya. The two men were drawn to each other: Will, a true pioneer, was the sort of man who made things happen, and Eliot, a true politician, was the sort of man who made other men offers to make things happen. Out in the bush one morning, Eliot put an intriguing proposition to my great-uncle: if he could bring in twenty families to Kenya, then the Government would allocate them free land on which to settle. Just that week, Eliot had received an order from the authorities back home to speed up the colony's development, to get on with expanding the single track beyond Nairobi and to get white settlers in to increase trade and the resources for the railway. The British Government had so far forked out around £5 million and they wanted to see some return, sooner rather than later.

The reason for Britain's involvement in East Africa was not actually Kenya itself – it was Uganda and the source of the Nile. The Government wanted to prevent the Germans or French jeopardizing access to the Suez Canal, as this was the British trade route to India, the jewel in the Imperial crown. Building the railway was a massive undertaking, and thousands of Sikh labourers from British India were shipped in to undertake its construction. The railway snaked its way through the diverse habitats of Kenya from the port town of Mombasa – through dense inhospitable scrubland leading on to open grassland plains, once the native Masai's best grazing land. Once the dominant tribe, their numbers had been depleted by smallpox during the late 1900s.

Great-Uncle Will was so smitten with the Kenyan bush, so captivated by the idea of actually living in this astonishing country, that he cut short his trip to return home, determined to recruit the families that Eliot required. He didn't need to look too far, as this branch of my family was full of prolific breeders. He himself had spawned seventeen children from his three wives, and they in turn had produced many others. Excited and alive to this opportunity, he did a good job persuading some of his immediate family to agree. Then he turned to his sister – my Great-Granny Aggett. She and her husband – and their not inconsiderable brood of eight children – were perfect targets. Things had not been going too well for Great-Grandpa Aggett. Having acquired a taste for alcohol and gambling, in cahoots with none other than the local bank manager, who saw to it that his mounting overdraft was conveniently overlooked, he was up to his eyes in debt. The family's precious old homestead and once prosperous farm in the Eastern Cape had been sold off and he was much chastened by the consequence of his addictions. Despite approaching sixty, he was keen to be rid of his tarnished reputation, to begin a new life. Will was offering him that lifeline and he rather gratefully signed up.

The Aggetts' eldest daughter, Ellen Margaret, had been widowed early on in her marriage. Left with two young sons, Stanley and Bryan, she had returned to live with my great-grandparents. Ellen was a feisty young woman, known for her fortitude and resourcefulness, and was more than willing to taste adventure. As it turns out, this decision was to have a direct effect on me: Ellen was my grandmother, and her seven-year-old son Bryan would eventually become my father.

Will was a marvellous storyteller, and his golden words conjured up the magnificence of Kenya, breathing life into his images of the land, the people and the wildlife. Quite simply, he saw Kenya as another Eden, the prospect of living there an invitation to paradise. In just a few months his powers of persuasion were enough to convince twenty families to want to up sticks from the Eastern Cape, to trek through the uncharted interior of Eastern Africa and begin life over. These were people descended from solid pioneering stock – stoical, adventurous, enamoured of Africa – the ability to uproot, survive and build new lives in their blood. They had listened to their parents' epic stories of crossing new lands and were somewhere hardwired to feel the desire to experience the challenges for themselves. I would love to be able to listen back down the years to what was discussed at Will's legendary planning meetings. To us, in these days of sophisticated travel when we can get almost anything we need anywhere in the world, an unimaginable amount of planning and thought had to go into the journey. Although the landing post in Mombasa was still the ancient coastal hub it had always been, and inland the railway had reached Nairobi, the travellers had to be self-supporting in every respect. There would be nothing to help them on the way – no roads, no shops, no doctors, dentists or chemists. They would be entirely responsible for keeping themselves, their babies, their children and their livestock alive and well.

It wasn't just a matter of a few provisions. When – and if – they arrived at the allocated spots, they would need a nucleus of breeding stock, as well as farm implements, seeds, tools, furniture and, most importantly, guns and ammunition to protect themselves and their property. The women had to decide on the bare essentials in the way of cooking pots, blankets, bedlinen, materials, haberdashery, medicine, clothes and toiletries. Of untold preciousness was the legacy of their settler ancestors – densely handwritten notes of practical hints on self-sufficiency, detailing how to make soap and candles; how to preserve and bottle foodstuffs; how to make clothes; how to educate your children on the go; how to use herbs, berries and wild plants to prevent and cure illness; and how to address emotional wobbles and the inevitable mood swings. Women back then were superb cooks, skilled seamstresses, tough and hardened to the perils of settler life, but for these families, the arduous nature of the journey and the harsh reality of starting life up all over again presented new challenges.

Eventually the day dawned when all the preparations were complete. There was no turning back. Lying in Port Elizabeth harbour, on the eastern seaboard of South Africa, was the chartered German ship the *Adolf Woermann*, waiting to receive the families and all their possessions. And what possessions there were! Once loaded, the great ship must have looked – and sounded – like the proverbial Noah's Ark. It conjures a vivid image in my mind, picturing my grandmother and her tiny children on board engulfed by animals of wildly varying sizes: prime stock, work oxen, riding horses, milk and beef cattle, sheep, milking goats, poultry, ducks, geese and turkeys, domestic pets of every sort, as well as huge wagons, farm implements of every description, precious pieces of antique furniture, boxes of books, bottles, jars and sewing machines. There was no concept of travelling light back then!

My children and grandchildren are so rooted here now, so settled, so much part of this land, that it touches me deeply to imagine the sheer emotion of the moment when the boat slowly drew away from the docks, with every single member on board waving a tearful farewell to all their loved ones on shore. None of them knew what the future held for them in a new land, and they must all have been conscious that there would be great dangers in the years that lay ahead. And they also knew that for the older members of the family this separation would be final, for they would be unlikely to set foot on their home soil again. It must have taken great courage, particularly on the part of the women, to launch themselves and their children on such a gamble into the unknown.

The *Adolf Woermann* sailed for two long months. The journey was not without its difficulties – dreadfully cramped conditions, illness and the inevitable death of livestock. But coming into the picturesque harbour of Mombasa against the backdrop of a splendid tropical sunrise must have been like the arrival in a promised land. As the adults transferred the contents of the ship to the docks, the children ran around in delight despite the punishing humidity and heat. Mombasa was a vibrant, noisy place, bright with the colourful goods of Arabic and Indian traders, the smells of spices, perfumes and exotic foods. The streets were lined with white frangipani blossom and coconut palms, and while the sun was setting there was time to stop and enjoy a meal in the old part of the town.

Before the journey inland could begin, all the livestock had to be swaddled in a protective hessian covering, leaving just a small opening for the eyes and nose, since they would be journeying across the notorious tsetse-infested nyika. This formidable and inhospitable barrier of arid scrub country was known as the Taru Desert, described in the 1870s by the Scottish explorer Joseph Thomson as 'weird and ghastly . . . eerie and full of sadness, as if here is all death and desolation'. Just one bite from an infected fly could be catastrophic, transmitting the wasting livestock disease trypanosomiasis, for which there was at that time no known cure. A few years earlier, most of the livestock used to transport materials to build the railway had been wiped out in this way and lessons had been learned. It must have taken days to cut the cloth and secure it around each animal. Not an enviable job.

Once the cattle were ready and the train loaded with myriad possessions, the next stage of the journey could begin. However, even the preparations necessary for a train to depart from a stop were complicated, for in those early days the wood-burning steam locomotives depended on a plentiful supply of both wood and water. There was no piped water in Mombasa, so supplies had to be drawn from two eighty-foot wells, or pumped from a river four miles away. Getting the train going was a big event. As a child listening to my father tell my brother, sisters and me the story of how our family came to be living in Kenya, I particularly loved the story-of-the-journey as it came to be known, and to this day I can shut my eyes and transport myself on board, catching the buzz of anticipation as the train drew out of Mombasa. There must have been a little shiver of apprehension running through some of the mothers in the group: the track had only recently been constructed, and although they were disembarking halfway along the route at Nairobi, they no doubt worried about some of the more shaky wooden trestle bridges and the deep ravines the train passed over. All the adults making the journey knew about the grisly deaths suffered by some fifty Indian and African construction workers in 1898 as they were building a bridge over the Tsavo River. It was this incident that had led to the lions in the area being dubbed the 'man-eaters of Tsavo', no doubt stirring fear in some of the less hardy members of my family.

While my experiences of life in Kenya are different in so many respects to those of my ancestors, as they woke to their first morning aboard the train they saw the same dawn unfolding in glorious brilliance, the sky washed with varying shades of crimson, pink, rust and gold, that I do to this day. Their tired eyes, rimmed with the red dust of the nyika, also gazed, as mine have, spellbound across the broad expanse of the great rolling Athi plains. From the windows, they could see before them the bounty of Nature – oceans of wildebeest, zebra, antelope, gazelles, giraffe, great herds of buffalo and even rhinos. The children were electrified by the transformation of the landscape, and the journey opened their eyes to sights they had never seen before. A pride of lions beside the track, lolling replete and lazy beneath a lone tree on the plain, prompted the driver to halt the train in order to allow the passengers a longer look. In fact most of the time Great-Uncle Will and others journeyed on a special platform on the prow of the locomotive so that they could see the passing game herds more clearly. Inveterate hunter that he was, Great-Uncle Will on numerous occasions actually stopped the train to embark on a full-blown hunt, when a particularly good trophy had been spotted near the track. The train would merely wait for the hunters to return, and the other passengers did not object to the delay, happy to take part in the fun as spectators.

How lightly my ancestors shot at animals. For us, now living in a different era, conscious of the decimation of wildlife and privileged even to glimpse such creatures in a wild situation, the actions of my forefathers appear shocking and difficult to understand. But at that time the maps of Kenya showed little on their empty faces, and beyond each horizon stretched another and another of endless untouched acres, sunlit plains of corn-gold grass, wooded luggas, lush valleys, crystal-clear waters. And everywhere there was wildlife in such spellbinding profusion that it is difficult for those who were never witness to this to even begin to visualize such numbers. At the time no one ever imagined that any amount of shooting could devastate the stocks of wild game, let alone all but eliminate it.

Once the train reached Nairobi, the passengers had to disembark, see to some administrative formalities and make their final preparations for the great inland trek. Nairobi, originally a pastoral area inhabited by the Masai, had been founded in 1899 as a supply depot for the Uganda Railway, becoming the capital of the British East Africa Protectorate a few years later. In 1907 Nairobi was in the process of being rebuilt, having been decimated by a recent outbreak of the plague. When my family arrived, it was still a jumble of sheds, shacks and Indian dukas cut by one tree-lined cart-track known as Government Road. Most structures were raised up on stilts to keep inhabitants from sinking into the surrounding swamps. There was dust everywhere – it coated every visible surface and tree. But it was busy and vibrant, teeming with Indian railway workers, street vendors, rickshaws and mule buggies, and the family were entranced. The elders of the group rested overnight in the one hotel – the Norfolk – which overlooked a swamp where the wild creatures of the plains came to drink in their teeming numbers. It was a perfect place for Great-Uncle Will. Never one to pass up an opportunity, on the first night he left a drink on the Norfolk verandah to dash out and bag a good trophy spotted at the swamp, and on another night he did not even have to leave his drink, but managed to secure a trophy from the verandah itself.

Soon enough, though, once the ox-wagons were loaded and ready, the family was ready for the trek inland. Dressed in their heavy khaki – the women tightly laced in and stockinged – heads protected by heavily fortified pith helmets, there was some trepidation as they moved off. While the Government allocation of 5,000 acres of virgin bush was a generous gesture on its part, the location of these new holdings, in Narok, situated in the very heart of Masailand, unsettled many of the group. Actually, they need not have worried. Even though the Masai had earned themselves a fearsome reputation in the 600 or so years they had been in East Africa, they had been advised by their witch doctor Chief Mbatian not to actively oppose the arrival in their land of either pale people or an 'iron snake', whose coming had been revealed to a girl in a dream. In truth, it was the wildlife in the land itself that was to prove the greatest threat to the family's beginning in a new land.

The journey took several months. There were no roads, just paths formed by the passage of wagons that followed wildlife trails through the thick scrub. Flies that accompanied the grazing hordes were everywhere, constantly landing on the face, and despite heavy, hot protective clothing, the thick dust of the land lodged itself in everyone's eyes, throats and lungs, making the children particularly prone to fits of prolonged coughing. Passing through areas inhabited by local tribesmen, many of whom may not have ever set eyes on a white face, their women often let out high-pitched screams as they saw the convoy approaching, causing the men to emerge armed with clubs, bows and arrows and spears. It was not unknown for spears to be launched at the wagons, before Great-Uncle Will bravely stepped forward to appease the local people with calming gestures. Predators were an omnipresent threat, though most of the time the teeming wild game provided a welcome diversion. The descent into the Great Rift Valley followed a trail blazed by earlier pioneers, as it twisted through the dense indigenous forests of the high ground, down a steep escarpment fault of the Rift and out into the open savannah of the valley floor. There the extinct isolated volcanoes of Longonot and Suswa stood sentinel over a string of alkaline and freshwater lakes, and the western wall of the Rift, the Mau Escarpment, provided a forbidding backdrop for those among the family who would have to hack their way up it in order to reach their destination.

But there were also moments of extreme beauty. Passing through cool shady forests into lush basins of glittering sunlight reminded the travellers of the rich variety of the land. For the amateur botanists, at every step there were new plants and flowers to marvel at – orchids, gladioli, hibiscus, and the jaw-dropping giant lobelia that grew up to twenty feet at high altitudes. For the keen ornithologists, there were birds of every conceivable variety: great flocks of fifty or more ostriches, blue-black glossy starlings, rainbow-hued superb starlings and brightly coloured sunbirds. There were pungent smells from remote villages; the smell of livestock and chargrilled meat; rich colours of cloth and beadwork; bewildering chatter and the braying of donkeys from remote villages. The Masai tribe were dressed in bright red blankets, their hair braided long with extensions of wool and dyed red with ochre-coloured clay, their bodies also painted with red ochre. They had elaborate beaded ornaments on their legs, arms and stretched hanging earlobes and the glint of their spears and daggers was a thrilling sight for the children.

My father remembered the journey well. I never tired of listening to him tell me how the herds of various animals would stand to the side to allow the caravan passage through, closing again behind them in what appeared an impenetrable curtain of living creatures. The thunder of galloping hooves and the voices of the animals provided the heartbeat of this new land. He delighted in trying to imitate the incessant cooing of doves, and the deep blood-chilling roar of lions never ceased to thrill. Meat for the pot was never a problem, and lion hunts were an almost daily occurrence that went hand in hand with long night-time vigils to prevent lions, hyenas and leopards taking a toll of the precious livestock. All the children loved watching Will as he galloped through the open plains on horseback alongside eland and giraffe to see if they could be outpaced by his horse.

These, though, were the carefree memories of my father, who was a child at the time. For the adults, the journey was fraught with difficulties and dilemmas on a daily, often hour-by-hour basis. Progress up the densely forested slopes of the Mau Escarpment towards Narok was painfully slow, since they had to hack a passage for their wagons through a tangle of almost impenetrable vegetation using only very narrow elephant trails. Every evening before the swift blackness of the dark descended, while the women pitched camp, the men had to erect brush bomas, enclosures for the protection of their livestock at night. And even when they finally came to Narok, they had to cross the Uaso Nyiro – today a mere trickle, but then a deep, wide, fast-flowing river. The only way to get to the other side was to swim the animals and float the wagons across – a logistical nightmare. But they were determined and they were capable, and finally, after a journey of four treacherous months, the families reached their destination. Great-Uncle Will's contingent had stopped near Lake Elmenteita, while the Aggetts faced a much more daunting challenge to reach Narok. There was a small trading and administrative centre in the embryonic Narok township, but their allotments lay further still beyond the river.

Of course, there was nothing there for them when they arrived. It is difficult to imagine – travelling for months in almost impossible conditions, trailing your life's possessions behind you, and then 'arriving' at your destination where there is nothing other than wilderness. I often wonder how they even knew they had arrived at the right place. There, having erected temporary grass huts, and stout thorn bomas to secure their livestock, the men had to begin the backbreaking task of clearing the land. It would take a while before they were able to construct more solid dwellings and create some sort of domestic order. Moreover, the location of their new holdings meant that the Aggett family was scattered and unable to help one another as much as they would have wished. For my great-grandfather, this was an unrelentingly difficult time – at fifty-nine, he was not in the best physical shape for such labour. If they had hoped for help from the Masai, this was not to be, for traditionally and culturally Masai men left all manual labour to the women while they tended and protected their cattle. But they were not hostile, watching quietly and with great curiosity as to the habits of the newcomers. They were mostly impressed by Great-Grandpa's tenacity and courage – attributes they valued among themselves.

We get stressed today if the shops are more than a half-hour's drive away, and when I go shopping there is always a little flicker in my mind as I think of Great-Granny Aggett, who certainly had her work cut out. Her nearest stores were at Kijabe – six days away by wagon. So out came the old family manuals, in between tending the animals, and fending off a host of furred and feathered predators by day and night, which laid siege to everything that moved. She made her own soap from homemade butter, ostrich eggs gathered from the plains and the caustic soda she had brought with her from home; candles by melting down wildebeest fat and pouring it on to tallow – the wick of a candle – in a hollow cylinder; and lotions and potions from wild herbs, mixed with beeswax. Meat was salted and sun-dried into biltong, while wild berries gathered in the bush were bottled and preserved. She worked tirelessly – and she too was nearly sixty.

For a while, my family threw all they had mentally and physically into making a success of their new life. George – one of the Aggetts' sons – spent a lot of time with the Masai and soon learned their language, becoming familiar with their way of life. My great-grandmother, her long thick hair a constant source of fascination among the local Masai women, found that her reputation as a healer soon spread far and wide. She was even trusted to treat the sick and maimed among the Masai, many with spear wounds and lion mauls, others with eye and skin infections. Her secret remedies lay in a combination of paraffin and the mildew from caked cow-dung as well as the herbal tinctures passed down through the generations.

As the rhythm of life settled a little, the family experienced moments of extreme satisfaction at their self-reliance and survival. Their souls were continually uplifted by the sheer magnificence of their surroundings: the wide open spaces, the magic of huge skies of the purest blue; the abundance of wildlife. But the extreme difficulties of daily life out there in the bush were exhausting and unforgiving. Farming was a process of hit and miss, Africa an enigma to the early settlers. Deceptively fertile-looking soil often lacked vital minerals for arable crops; the altitude and the short equatorial daylight hours influenced growth; the rains yielded either a feast or a famine, always too much or too little – and often torrential hailstorms flattened everything in sight. There were diseases of cattle not encountered before, all the natural hazards posed by wild animals, plus swarms of locusts and 'army worm' caterpillars that descended on crops in voracious multitudes, devouring everything.

It was tough going for my ageing great-grandpa. On one particularly ill-fated morning, he rode out as usual on his favourite horse, Princess, leading his second mare, Daisy, who needed exercising. He tethered Princess in the shade of the large trees that lined the banks of the Uaso Nyiro River, leaving Daisy free, confident that she would not stray far from her companion. He then walked out to his irrigation furrow, which by this time was quite a long way from the river. He had been digging this for some time, in an attempt to bring water from the river to a vegetable patch he was cultivating. On this particular day he returned at dusk, spent and exhausted, only to find to his horror that his precious Princess was in the process of being devoured by a huge black-maned lion, crouched menacingly over its kill, while Daisy nervously circled the attacker at dangerously close quarters. On this one day, Great-Grandpa had broken his golden rule and not brought his gun, so there was nothing for it but to try to catch his surviving horse.

The lion meanwhile was becoming more and more angry, pivoting around on its haunches, growling and snarling and lashing its tail ominously, following Great-Grandpa's every move with blazing eyes. It seemed that time stopped as my great-grandfather willed Daisy to stand still just for a moment so that he could scramble aboard. Finally he sensed that it had to be now or never, and with one last herculean effort he lunged towards her and somehow – he never knew how – managed to get himself across her back, jamming his heels hard into the horse's flanks. At this very moment the lion charged, letting out the most spine-chilling roar, and Daisy was just able to leap clear, barely escaping the lion's cleaving claws.

It was a very shaken, tired and broken old man who stumbled into the house that night, for quite apart from his ordeal he had loved Princess dearly, as can only a man who is totally reliant on his horse. Princess had carried him faithfully many hundreds of miles both in South Africa and Kenya, and between them they had developed that almost tangible telepathic rapport – an empathy, binding and strong, that defied definition. For the first time he acknowledged that he was beaten and could battle no more against such insurmountable odds. I suspect he also wished that he had never left South Africa. That night, he and Great-Granny Aggett hardly slept a wink, mulling over their predicament, and by the next morning they had made up their minds. There was no way they were going to make it where they were: they had to move. The next day Great-Grandpa Aggett saddled Daisy and rode off to Nairobi to seek advice from the colonial Government.

In fact, it had already dawned on the authorities that the isolated and vulnerable white settlers of Masailand would have to be moved elsewhere, and negotiations with the relevant elders and chiefs were already under way to bring the Masai people from around Kenya to the area around Narok so that they were settled in one place, away from their enemies, the Kikuyu. By the time Great-Grandpa arrived in Nairobi, the decision had already been taken to move him and his family out of Masailand, and offer them alternative holdings on the Laikipia Plateau. This was prize ranching country, where wildlife also abounded in numbers that matched the endless herds of the Athi plains and the Masai lands of Narok.

And so once again the family loaded up their wagons and were on the move, laboriously retracing their steps, with what remained of their livestock. At the same time, the Masai living on the Laikipia Plateau filed down into the Rift, led by thousands of warriors in full battle regalia and accompanied by 100,000 head of cattle, half a million sheep, and hundreds of loaded donkeys. The women, children and elders walked slowly beside the donkeys that carried their few possessions, while another vanguard of warriors brought up the rear – all overseen by a contingent of the King's African Rifles, just in case the warriors caused a diversion on the way. It must have been an unforgettable sight, this exodus of the Masai from Laikipia back to Narok, which coincided with the move to Laikipia of most of my Aggett relations.

The younger generation were excited and eager to establish themselves in their new holdings, but my great-grandparents, physically and emotionally drained by the past few years, settled on a small-holding seven miles from the lakeside town of Naivasha. There they set up a home that was to become a warm, hospitable focal point for the rest of the clan, offering unfettered freedom for the children to roam the great expanse of the plains that bordered that freshwater lake within the Great Rift Valley.

Meanwhile my father, Bryan, was growing up fast in Nairobi. His life had changed somewhat since the arrival of two younger half-brothers, Fred and Harry. His mother, Ellen – widowed when Bryan was so young – had subsequently married Ernest Nye Chart. She had established Nairobi's first grill room in the Grand Hotel, and now she and Ernest were taking over the management of the hotel itself, having achieved some success as local entrepreneurs. And despite all the initial hardships, my father's uncles and aunts were also becoming established and successful in their new homeland, setting up professional hunting parties, cattle-ranching establishments, farms, hotels, transport and trading companies. Bryan moved effortlessly between his extended family, his aunts, uncles and numerous cousins, enjoying a warm welcome and wonderful hospitality at every visit, for he was a very popular member of the family.

My father was one of the two very first male candidates to sit – and pass – the school-leavers' exam set by Cambridge University. His academic ability probably saved his life during the First World War, as he was sent to work in an office rather than to fight on the front line. However, like thousands of others, he succumbed to the deadly Spanish flu and was sent back home. Great-Grandma Aggett nursed him back to full health and, once he was strong enough, one of his uncles offered him work. Uncle Boyce, an enterprising settler, had many irons in the fire – a hides and skins trade, a safari business, a store near Narok and a handful of farms. My father excelled in all things practical and proved a great asset to his uncle's safari business. In those days safaris went out for five or six weeks at a time, and Bryan was adept at giving the clients a memorable and varied time in the bush.

My grandmother, Ellen, was ambitious for her second son and did not approve of him 'fooling around with lions'. She urged him to invest in livestock. Always dutiful, Bryan used his £100 of army savings to buy eight cows and three calves, which he then lodged with my great-grandparents while he looked for some suitable land. More and more new settlers had arrived in Kenya after the Great War in response to soldier settlement schemes, and my father and his brother Stan wanted to get in there before things became too competitive. Bryan and Stan farmed sensibly, planting their crops in good time, devising new ways in which to keep them out of harm's way. However, things did not go quite according to plan, and to add to their woes, at the time of harvest the land they had cultivated went up in smoke. Once again Bryan secured work with another of his uncles, this time hunting buffalo for their hides. And once again Ellen signalled her disapproval, this time taking decisive action: convinced that Bryan needed refining, she shipped him off to South Africa.

Actually, Bryan was a willing participant in this scheme, as his brother Stan had already been dispatched for a bit of Ellen's civilizing process and had sent back glowing accounts of rather beautiful – and eligible – women. And so it was there that my father met Marjorie Webb, a slender, immaculately turned-out young woman. He was smitten with her at once, falling in love with her inherent grace and bouncing blonde curls. And the feeling was mutual: Marjorie told her friends it was love at first sight. By the end of his stay – much to the horror of her parents – Marjorie and Bryan were so deeply in love that they wanted to get married. Her father, in particular, had issues with the Aggett contingent, considering them to be uncultured, rough and domineering. He was not keen for his daughter to spend the rest of her life in 'darkest Africa', and even though he liked Bryan – everyone did – he did not think him 'good enough' for his precious daughter. He was canny, though, knowing that to deny their request would be counter-productive, and he bought Marjorie a ticket to Kenya so that she could accompany Bryan on his return journey and experience life in the raw for herself for a couple of months.

Far from being put off, Marjorie fell in love with Kenya. She was enraptured by the majestic beauty of the land and the thrumming diversity of the country. She returned to South Africa more determined than ever to marry Bryan. And what a sense of purpose she brought to my father! Fuelled by love, over the next two years Bryan worked as never before, eventually purchasing 770 acres of land near

Gilgil. Using the farm's quarry for stone and cedar trees for timber, he built a house on the land. He installed a sawmill on the farm and set up a small timber concern. Touchingly, full of hope for the future, he named the farm L'Esperance. When news reached Dick Webb of Bryan's achievements, he knew that he could no longer hold on to his daughter.

Two years after they first met, Marjorie – not without a touch of trepidation – steamed out of East London harbour to be reunited with Bryan. As soon as she saw him on the Mombasa quayside, eagerly scanning the faces on the deck, she knew her decision had been the right one. Poised on the brink of a lifetime together, their journey inland was magical, reminding her of the wonders of Kenya. Marjorie was never to forget arriving at the farm, the smell of the cedar oil pervading the beautifully panelled and polished rooms that my father had built and furnished for her.

The wedding party was a joyous celebration. The huge Aggett clan travelled from far and wide and the party went on for some days. Marjorie was instantly welcomed into the heart of the family – even Ellen (almost) approved – and she settled happily into life on the farm. A talented homemaker and artist, she set about adding some feminine touches to the house. She also cultivated the garden that in later years was to become one of the most beautiful in the district. Marjorie was a gracious host and soon she and Bryan were entertaining family and friends, the farm filling with life and laughter. In 1930, a year after their wedding, she was to become a mother – a son, Peter, followed eighteen months later by a daughter, Sheila. And then, three years later, in June 1934, I was born. Our little sister Betty arrived four years after me. By this time, my father had built a house for his mother, Ellen – known to us children as Granny Chart – near Gilgil and another for his newly arrived in-laws, Granny and Grandpa Webb, about five miles from our house. They had decided that they wanted to be a part of their grandchildren's lives and emigrated from South Africa. Our family was complete.

Nearly thirty years after leaving the Eastern Cape, some of the prominent members of the pioneering vintage had passed away – Great-Uncle Will, Great-Grandpa and Great-Granny Aggett among them. While I was too young when they were old or dying to remember them in person, I am forever indebted to their spirit and determination, the sacrifices they made to ensure the security of the next generations of the family. Thanks to them, my immediate family was secure enough to begin to put down their roots in the land – to feel the powerful stirrings of belonging.

2. Childhood

'O Lord of love and kindness, who created the beautiful earth and all the creatures walking and flying in it, so that they may proclaim your glory. I thank you to my dying day that you have placed me amongst them.'

— St Francis of Assisi

My life-long involvement with animals began with a mother cat and her kittens. My mother told me that I was an inquisitive child, always on the move, wanting to get in on the action. To stop me disturbing my brother and sister during their lessons, my mother would wedge me into the cat-box, the only place apparently where I was guaranteed to be as good as gold. She told me later: 'You would stay there for hours, sucking your thumb, with a kitten or two snuggled in your lap.' I was then just a toddler.

Animals were everywhere, their sounds, their scent, their behaviour part of the everyday fabric of life on the farm, and as soon as I could walk, I would toddle out to the back of the house and squeeze myself into the chicken run so that I could watch the tiny newly hatched chicks. I loved the furriness of them, their little cheeping sounds, and I would babble away at them. I thought it was completely normal when going for a walk in the forest to be accompanied by a huge retinue of humans and animals — as we left the house my mother, father, brother and sisters and I would be joined by all our dogs, Bob the impala, Daisy the waterbuck and Ricky-Ticky-Tavey, the little brown-furred dwarf mongoose who always ran on ahead, leading the way for the rest of us. He was a great favourite and a wonderful pet, always busy and inquisitive. Dwarf mongooses are carnivorous and also love eggs, which they manoeuvre up to a tree or rock and hurl between their back legs to break open. We used to tease

Ricky-Ticky-Tavey by giving him a ping-pong ball instead of an egg and this drove him nuts, because it wouldn't break as he thought it should and he would growl angrily at it. Usually, though, he would make a friendly chirruping birdlike peep as he went about finding food for himself: insects, reptiles and rodents. He had little ears, a long tail and short limbs, and was so gregarious that he wanted to be involved in whatever we were doing. We used to love cuddling him under our jumpers to keep him warm.

This daily excursion, the vibrancy and chatter of family and animals, was so much a part of me that from a very early age I had no fear of animals whatsoever, more familiar with them, as it turned out, than my own shadow. It's an old family story how once, when I was about sixteen months old, I thought something dark and sinister had attached itself to me as I tottered on to our verandah through the shade into a brightly sunlit highland morning, followed by my shadow. Apparently I bellowed with such gusto that people erupted from every door in the house. Fearing venomous safari ants, spiders or snakebites, my mother upended me for inspection, but there was nothing evident to account for my screaming. '*Na lia bure*. She cries for nothing!' confirmed Sega, our Kikuyu cook. 'Show us, Bay,' urged my brother, Bay being the pet family name by which I was known (short for 'Baby') until Betty was born. I was set down and with trepidation pointed to the shadow behind me. There followed a great burst of laughter that was a mixture of relief and mirth. 'Oh, Bay. You drip! It's only your shadow,' exclaimed Sheila. Oddly the first glimpse of my shadow remains starkly vivid, imprinted on my mind to this very day: that horrible sense of panic at the unknown.

I was close to my siblings, for we were together daily in early childhood, tangled up in each other's games and schemes. We spent most of our days outside. I doubt there are few places on earth as stunning as the East African stretch of the Great Rift Valley, born of movements and fractures of the earth's crust some 15 million years ago. It has been said of the Rift that although it might have its counterpart on another planet, there is nothing like it on earth, for all the other rift valleys of comparable size lie deep beneath the oceans. Some 4,500 miles long and in some places fifty miles wide, the

African section of this mighty geological trench runs through the Ethiopian highlands, clear through the highlands of both Kenya and Tanzania, to a point in the south of Tanzania near Mozambique, where it becomes obscure. It is studded with both ancient and recent volcanoes and with beautiful fresh and alkaline lakes, both types of which were within easy access of my father's farm, situated as it was on one of the outcropping spurs of the Rift's eastern wall at the foot of the Aberdare mountain range. The altitude of our farm was a little over 7,000 feet, so the temperature was always perfect: sunny days and cool crisp nights.

My mother kept hundreds of chickens, which were confined in large bomas during the morning so that they would lay their eggs in the boxes provided for the purpose rather than in secret nesting places in the bush. It was the Chicken Toto's job to keep the poultry out of the garden and vegetable patch when they were let out of their bomas to range free each afternoon, for the garden and front of the house were out of bounds for the feathered members of the farmyard. One of my favourite spots was a small wire-covered chicken run, where the broody hens sat on their clutches of eggs in little tin huts and the tiny newly hatched chickens and ducks followed their clucking mothers, miniature bundles of fluff that I could spend hours just watching. In another small covered run, near the garage, were our pet angora rabbits and these, too, were very special to me. Whenever I got exasperated with my siblings – a daily occurrence – I would run to the rabbits, ducks, chickens, the broody hens or the mother cat and her kittens in the cat-box and pass a comfortable, peaceful hour or two in their company.

Like most colonial homes of the period, the rooms at each end of the house had large symmetrical bay windows open to a gorgeous garden and spectacular views and joined by a spacious verandah. My favourite room was our main living area, known as the sitting room. The walls were panelled in polished cedar and hung with lifelike paintings of buffalo, lions and a lone bull elephant. The curtains, easy chairs and settees were covered in floral patterns and the room was airy and light, perfumed by the wonderful scent of roses from the garden, which filled every available vase and were of every conceivable colour. Instead of carpets, leopard-skins lay on the floor, and apart from the piano the most cherished thing in the room was a large hand-carved mvule table, fashioned from one enormous plank of the valuable hardwood, which had been a wedding present to my parents. A windowseat with a lift-up lid, covered in brightly coloured cushions, ran along one wall, and became known as the dungeon – an ideal place for storing things, or in my case, a place to hide from Sheila when I had messed up her dolls' house.

My other favourite spot in the house was the kitchen – Sega's domain – and Peter and I loved nothing better than hanging around the back door trying to get a bit of his delicious irio, a mixture of mashed potato, pumpkin leaves, peas and whole maize. As a reward for all sorts of endless errands, he would allow us a taste, though if we were feeling wicked and daring, we would help ourselves to a chunk when he wasn't looking. The kitchen was detached from the main house, as a precaution against fire, and was accessed through a covered walkway. It was dominated by the Dover stove, which swallowed wood constantly and on which, in among the simmering brews of soup and other cooking pots boiling the leftovers for dogs and chickens, sat the flat irons used to straighten out our clothes. A small high opened window overlooked the woodpile outside, where, once a week, the African wives of workers on the farm brought a load of wood on their backs in exchange for a weekly portion of maize-meal and the two-acre plot on the farm for each family of workers, which they could cultivate and where they could graze a maximum of thirty goats and sheep. These smallholdings were known as shambas and were set a small distance from our house, and they were alive with the sounds of our workers' families and smelled of smoke and cooking. Traditionally, the women of the Kikuyu tribe were the load-carriers within the tribe, so it was as normal for them to bring wood to our kitchen as to their own homesteads. The leather straps that attached the huge loads to their heads wore deep grooves into their skulls, and invariably perched on their backs was a toddler or two, while slung in folded hide hanging from the women's necks would be a tiny suckling baby attended by hordes of flies. We were always incredulous at the weights these women carried on their backs and were fascinated also by their children and babies, who would stare at us as solemnly as we would regard them.

During the day, ours was a busy, often noisy household. Apart from the sound of animals, there were the endless arguments between Granny Chart and Grandpa Webb. Ellen was not happy about this, and whenever she visited our house at the same time as them she would flounce like a tornado through the rooms, banging doors, keen to show her displeasure at their very presence. She was a large, well-endowed woman, made of the stuff that created the Empire – a formidable old force. Grandpa Webb was no pushover either and his wicked sense of humour got him into frequent trouble, especially when he was caught – often! – in exaggerated but accurate mimicking of Granny Chart's tantrums. Days would pass in frosty silence and it would take all the tact of my softly-spoken, gentle Granny Webb to try and smooth things over. As children we used to watch wide-eyed as these adults shouted and sulked at each other, and as soon as things became heated my mother would try to shoo us out of earshot of their noisy exchanges.

My parents worked extremely hard. Like the women who had trekked from the Eastern Cape to settle here, my mother had to be proficient in just about every aspect of farm-life and homemaking. She was always on the go, responsible for all the farmyard animals including the large numbers of pigs on which we depended for some of our small income; the general running of the home and the domestic helpers we employed; making all our clothes; teaching us children for two hours a day; and tending to our much-needed vegetable garden. But she was always loving and even-tempered, managing to find time for her passions – painting and making our house beautiful. She was a brilliant artist, known for her skilful murals, so nursery rhymes danced off our bedroom walls and hand-painted sunshine birds of Kenya adorned silk lampshades. I thought of my mother as an angel, and at bedtime each evening when we knelt to say our prayers she was always there beside us. I loved the flowers, especially sitting in the jonquil patch enveloped by their heavenly scent, and I spent a lot of time staring at the 'floating bowl' in the sitting room, in which stood a pale-blue cut-glass mermaid with long flowing hair surrounded by cut roses from our garden, lost in my own thoughts and dreams.

My father was more remote, in contrast to my mother. He wore his emotions on his face, an almost constant expression of worry and concern, for it was difficult in those days to make ends meet. We didn't see much of him during the day, as he was always busy, involved somewhere on the farm. It was difficult to make a go of a farm and there was always something worrying him – a sick animal that he had to attend to, pestilence, the killing of one of his precious animals by a marauding leopard. The nearest vet was over 150 miles away and the farmworkers did not yet possess the skills needed for European-style farming. My father had a contract to send butter to Nairobi and made 300lb a week, fetching the equivalent of 6d per pound. Our pigs were hard to market, so he made ham and sausages himself on the farm, the ham fetching the princely sum of 1d per pound. Sometimes it was so difficult to generate enough money to keep us going that my father hired himself out, building dipping tanks for neighbouring farmers or transporting other people's produce on our ox-wagons. Although much had been learned since the first settlers arrived, farming in the Rift Valley was still unpredictable – the periodic droughts impacted on grazing for the cattle. Between this and endemic diseases, about which little was known in those days, whole herds of livestock could be wiped out.

And the locusts! Memories of the despair on my father's face as a swarm approached remain vivid in my mind. If you have never seen locusts descend, it is a sight to behold. Like large grasshoppers, they come in a dense black cloud that blocks out the sun and they devour every blade of green for miles around, leaving vast areas bare before they take off to wreak havoc somewhere else. Mostly I remember the panic that preceded their arrival, for whoever first spotted the swarm had to warn everyone else so that they could grab tin cans and beat them as loudly as possible in an attempt to divert the swarm. For a few moments it felt as if the world would never again be quiet, the symphony of their flight making us quicken our beat on the tins – a sort of atonal premonition of the chaos to come.

But the locusts were not all bad news. For Sega they were a

culinary delicacy, and we would watch in horrified fascination as he pulled off the legs and heads, tossed the torsos in hot butter as he roasted them over coals and crunched up the browned bodies with obvious relish. My special friend – one of our gardeners from the Mkamba tribe, whom I used to beg over and over again to show me how he could pull out his filed front teeth and put them back in again – persuaded me to try some one year, which I bravely did, just to please him. I don't really recall the taste, but I do remember Peter sneaking on me and my mother telling me not to eat insects ever again.

In contrast, during the rains all the anxious creases on my father's brow disappeared. He would stand on the verandah, hands outstretched, looking out over the Great Rift Valley, and watch as the first raindrops fell, soaking the earth, breathing in the scent of the air. Meanwhile my brother and sisters would be praying for hail, despite the fact that hail meant doom for our father's crops. But for us it meant one thing: ice cream.

We had no refrigerator and so we could never keep anything that would melt. At the first hint of hail, then, we would dash outside to frantically scoop up the hailstones as my mother rushed into the pantry to prepare the mixture for ice cream. This was placed in a sealed container, surrounded by the hailstones and salt and lowered into a bucket, which we then had to roll up and down the back verandah until the ice cream had frozen. Meanwhile those of us not rolling the bucket would be jumping around with mouth-watering anticipation. Hail only came about once every three years, so tucking into the frozen ice cream some hours later was as good as it got. No ice cream has tasted as delicious ever since.

Although we were a self-contained family, there were of course plenty of visitors to the farm. My parents were known for their hospitality, and apart from our grandparents, friends from neighbouring farms often popped in without notice. My father came alive when we had visitors, regaling them with amusing stories, and he was deeply appreciated by his friends and neighbours, who knew they could come to him at any time for help in any one of the many areas in which he was skilled – carpentry, construction, mechanics, farming, animal husbandry . . . the list went on. Despite the fact that my father was teetotal, we children used to love to watch the change that came over him when he was relaxing with my mother or with friends. He would go from being preoccupied with farm-related problems to being chatty and funny, and we were always happy to see him sitting down in our living room, talking and enjoying my mother's delicious non-alcoholic ginger beer.

Among my parents' close friends were the Higginsons, who lived on a small farm just outside Gilgil with their two sons, Michael and Philip, who were close in age to my brother, Peter. Mr and Mrs Higginson (or the Higgies as they were affectionately known) were a lively couple, full of banter and often at loggerheads with each other. This was illustrated perfectly one rainy evening soon after my parents had met them, when there was a knock at the door as my mother was bathing Peter and Sheila. Due to the appalling conditions of the roads during the rainy season, visitors after dark were few and far between, so my mother hurried out fearing that something must be very wrong. There was Mrs Higgie, dripping wet, with her two small sons in tow. She explained, in a rather harassed tone, that their old Rugby car had got well and truly bogged in the mud at the bottom of the road, so Mr Higgie had suggested that all the passengers, including the two little boys, get out and push. After a great deal of effort, they managed to dislodge the car from the mud, whereupon Mr Higgie simply roared off, leaving them all behind, caked in dirt. My mother was horrified that any husband could behave in this way and called for my father to drive them home. Reporting back afterwards, my father was equally aghast to have arrived at their farm only to find Mr Higgie with his feet up in front of a roaring fire, calmly perusing the newspaper and not a bit concerned for the rest of his family. Nor apparently did he pay the least bit of attention to the tirade unleashed by his wife, simply glancing up over his spectacles nonchalantly before becoming absorbed in his newspaper again!

Actually Mr Higgie was a highly decorated soldier, a good and amusing man. We all liked both him and Mrs Higgie very much. Mrs Higgie was our greatest source of local gossip, and in those days, when children were very much 'seen and not heard', Sheila and I would tiptoe and hide behind the door to the dining room to eavesdrop as she recounted the comings and goings of the Happy Valley set. Neither my parents nor the Higgies were part of this small community of aristocrats, who lived raunchily in the Wanjohi Valley on the eastern wall of the Rift, but everyone enjoyed hearing about their debauched sexual antics and permissive lifestyle.

The Higginson brothers were my brother's constant companions, cycling over most days to join in our games. Most of the time we played well together, as Sheila and I were also tomboys in our childhood and we enjoyed climbing, scrambling and exploring with the boys. However, as we got older, the boys began to pull rank and us girls found ourselves somewhat marginalized from their close-knit friendship.

There were frequent excursions out into the surrounding areas, especially trips to Gilgil town, three miles away. At that time, my father's single most prized possession was a T-model Ford car. He had bought it as a surprise for my mother when Peter was born, as he did not want to bring her back from the nursing home by ox-wagon. The car came to be known affectionately as Never Die. Up the road lived an old settler named Mr Worthingham, who decided that because petrol was expensive, he would use four oxen to pull his new car along. Seeing him sitting solemnly behind the wheel, steering a car that was being hauled at walking pace by oxen, made many people smile. At least Never Die was driven in the correct manner, albeit sometimes fuelled with paraffin.

My mother instilled a great love of Nature in us, beginning with the flowers in our garden that we watched blossom and bloom year on year. The entire outside of our house was covered in Kitale creeper, its deep blue convolvulus flowers festooning the walls all the year round, and the garden was a joyous rainbow of colourful roses, Barberton daisies, dahlias and jonquils, among many other beautiful blossoms. Three entire beds were devoted to the sweet-smelling roses that were my mother's pride and joy. On the other side of the rose terraces was the orchard where she planted the almond seeds that she had brought with her from South Africa. There were peach trees and some rather unyielding grapevines, plus a tall barricade of prickly pears, which was such an attraction for the mouse-birds that Peter used to scare off with his airgun.

But it was during our weekly walk through the nearby forest, to visit Granny and Grandpa Webb in Gilgil, that my mother became truly animated, zealous in her love of what she termed 'the matrix of life'. Something within the forest stirred my soul, and the background music of the river enhanced an almost spiritual experience for me. In a sort of reverential hush, we would take our time through the glades, spotting as many animals as we could. You could always tell when a pack of monkeys was around, as there was a musty smell in the air, but you had to be quiet in order to spot them. Once you saw one move, suddenly the air would fill with their movements and sound and we would crouch down low, still as statues, as they leapt into life. We loved watching the Colobus most, those beautiful black and white forest monkeys that soared through the trees with effortless jumps, fur flared out to assist their passage aerodynamically. Their tiny black hands were not unlike our own, except that they didn't have thumbs. My mother told us that this was because they had been removed by evolution, thumbs an encumbrance that used to snag against the branches and twigs and slow down their progress. It was their voices that intrigued us the most, for when they called to each other it sounded like motor-bikes revving up. I was entranced by the variety of animals we saw in the forest. Most of the bushbuck, duikers and suni had hunched backs to make it easier to move through the undergrowth, and spotted or streaked coats to enhance camouflage in a world where sunlight streaks rather fleetingly through the herbage. The birds of the forest were both wonderful and plentiful – hornbills, touracos, starlings, parrots, barbets and bulbils, thrushes, babblers and flycatchers all abounded and everywhere their song interrupted the silence.

We learned to distinguish different species of birds by their calls, and I loved the maiden-ferns that waved their feathery arms at me. I was convinced that the little moss-covered boulders surrounded by toadstools and tiny wild flowers were the very entrance to fairyland itself. I firmly believed in fairies, and would approach them very, very slowly and very, very quietly, blaming the fact that I never saw one on Peter and Sheila, who would make as much noise as possible the moment they saw me on my tiptoes.

My mother likened the forest to a giant's sponge, retaining water and releasing it gently to the lower regions consistently and faithfully throughout the year, year in and year out. She said: 'If you remove the forest, then the slopes will stand bare and rocks will stick out like the bones of a skeleton with all its flesh gone.' She felt acutely the therapeutic value of the natural forest and taught us to unwind, to release our minds so that we could appreciate the soothing tranquillity of the dim green twilight. Through my mother's patient and passionate love of the forest, I came to believe that plants have all the attributes of other living creatures, though in a different form, for they react so certainly, so variously and so promptly to the outer world. While we cannot decipher all plant responses, not understanding what they 'say' to one another or what they 'shout' at us, by observing them closely we can see the most amazing things. Carnivorous plants will grasp at a fly with infallible accuracy, moving in just the right direction at just the right time; some parasitical plants recognize and even react to even the slightest odoriferous whiff of their victim, overcoming all obstacles to crawl stealthily in the right direction. There are those plants that seem to know which insects come only to plunder their nectar and so shut themselves up when a thief is about, opening only when the dew on the stem is sufficient to foil the marauder. Other more sophisticated types actually enlist the help of certain ants in a protective role, rewarding them with nectar in return for their warding off harmful insects and herbivorous mammals. My mother showed us some orchids that grow petals to mimic the species of a fly so perfectly that the male attempts to mate with it and in so doing pollinates it. The night-blossoming flowers around us were pure white in order to attract night moths and night-flying butterflies more easily, exuding a stronger fragrance at dusk to lure them, and rather than the delicate perfume of its type, the carrion lily made itself smell awful, like rotting meat, so that it would attract flies in areas where only flies abounded. There was so much to observe and learn, and later I believed that I could have devoted my life to the close investigation of the structural ingenuity of plants.

As we wandered through the forest, I loved searching for and picking my favourite flowers, the beautifully scented wild *Carissa edulis* blossoms that I would, on arrival, give to my Granny Webb. It wasn't long before those flowers became known by the family as 'Daphne flowers', and even now they conjure the memories of our weekly forest walks and all that my mother taught me.

Wednesdays at Granny and Grandpa Webb's house were special to us, for we could do almost anything we wanted. First, though, we had to line up against the wall for Grandpa Webb to 'measure' us to see how much we had grown. We were then 'straightened' and lectured about how to carry ourselves properly. Once released, my first port of call was the linen cupboard in the bathroom, where Granny kept her soaps that smelled of cedar, lavender and roses all rolled into one. Then I would ask if I could wear her jewels. Bouncing into her room, I would sit on the bed. There was one stipulation for trying on all her jewellery, and that was that I had to remain seated on the bed during the process, Buddha-like, with rings, bangles, necklaces and brooches festooned around my neck, arms, legs and fingers, her precious gold watch ticking quietly on my wrist. To this day each item is still imprinted in my mind, and some I now own. It was the gold watch that fascinated me the most, because I knew that I would have to wait until my fifteenth birthday in order to possess a watch of my own.

I would sit on the bed happily for an hour or so, examining and marvelling at every piece, not moving off the bed until I heard my siblings calling for me to join in the shop-keeping game, which involved dressing up in all our grandparents' old clothes and 'shopping' for the items on the pantry shelves. The morning would come to an end when we were called for lunch, when there would always be my favourite sago pudding, tinted pink or yellow, fluffy and delicious, topped by meringue in the shape of Mount Kenya, or Grandpa Webb's famous potato scones, for which I still have the recipe written in his own hand. Wednesdays were, without doubt, very special days of my childhood.

As I turned four, Peter and Sheila went off to boarding school, initially to a school near Nakuru. Betty was just a baby, no good for exploring outdoors, so without my two older siblings I was bereft and lonely. To make matters worse, just before they left,

Ricky-Ticky-Tavey had decided to explore the nooks and crannies of Never Die's engine and my father, completely oblivious to our favourite mongoose's whereabouts, had wanted to use the car that day with tragic results. The entire family was plunged into mourning that treasured little friend. As usual I busied myself with my special rabbits, cats, chicks and ducklings. But then, overnight, my life changed: I was given the responsibility of caring for an orphaned baby bushbuck. I named this little forest-dwelling antelope Bushy and I loved him totally, right from the very first moment he arrived.

Bushy was the first creature to provide me with an insight into the wonders of the wild animal kingdom. He was gorgeous to look at, with large soft ears and beautiful liquid eyes, his skin of a rich chestnut colour with white patches on his throat and vertical white stripes and spots on his body. I could spend ages just stroking and cuddling him. My gardener friend helped me make a retreat for him, laboriously cutting brush and stacking it in a corner of the chicken run. This was a great success, Bushy immediately hiding himself inside, emerging every four hours for his bottle-feeds of diluted cow's milk. At first I was disappointed that he hid himself away for so long, since I wanted to play with him as much as possible, so I would try and drag him out, but my mother explained to me that as a baby, before Bushy was orphaned, his mother would have hidden him away for his own protection and being so young he only really felt safe when hidden. She told me that because I loved him and didn't make him do things he couldn't yet do, as he grew up he would start to spend more time out of hiding. So at first I sat beside his new home most of the day, just to keep him company, and at night carried him to the little schoolroom so that he could be with the cats and safe from the leopards. Granny Webb's friend Mrs Hansen gave me a little bell that I tied around Bushy's neck, and from then on I could always locate him as he later spent more time frolicking around the garden. As he grew up and became more independent, Bushy became more responsive. I would talk to him endlessly, absolutely convinced that he understood everything I said to him.

But wild animals are wild animals, more ancient and sophisticated than us. Knowledge vital to survival is instinctive – what to eat, what to fear, who they are and how to behave in their ordered communities is knowledge imprinted at birth, so that they come into the world already programmed to a certain extent. In hand-raised animals, however, natural instincts lie latent, suppressed by soft and safe living, so they must be honed by exposure to a wild situation.

This is one of the most difficult aspects of raising wild animals – knowing when it is the right time to open the stable door at night and expose your hand-raised baby to natural dangers and finding the courage to do so, knowing that its future is now at Nature's mercy. But it is an essential part of rehabilitation. Only then does everything begin to fall into place, and what was once your garden pet becomes what it was destined to be – another member of the wild community, faced with the spectre of Nature's most powerful tool, natural selection.

Through exposure to the wild, an animal learns a number of vital lessons: the early warnings of danger in the language of birds; the alarm calls of monkeys and other animals; the hidden messages in scents on grass stems, in dung piles, in the wind and, most importantly, the rank and status within its own hierarchy. Such things cannot be taught by a human foster-mother, for we humans are too far removed and remote from Nature and have lost the skills that once, long ago, we must have possessed in common with others of the animal kingdom. All a human foster-parent can do is provide the right circumstances and a secure base from which an orphaned animal can begin to explore and to which it can return, if threatened, until it finds its own niche in the wild community. You should not raise an orphaned animal unless you can be certain that it will be able to enjoy a good quality of life at the end of its dependent years, or unless you are sure that you can be unselfish enough to grant it freedom when the time is right.

This much I now know, but at four years old I loved Bushy so unconditionally that I would have given all my hailstone ice cream to him. As far as I was concerned he loved me back and we were going to be together for ever. I knew that I had to be gentle with him and I loved to be with him, chatting to him incessantly, trailing him around the garden, feeding him, settling him and fondling him. I could see that being confined made him unhappy, so I let him out to roam outside the chicken run. There was nothing I would not have done for him, and I mistakenly thought that his affection for me was such that he would never choose to run away.

He vanished on the same day that one of my grandparents' friends, Mrs Hansen, passed away at their house. I was inconsolable and shed tears of bitter loss. Later, when I understood that a wild pet is simply on loan for its dependent years before that mysterious inherited genetic memory we call 'instinct' manifests itself, with hindsight I knew that Bushy did what was only natural, but aged four I felt as if my heart would break. As for Granny's friend, Mrs Hansen, I was confused. Later that day we were bundled into Never Die and taken to Granny and Grandpa Webb's house. I pleaded with Granny Webb to let me see her.

'She has gone to God,' whispered Granny, tears welling in her eyes.

'No, she hasn't,' I said. 'I can see her there in the bed.'

'That is just her body in the bed, her spirit has flown off,' said Granny.

I looked up at the ceiling to see if anything was flying around but there was nothing there, so I cried anyway, but more for Bushy than for Mrs Hansen. Life seemed unbearably sad.

Nevertheless, with a child's resilience, it wasn't long before I cheered up, for it was soon a favourite time of the year, entailing the annual and much anticipated journey to Granny and Grandpa Webb's seaside cottage at Malindi. They had bought this as a holiday home for the family, eventually moving there from Gilgil some years later. Memories of going there as a child, of packing up at the farm, of the always adventure-filled journey, and the excitement of the first headlong run into the sea, remain so sharp in my mind that whenever I return each year, I can still see and hear myself and my family in the house, on the beach, and body-surfing in the sea.

In the summer of 1939, when I was five years old, with the clouds of war gathering and the air thick with uncertainty, my parents decided we would make the journey again by road while we could. Preparations started weeks beforehand – my father making hams, bacon and sausages and my mother baking endless biscuits and crackers, stacking them up in a huge wooden box; oiling dozens of eggs to keep them fresh and making biltong, the salted spiced meat that she doused in vinegar and hung out to dry. My father converted the back of an old Ford V8 lorry into a reasonably comfortable space for us children, though there was such a lot that had to be taken with us that we had to squash up together most of the time. We set off at 4 a.m., hardly waking from sleep as my father carried us from our warm beds, but when the dawn lit the sky in a blaze of colour as we approached Nairobi, we awoke from our dreams to the thrill of a real life adventure.

Nairobi was the very apex of civilization to us, back in those days. First, my father stopped the truck on the outskirts of the town so that we could change into our best clothes, because my mother wanted us to all look smart, in case we saw someone we knew. Nairobi was a wonder to us children: huge crowds of people; shops and stalls piled high with goods; a cacophony of alien sounds, so different to those of the natural world. We talked about what we had seen for days afterwards as we journeyed on to the Athi plains, where we set up camp for the night. Our parents slept under a tarpaulin attached to the back of the truck, while we stayed in the back, the canvas replaced by a large mosquito net through which we could see the moon and the stars. The night chorus of the Athi plains was always marked by the incessant background symphony of thousands of wildebeest and zebra, interspersed by the eerie howl of hyenas and the barking of jackals, while the deep-throated roar of a lion triggered a brief hush.

The journey was like no other, each step revealing something new. My favourite stop was in the heart of the nyika, near Mtito Andei, 'the place of the vultures', where the soil was red and sandy and the sultry air was filled with the fragrance of earth mingled with wild sage. The scenery here was rugged and spectacular in its vastness, reflecting in its expanse a sense of eternity. The skies were a crystal-clear blue, and the towering dome of Kilimanjaro lent majesty and power. The sun beat down, baking the blood-red earth with intensity, and the air was filled with the excited and urgent chatter of bright yellow weaverbirds as they hung upside down along the branches of the acacia trees, building their intricately woven nests. We camped beneath the twisted branches of a massive baobab, the tree that many Africans regard as the home of their ancestral spirits and whose flowers last for such a short time. There was life in the folds, indentations and wrinkles of its pith bark, the nest of a pair of hornbills deep inside, having walled themselves up, closing the fold with mud, leaving just a small slit for the male bird to pass grasshoppers and insects to his wife inside. There were chameleons, lizards and back-fanged arboreal boomslang snakes searching for hatchlings and eggs. In the evening we saw enchanting little bush-babies with large, round, liquid eyes – nocturnal monkeys with eyes like orbs, and yellowish limbs and tails, that were constantly on the go. Small black-and-white-spotted genet cats, which were actually more like mongooses than cats, ran across the boughs with amazing agility, thanks to little suction pads on their feet. We took some of the white pulp of pure cream of tartar from the baobab's big hanging fruits and saw how the emptied capsules could be used as water dippers. My mother explained how the fibrous wood was used to make paper and bags and the roots a red dye. Many of the trees, she told us, were deliberately hollowed out to serve as water storage tanks, trapping rainwater in their giant bowls, where it kept pure and fresh for months afterwards. This giant tree with a life expectancy of thousands of years was a world in itself. Lying under it at night I felt secure, as if the tree was exuding safety as well as shelter.

As we journeyed on and came nearer and nearer to the sea, we argued happily in the back of the lorry as to which of us could spot the first coconut palm and then the sea itself. At Mariakani, on the outskirts of Mombasa, we cracked our first coconut and ate the first mango of our holiday. We children could not stop staring at the women from the Giriama tribe, who strode around expertly balancing receptacles on their heads, bare above the waist, with their breasts swinging above short, heavily pleated calico skirts, some with a baby slung across their backs. At Mombasa we stopped to get Betty and our grandparents, who had travelled down by train and had had a much smoother ride, albeit less exciting, than ours. My father then had to negotiate a taxi to take them on the last stage of the journey to Malindi, his dialogue in Swahili constantly interrupted by Granny Chart, who was a more formidable haggler. We spent a night in Mombasa, which had an atmosphere all of its own, the smell of spices and frying fish mingling with the heady scent of the ocean.

The final leg to Malindi was just a rough sandy track with two creeks that had to be crossed by ferry, and this took all day. The highlight was the ferries, each of which consisted of a huge wooden platform supported by floating drums that could carry about three cars as well as our lorry, all elaborately coaxed aboard by an old foreman who waggled a ping-pong bat furiously to position the vehicles just right, even though it was puzzling trying to understand what the signals meant! When everything was to his satisfaction, the leader of the ferrymen made a series of loud honking blasts on a conch shell, a seemingly crystal-clear signal, because almost at once a wonderful rhythmic stamping dance and elaborate song about the passengers started up. At first I was mesmerized by the rocking of the ferry, for the ferrymen seemed to want to outdo each other in how much they could stomp. Soon, however, I was listening to the words of the song, for by this age I understood and could speak Swahili. The men started singing about my father and his family, pointing at us children, and this made us feel really important, being singled out for special mention.

Eventually we reached Malindi, and as our beach cottage came into view we were already stripped down to our costumes so that we could leap over the dozens of large pink ghost crabs and jump straight into the sea. Grandpa and Granny Webb's cottage overlooked the best section of the bay, where the beach sloped gently into the surf and the currents were benign, so the bathing was safe. However, when the tide was low, the waves turned into what we called 'dumpers', and these needed to be treated with great caution. Huge swells that coasted silently in long lines towards the shore suddenly reared up in a curling arc of translucent green to thunder down in shallow water, throwing spray high into the air and stirring up the sand of the seabed. It was one of these savage 'dumpers' that broke my father's nose, picking his surfboard up and hurling him with incredible force into the sand face-first, so that he stumbled to the shore barely conscious, with blood pouring down his face. 'It must have been a shark,' whispered Sheila to me, Peter and Betty, as my mother ran down the path from the house to reach him. In fact, no person to my knowledge has ever been taken by a shark in Malindi Bay, but our parents used the threat of them, saying that they fed at night as a way of making sure we did not go into the sea after dark.

The time we spent at Malindi was magical. My parents were relaxed, away from the sweat and toil of the farm; Grandpa Webb and Granny Chart settled into their annual ceasefire and my brother and sisters and I spent our entire time either in the sea or on the beach. The cottage was also almost outdoors, its roof Makuti matting fashioned from palm leaves, so that the ocean breeze could blow free under the wide eaves. The toilet facilities were the same as at our farm – 'a Long Drop' behind the house, with a wooden box over a very deep hole, hollowed out to form the seat, under which were huge cobwebs, massive spiders, unblinking geckos and perhaps even a skulking snake – so I chose to use the chamberpot as much as I could, even though I had to withstand the constant jibes of my siblings.

After the initial days spent swimming in the sea and playing in the sand, I would beg my mother to take me to the local coral reef so that I could catch some of the brilliantly coloured baby coral fish to start up my own little aquarium. Armed with nets and buckets we would follow the tide out, treading carefully over the flat surface of the reef, covered in sea grasses and bright green sea lettuce, to avoid the hermit crabs that were busy carrying their shell homes on their backs, while mudhoppers used their pectoral fins as tiny legs to shoot across the shallows. We also had to look out for the black waving arms of many different kinds of brittle stars, which protruded from every nook and cranny, as well as the sharp spines of the sea urchins, which could penetrate our tennis shoes. On the shore side of the far reef there was a deep channel where the corals grew undisturbed, breathtakingly beautiful in a variety of shapes, sizes and subtle colours. This was a whole new world, with multitudes of fish of every hue and shape. The far reef was the most fascinating of all, for here, embedded in the coral and covered in barnacles, was the wreck of an old ship.

It was the Blue Lagoon at Watamu, the ocean to the south of Malindi, that gave me the greatest pleasure. Unlike today, the lagoon was remote and untouched, frequented only by fishermen from a small Giriama settlement inland from the sea. There were twin lagoons, separated by an ancient coral headland, whose rugged walls had been hollowed out by the sea to create cool shaded caves that became exposed at low tide and provided ideal shelter in the heat of the day. In some of the caves the retreating tide left little pools, and the sunlight filtering through the orifices in the headland above would create prisms that reflected all the colours of the rainbow. The effect was magical. Depending on which monsoon was blowing at the time, one or other of the lagoons would be choked with an enormous pile of seaweed, but always one would be clean, its sands pure white, comprised of minute particles of pounded shell. Here, the coral heads, viewed through our goggles, were even more beautiful than those at Malindi's coral reef, and the fish more brilliant because the water was so clear and not sullied by the silt-laden waters of the Sabaki River. Shining blue and red parrot fish pecked at their coral castles, black and white scorpion fish skulked in their hideaways, butterfly and surgeon fish floated and darted, while bright red starfish and shells of all sizes, colours and shapes littered the ocean floor.

The lagoon and its magical spectacle of marine life was the nearest I ever got to the fairyland fantasies of my childhood. I remember it with deep nostalgia, and it always makes me think of Karen Blixen's words: 'Yes, this is how it was meant to be.'

It was my last summer of innocence.

3. Growing Up

'I stand enriched, endowed with a priceless heritage that is my very own.
While on this earth no man can take away from me the sun, the sea, the
warm south wind that softly whispers by.'

– My mother, 1950

After my near-perfect early years, life changed and I had to grow up
rather swiftly. As the Second World War got under way, the Government needed to find a way of feeding the British and Kenyan troops
fighting in Abyssinia (Ethiopia) and deployed in Burma, as well as the
Italian prisoners-of-war captured in Abyssinia and the German prisoners captured in the Middle East. In order to provide food, thousands
of animals had to be massacred, and for this task my father was chosen to shoot wildebeest and zebra in the Southern Game Reserve, at
a place called Selengai. This area covered over 10,000 square miles of
prime game country that encompassed the eastern edge of the Loita
plains near Narok, swept over the Athi plains beyond Nairobi, to
Amboseli at the foothills of Kilimanjaro, stopping at the fringes of
what is now Tsavo West National Park. The terrain consisted of forest, high and low bushland, savannah and an unforgiving thorn
scrubland. It was an area teeming with wildlife.

My father had no choice but to accept the assignment and he did
so with a heavy heart – not only because he had to leave the farm for
six weeks at a time but also because of the destruction he was going
to have to cause. By the end of the war he had shot thousands of
wildebeest and zebra, and I know just how devastating this was for
him. At least, if there is any comfort to be had, there was no one better than my father to carry out such work. He was a sensitive
naturalist, a man who cared deeply about wildlife, and he ensured

that no wounded animal was ever left to suffer the agony of a painful and lingering death. And he certainly helped keep the troops and prisoners-of-war alive, sending over 100 sacks of food every day to Nairobi from Emali, the nearest railway siding to his camp. Disappointed at first that as a farmer he had been assigned a non-combative task, he joined the Kenya Defence Force for part-time duties, but of course my mother was secretly delighted that he had not been sent to the front line, as was his mother, Granny Chart.

Although I was young, I could tell that the war was of grave concern to the adults. My father would be glued to the radio every time there was a news bulletin, and all the grown-ups would be continually absorbed in deep conversations, their voices low and their expressions troubled. Only Grandpa Webb seemed to be energized, polishing brass buckles and his First World War medals – 'Getting ready to fight the Germans,' he told us, with great pride in his voice. Grandpa Webb had a bad leg, and I was very worried about how he was going to manage if he met a German soldier: 'You will only be able to kick with one leg,' I pointed out. With his characteristic humour, Grandpa Webb was not to be deterred and took to showing us how he would fight, hopping around on one leg using his fists as a decoy. Later though, in a more deluded moment, he presented himself for call-up to the authorities, resplendent in khaki and with an old-fashioned topi on his head. He was pretty incensed at being told that he was too old to be of much use this time around.

Aged six, I joined my siblings as a boarder at the school in Nakuru. Mostly I liked school, and though sad when we were dropped off at the start of each term, I soon got used to the routine and to sharing my life with so many others. In that childlike way of wanting everything to fit nicely into place, I remember being confused by the words of the school song, which included a description of Lake Nakuru as 'the placid lake below', stating that I thought a lake needed to have water in it in order to be a lake! When we had stopped to take a look on our way from Gilgil, it had been a dry dustbowl where powdered soda soil was picked up by whirlwinds and showered like a sprinkling of acrid-smelling talc all over the town, including, as it turned out, the school. Fortunately, however, a little while later the drought broke and the rains transformed it, tranquil and beautiful; I watched in wonder as the birds came back – over 400 species in all, we were told – to join the pink spectacle of the resident flamingos. The flamingos lent what can only be described as an ethereal presence to the lake, like ballet dancers, their graceful necks bent delicately as they filtered the algae from the surface of the water. The pelicans and the shoals of fish, the little tilapia fish in particular, were equally interesting. At the lakeside you could see the males busily excavating their tiny breeding pits by picking up one particle of sand at a time, spitting it out over the rim and bombarding rival males with invisible jets of water. Whenever a female showed any interest in a pit, she was treated to an eager display by the male, side on, so that the light could reflect the pretty body colouring of the flanks. Mating took place above the pit, but as soon as the eggs were laid and fertilized, the female scooped them into her mouth and there, in due course, they hatched, the fry safe in the haven of her mouth until they were about half an inch long and ready to fend for themselves. Whenever my parents or grandparents came to take us for a picnic outing on the shores of the lake, I would spend ages mesmerized as I studied the fishes' quaint habits.

I was less enamoured of the 'sick-bay' routine at school. Every day after breakfast those that had to lined up for 'treatment', which was meted out by one of our ferocious teacher-spinsters. This was Miss Chart, the Matron, severely clad in starched white and with the gruff voice of a man. When I had first learned her name, I was terrified that she might be a relative of ours, but Granny Chart had assured me that she wasn't. I was always in the line-up because my mother had arranged that I had to have extra milk, Virol and Scott's Emulsion in an effort to put some more flesh on my bones – something that today is quite a family joke.

Our headmaster, Mr Whiddett, dominated our schooldays, meting out the most humiliating punishments – acts that thankfully would not be tolerated today. I can still remember the feeling of dread as he prowled around the room like a leopard looking for pupils who had scored less than five out of ten in the weekly mental arithmetic test.

Once spotted you would be hurled into the corner and made to declaim 'I am stupid', or literally picked up and thrown outside the door. On one occasion, we had to open our desks, put our heads inside and wait for him to slam down the lid. I ended up with a chipped front tooth but consoled myself that it was better than his usual treatment of girls, which was to fumble our breasts and mutter, 'Coming along nicely.' What made my parents invite him to our summer safari one year is something I have never been able to understand. I suppose in those days we did not realize that such behaviour was entirely unacceptable, nor talk as openly to our parents as children do these days.

Of course there were kindly members of staff too – my class teacher, who took us all the way through primary school level, was a lovely bald-headed Welshman whom we called 'Pop Davis', and Sheila's class teacher was Arthur Brindlay, a tall, genial Englishman. In an incredible turn of events some forty years later, Arthur was to become Sheila's lover following the break-up of her long-standing marriage, something that floored even my parents!

In 1940, as soon as the first long holiday came around, my mother took us to my father's camp at Selengai. As soon as I saw the location of the camp I thought, 'This is how I would like to live, out here among the animals under the sky.' My father had established the living area in a grove of tall yellow-barked acacia trees that cast a deep shade over about an acre of land, and he had managed to utilize the area so that it was contained but appeared spacious. A large mosquito net, strung from a branch, covered our dining area, while on the outskirts of the shade was my parents' sleeping tent with a cot for Betty, each space covered by nets. Peter had his own tent, which the Higginson brothers shared when they joined us, which seemed to be always. Our bathroom was a small enclosure of cut thornbush in which was a canvas bath, and the kitchen was situated to the side of the dining area with an eye to the prevailing wind. My father had made an ingenious safari stove from an upended army gallon drum and it even had a chimney, which meant my mother could bake the things we usually ate at home.

Aside from drying the meat into biltong – sun-dried meat first soaked in tubs of briny salt water – my father knew exactly what to do with every usable part of the animal. He had set up a 'biltong factory' along with his indispensable aides, two Italian prisoners-of-war: Dario, a mechanic who spoke a bit of English and loved to make spaghetti – which, incredibly, he hung out on the washing lines to dry – and Ferrara, who spoke no English but was a skilled hide and skin tanning expert. I was a regular visitor to the 'factory', though I balked at the sight of the massive slabs of meat laid out on giant wooden boards. It was there that the forty employees of the Wakamba tribe, wearing their distinctive grass hats with zebra chinstraps and singing at the tops of their voices, soaked the cut-up meat in huge tubs of brine, salt, pepper and vinegar, leaving it overnight before hanging it to dry in strips on an extensive shaded network of wire lines. My father told us that all parts of the animal were put to good use: the hides of the wildebeest and zebra were bagged separately, bound for America, where they were made into machine belting; the bones were ground down into bonemeal for animal feed and fertilizer; the hairs from the manes and tails were turned into bristles for brushes and brooms. There was also leftover fresh meat – the offal in particular, which was not suitable for biltong and which my father gave to the Wakamba workers. There had been a drought in their arid tribal land, and by working at the 'factory' they were able to take back nourishment for their hungry families. They regarded offal as a delicacy.

Compared to the sprawling nature of our farm and the winding corridors of my school, the camp was a perfectly organized enclave and I loved the different sections – the mess tent and kitchen area, our sleeping area, the biltong lines and the staff tents – and having all my family so close by. When we had visitors, Sheila and I had to vacate our tent to sleep under a tarpaulin open at one end, where my mother erected a barricade of camp chairs, its sides anchored by two planks of wood. It was at these times that my sister and I became somewhat edgy when darkness set in. The smell of meat attracted predators of all shapes and sizes every night, not least lions. Their roaring kept us awake, but what truly scared us, lying there in the pitch darkness, was the rhythmic rasping of their tongues as they licked the sides of our sleeping shelter. The lions could not resist the flavoursome tarpaulin, which had previously been used to carry salt. The thought that only a flimsy piece of canvas separated lions' faces from ours was daunting, to say the least, and Sheila and I both wriggled up as close to the middle as possible, often ending up shoving each other out of the way while trying not to disturb the lions. We were much less wary of the resident leopard that lived around the camp, while the eerie calling and laughing sounds of the hyena didn't worry us at all, for those epitomized the African night. Eventually, however, we would fall asleep, and would wake to the chorus of birdsong and a refreshing silence once all the predators had dispersed by sunrise.

Every morning before the day's activities began we had to endure the ritual of tick prevention. Ticks were everywhere and they got into every part of our anatomy, but although they irritated us like mad, I couldn't help being fascinated by their splendid variety – striped legs, spotted legs, red legs, yellow legs, spotted legs with green stripes, so it went on. We didn't have any insect repellent or sunblock in those days, so my mother rubbed Great-Granny Aggett's good old cure-all combination of paraffin and oil over us. It didn't make much difference, if truth be told, and in the evenings we had to stand still for what seemed like ages while we were ceremoniously de-ticked.

Days in the bush were full of adventure. I was impressed with my mother as the driver of the carcass-lorry, and we would set off each morning with my father and Muteti, his Wakamba gun-bearer, who was an expert tracker and bushman. He and Muteti would jump out to stalk their quarry on foot, leaving my mother and us children in the lorry. The vultures learned to follow the lorry, knowing it would lead to a kill and a meal, and they would circle overhead eyeing the meat. My father could look up from wherever he was and, from the position of the vultures in the sky, know exactly where we were. I thoroughly enjoyed the thrill of the occasional rhino chase, for this caused a real adrenalin rush. If we stumbled upon a rhino at close quarters and it turned to charge, my mother would have to drive away at a ferocious speed, bouncing over anthills and pig-holes, threading a tortuous route through stunted thickets with an angry rhino huffing and puffing hot on our heels. I can only imagine that her heart must have been racing faster than the engine.

We were at the camp for the full six-week cycle. I would often remain behind in camp and jump on the lorry heading down to the Sand River – the lifeblood of the area – to fill the drums with water drawn from a deep hole excavated in the sand. The water in this hole was clear and pure, having been filtered through the riverbed sand, and we all drank it without a second thought. We sat in the cool shade, from where we could watch the game come down to drink in the shallow pools: the sand grouse settling in soft sandy clouds to drink, and the little dwarf mongooses that reminded me of Ricky-Ticky-Tavey busily scuffling in the debris beneath the trees, looking for insects and disappearing down the holes of the anthills when disturbed. The Masai would bring their huge herds of cattle to drink at the river, and because of the dry sand it would take the entire morning to get all the animals watered. I was calmed by the patience of two of the young men, who organized them in such an orderly way. Back at camp, local Masai men and women would come round to touch our hair, truly puzzled as to how we made it and attached it so firmly to our heads, but we weren't really able to talk to them to explain! And when we were playing music on our wind-up gramophone, they would turn away, startled by this talking contraption which for them bordered on magic. For me, as well, it seemed close to magic, for I could not yet fathom how it worked either. Sitting for hours by the water we children were able, through gestures and expression, to communicate with these young Masai men. They seemed to like children, for every few days they would come to the camp and offer my parents and us a calabash of milk and blood, which had a strong smell of smoke. The blood bit did not appeal to us at all, but we thanked them politely and in exchange often gave them empty bottles, something they truly appreciated as receptacles for milk.

These were days of discovery. That is how I remember Selengai as a child, but later, when I heard my parents talk of this period of our lives, I realized just how difficult the upheaval was for them and what a grim toll that work took on my father. For me, the hours of observing the habits and patterns of such a wide variety of wildlife at such close quarters contributed hugely to my lifelong connection to

Nature. I learned a great deal, not least from an orphan of the time named Punda, a tiny zebra foal. Out one day on the plains, a heavily pregnant mare fell to Dario's gun, and when one of the helpers immediately opened up her stomach cavity to haul out the viscera there was a uterus in which a foetus was stirring, obviously waiting to be born. A quick slash of the knife opened the bag and the baby, all wet and sticky and kicking feebly, gasped to draw its first breath. It had entered a cruel world in a tragic way, and when my father arrived on the scene he extracted some of the vital colostrum milk from the mother's still warm udder to reinforce the foal's natural immune system. We were the first moving objects that the baby saw, and, having staggered on to wobbly legs, he walked straight up to me with an innocence and an implicit trust that touched my heart and made me want to protect him for ever. We lifted him on to the lorry, where he snuggled up beside me, and as soon as we got back to camp, my mother and I mixed the colostrum milk with some sweetened condensed milk in a baby's bottle and I fed him with as much love as I could show. Thereafter, observing Punda develop from the moment of his birth allowed me a valuable insight into zebras, as we brought him back to the farm with us where he settled in well, making friends with everyone, especially the dogs. Sadly, this was to be his undoing, as several months later he followed the dogs down to the sawmill in the forest and was never seen again.

And so, as I edged into double figures, the war years passed. Near Gilgil town there was a large army staging depot, which was always a constant buzz of activity as supplies and soldiers came in and out. My parents offered our farm as a retreat for injured servicemen and women from the fighting in neighbouring Abyssinia or Italian Somaliland, and I can still vividly recall some who stayed with us – not only because they spent so much time recounting their experiences but also because they brought us treats of imported biscuits and sweets. My parents formed deep and lasting friendships with some whose paths would never have crossed with ours in less forbidding circumstances. When peace was declared, even though the main fields of battle were so far away in Europe and Burma, there was much talk in our community of the atrocities of war, the loss of so many valuable lives, of lessons being learned, and prayers for a better future for our generation across the world.

Back at school, I did well at the academic side and applied myself diligently to the curriculum. My mother had given us a good grounding. When news came from home that my father's biltong location had been changed to the Narok district and our safari would now take place in the Mara – a lush area that benefits from Lake Victoria and higher rainfall, providing a good habitat for animals – Sheila and I ran around in great excitement, but when my sister turned the page over to read on, her face fell. 'They have invited Mr Whiddett to come too,' she said, and in the look we then exchanged, it was clear that we were appalled and would not be going to make things easy for him.

However, even this blow could not spoil our excitement as the holidays drew near again. Today the Mara is the most famous tourist wildlife paradise on earth, but back then it was undeveloped and untouched, pristine and beautiful, with a greater abundance of animals than even the Southern Game Reserve. Our camp was near Subutai, a sugarloaf hill in an extensive grove of tall yellow-barked acacias about thirty miles from the Uaso Nyiro River. We thought it might even have been on Great-Grandpa Aggett's original holding, and were entranced all over again by my father's stories of his pioneering family. Setting up camp, Sheila and I made sure we were as far away as possible from Mr Whiddett, managing with a bit of prompting to get his tent erected way out on a limb on the far side of the camp.

It was exciting to explore this largely unexplored country. We travelled in the lorry slowly across the endless plains in order to avoid the large aardvark holes, each new plain a spectacle filled with animals – wildebeest and zebra, topi and kongoni hartebeest, Grant and Thomson gazelles, their tiny tails busily flickering like windscreen wipers. Herds of buffalo and elephants moved in and out of the thickets along with rhinos, some accompanied by a calf at foot. Each plain seemed to hold a resident pride of lions, and each lugga its own leopard. Warthogs popped up wherever we went, running along with their tails erect like flagpoles, and hyenas, disturbed by our passing, loped from rain-filled puddles in which they sat casting an appraising eye over the night's menu.

I had recently developed an interest in wildebeest – known affectionately as 'the clown of the plains' and the most advanced of the ungulates. We had learned from my father about the nomadic lifestyle of the Serengeti wildebeest and zebras, whose annual wanderings in search of fresh grazing encompassed 300 miles. Now I was able to observe them in their natural habitat – to see for myself how they lived in such close association, yet had almost no physical contact with each other, even when resting; how the bulls seemed to fight more for the acquisition and possession of territory rather than the proximity of a receptive female, and how often frenzied but short-lived ritual scuffles broke out among the males.

So it was with some sadness this time that I regarded the biltong lines, festooned with strips of drying wildebeest meat. This was no holiday for my father, Dario and Ferrara – they had a job to do – and the killing, cutting, drying was in full swing all over again. However, a problem soon arose. Here in the Mara it became clear that the newly recruited team were not half as efficient as the old, many of the workers not being cut out for this type of work and deserting their posts. My father began to despair of being able to fulfil his contract deadline, until one morning when the most unexpected thing happened. It was Peter who first heard the distant but familiar singing and called to us to come and listen. Soon we could just make out a distant line of about fifty men jogging towards us, and as they came nearer, we heard the familiar words '*Ngaw, Ngaw Mama, Ngaw Ngaw miwe!*' We simply could not believe it. The old Selengai team, headed by Muteti, had arrived as though in answer to a prayer. They had managed to pay their own train fare to Kijabe station, then walked and sang the remaining eighty miles to camp.

My father was so moved that words failed him as the men clustered round, smiling, trying to shake our hands, which were pumped up and down energetically. Soon my father was smiling as broadly as the men, amid much cheering and singing. But then he had to tell Muteti that he could only employ twenty men. There followed a spirited discussion among the group, who decided, with extreme good nature, that this dilemma could be easily solved by a running race and the top twenty runners would stay. We were enthusiastic spectators, leaping up and down and shouting encouragement as the runners sprinted off in a cloud of dust across the plains, and from that moment on everything went as smoothly as it had at Selengai.

For us children, the rest of the safari passed by all too quickly in a haze of days, and a wealth of new experiences: creeping through the bush at the Barakitabu hot springs to spy on Mr Whiddett taking a bath; collecting the soft belly feathers of the Marabou storks; becoming more proficient along with my brother at target practice and even being allowed to spend a night in my brother's game blind – a hide he had fashioned where we could sit hidden from view and observe the wildlife at close quarters – even though Sheila and I were frog-marched back to the camp when we got the giggles; travelling three full days to Jagitiek to try to find the legendary black-maned lions and then, best of all, returning to camp to hear that the war was over. It surprised us that Dario and Ferrara were upset – 'We will have to be returned to Italy and we will miss you.' However, the rest of us were jubilant, and I breathed a prayer of thanks that there would be no more prisoners to feed, and no need to kill any more animals for biltong. We celebrated with a huge bush banquet, afterwards enjoying the most memorable and competitive game of 'kick the tin' ever, our version of hide and seek, played in the late evening in failing light and involving a lot of noisy excitement as players exploded out of hiding places. We returned home to our farm some days later when we had to take Dario and Ferrara to the army barracks in Gilgil for repatriation back to Italy. This was difficult for all of us, as we had got on so well together. We often envisaged them recounting to their grandchildren tales of their wild time in Africa.

Towards the end of the war a terrible drought depleted the farm's cattle herd and my father was forced to think of a new way to generate income for the family. Ever resourceful and keen to sell milk in good quantity, he imported some pedigree Ayrshire cattle from Australia – four heifers and two bulls – and did this for two years in succession. Although imported livestock were particularly susceptible to Africa's tick bovine diseases, ours actually flourished and within time bred over fifty calves. Some of the milking cows yielded up to four gallons a day, which guaranteed us a regular income, as did the sale of the bull calves. The new additions were the inspiration behind my father's inventive 'spray race' – a neat alternative to the conventional dipping tank. Not wanting his aristocratic bovines to risk injury by jumping into a tank, he constructed a shower that sprayed them with insecticide as they walked sedately through. The first 'cow' to brave the invention was Sheila – sprayed with water – and it proved to be an enormous success, adopted and adapted by many of the local farmers.

When I turned thirteen I joined my older sister at the Kenya Girls' High School in Nairobi, where I settled in relatively easily, making close and to this day lasting friendships and distinguishing myself in the science as opposed to the arts stream. In adolescence, my previously straight and straggly hair turned thick and curly and was tamed into a bob, and my figure turned feminine for the better. In tandem with my classmates I was to acquire a 'Patch' boyfriend – 'Patch' being the nickname given to the Prince of Wales School, where my brother, Peter, had completed his secondary education. In those days further academic tuition at university level was an option only for those aspiring to be a doctor or vet, for which a university degree was essential. We knew that our father could not afford the fees, quite apart from the fact that none of us girls even entertained the idea of becoming academics. We were much more practical, anxious to earn our own money in order to relieve the burden on our parents and get on with our lives; eventually getting married, with a family of our own and living happily ever after, as had our parents. As it turned out, I was smitten early even by the standards of the day, for at the age of fifteen I fell madly in love with Bill Woodley, an ex-Patch boy, who at the time was working as a junior assistant warden in Nairobi National Park alongside my brother, who had also joined the new National Parks Service. We had a lot in common – he was Kenyan-born, crazy about wildlife and committed to Nature. Rather amazingly, he fell in love with me, much to the envy of my friends. On days when we were allowed out, he would pull up outside school in his lorry, named Lena, which had been left to him in a legacy, and toot for me to join him; dressed in his bush jacket, he looked even more handsome than usual. Aged twenty, he was considered sophisticated and worldly, a catch above the usual schoolboys my peers dated. By now I was a school prefect, charged with keeping order in my 'house' and setting a good example to the younger pupils. I was obsessed with being in love with Bill, and during the holidays I tried to acquire items for my 'bottom drawer', nice linen and other household items, something that was fashionable in those days to set one up for married life. Both Granny Webb and my mother, with all their gentle tact and wisdom, cautioned me about becoming too involved too young – 'There is no hurry, Daphne, no hurry at all' – but Bill and I were so wrapped up in each other that I could barely even wait around long enough for her to end her counsel. As far as I was concerned it was only a matter of time – I knew I had to finish school at least – before Bill and I would be married.

As we passed into the 1950s the fabric of life began to change, unrest among Africans gathering, slowly but surely. At first the turbulence was minor – negligence in work, small incidences of theft – but then, in a matter of months, it was clear that the unrest had moved on from local issues to something political and territorial. There were signs that the Mau Mau, who were an underground group of members of the Kikuyu, aimed to remove from Kenya British rule and European settlers, who they felt had dispossessed them of their land. The local policeman told us that clandestine meetings were becoming commonplace, as these activists went around gathering support for their cause with promises of land, houses, cars and all that the 'White Tribe' owned once they had been driven out or killed. Oathing ceremonies involving obscene rituals began to take place surreptitiously, often imposed under duress, some said to be so barbaric that the details were spoken of only in hushed whispers. The increased attacks on the livestock and property of the white farmers, plus an escalation in lawlessness, were all symptoms of the changing climate.

There were many discussions and firmly held views in my family and among our friends. It was impossible for Granny Chart, or any of us white Kenyans for that matter, to accept the Mau Mau view of the settlers as illegal intruders. Rather than brutal foreign colonizers, we and our ancestors were humane and totally honourable pioneers who had braved the unknown and, with blood, sweat and toil, brought progress to darkest Africa, promising law and order and good governance under benign British rule. Those in the know urged the British Government to quell the Mau Mau before it had time to turn an entire generation of youth, but these warnings went unheeded by Whitehall, and the intimidation meted out by the activists against those who gave witness against the organization, or who refused to take the secret oath of allegiance, became more brutal, barbaric and savage, with murder and mutilation turning into almost daily events.

At first, everyday life was not radically affected, but then as the evidence of carnage shifted – from strangled cats and headless dogs hung from trees, to white farmers brutally murdered – we had to restrict our movements. No longer could we stay out in the forest, and doors had to be locked by nightfall. My father moved his pedigree stock nearer the house and employed tribesmen not aligned to the Kikuyu, Embu and Meru to guard them at night.

It wasn't long before the horrific reality of the Mau Mau attacks struck at the heart of my family. In the dark depths of night, Grandpa and Granny Webb were robbed and badly beaten during a raid on their house by thugs suspected of being Mau Mau initiates. Actually, they were 'luckier' than neighbouring victims, who had been hacked into little pieces. Both my grandparents were assumed dead, clubbed into unconsciousness and left lying in pools of blood. Fortunately they suffered only relatively minor injuries and concussion, but the savagery of the attack, the hatred wielded upon them, left its emotional mark on them. There were no telephone links on the farms in those days and only a few people had radio communication. Unwilling to give up their independence by moving in with us, my grandparents were persuaded that they would be safer in their seaside cottage at Malindi. It was almost unbearable to think that we would now see each other only a few times a year, but this brutal attack left indelible scars on both my grandparents. Even Granny Chart was sorry to see them go, though remaining adamant that she would be staying put, and going nowhere, no matter what! She even refused my father's eminently sensible suggestion of taking in a police reservist as a lodger, saying that she did not want to have to look after him as well as herself. Fear was not a part of Granny Chart's DNA.

However, apprehension became a way of life on our farm. Our staff were nervous and edgy and no one ventured out after dark. One of our most joyful Mkamba workers (an individual member of the Wakamba tribe is known as a Mkamba), whom we nicknamed Kinanda, or 'the gramophone' because he was always singing, began to waste away. His behaviour changed, the singing stopped, and he became morose and withdrawn. All of us were worried, thinking some terrible illness was consuming him, so on the pretext of some work in the town, my father managed to get him into Never Die and drove him to the doctor in Nakuru. The outcome of extensive tests was puzzling, for the doctor could find no physical cause whatsoever for his decline. Upon returning home, Kinanda began to talk, but all he revealed was that he was doomed to die and there was simply nothing anyone could do about it. He wanted to continue to work for as long as possible, then go back to his ancestral land, where his bones would be laid to rest. We were devastated that he would want to give up his life like this and did our best to talk to him, but it was to no avail. My father suspected that a spell had been cast over him, so a succession of witch doctors were brought in, in the hope of countering anything sinister, but nothing worked. Kinanda continued to fade away before our very eyes, professing ignorance all along as to why he had lost the will to live. Finally he declared that it was time to be taken home to die, and with tears streaming down his sunken cheeks, and tears streaming down all our faces, we bade him farewell, knowing that this was the last time we would see each other.

Kinanda died shortly after. On his deathbed, he asked that a message be relayed to us. In an enforced Mau Mau oathing ceremony he had been ordered to murder us all, and because he refused to do this, loving the family too much to kill us in cold blood, a death curse was cast on him. His refusal to murder us had cost him his own life and that disturbed us unbearably. Kinanda's sacrifice is something that deeply affected us all and is still lodged inside me to this day.

*

I left school at sixteen, convinced I had fluffed the Senior Cambridge School Leaving exams, but as I was confident that my future was going to be with Bill, I decided that the most useful thing I could do was to acquire some skills about how to run a home efficiently. My mother was of like opinion, not because she thought I should be marrying Bill just yet, but because being a competent housewife was in her view an essential skill for life. Under her expert tutelage I embarked on a hectic three-month in-house domestic training course, learning how to organize a household, how to cook, how to clean, how to polish and garden. Family secrets, including Great-Granny Aggett's candle- and soap-making, were gifted to me, as well as tried and tested herbal cures for low-level illnesses and injuries. I also took this time to learn how to drive, suspecting that I only obtained my licence because the policeman conducting the test suffered whiplash when I did a rather jerky hill start and he probably never wanted to repeat the experience again. During those three months I acquired lifelong knowledge and skills that in turn I have passed on to my daughters, Gillian and Angela. I derive much pleasure, and a feeling of continuity, in seeing them follow the old pioneering recipes, even if some of the ingredients or methods have been updated in the interim.

It mattered to me and came as quite a surprise that I actually did well academically, even though I had been distracted. I passed my School Leaving Certificate with flying colours, placed eighth in the Colony and awarded a bursary that qualified me for free university education. My headmistress, Miss Stott, was convinced I should pursue a career in medicine, and my parents and grandparents took this very seriously. However, I knew this would mean a seven-year exile to study in England and that was the last thing I wanted, over and above being parted from Bill. I could not see myself living anywhere other than Kenya, so I told my parents that my heart would break and that if they made me go, I would elope.

They could tell that I meant it, and after much cajoling the subject was dropped. Instead, I joined Sheila in the YWCA in Nairobi and began a secretarial course at the same college as my sister. Bill had been given the extra task of grading the Nairobi Park roads, over and above his other Park warden duties, and so we were together a lot, spending all weekend doing his rounds on his enormous Caterpillar Grader, on which he had painted the name 'Daphne' in large letters at the side. But soon Bill was informed that he was being transferred to the as yet undeveloped but newly gazetted giant Tsavo National Park. By coincidence, Peter was being sent to the western half of the Park and Bill would be in the eastern section. For Bill and me this posting was a calamity, Tsavo being 200 miles from Nairobi, so we decided to become engaged. At my seventeenth birthday party, with the family gathered, Bill asked my father for my hand in marriage. Taken completely aback, my father mumbled: 'Yes, yes, of course, one day, no hurry,' but when the ring we had chosen together in Nairobi was lovingly placed on my finger, my father had to take the request more seriously. Grandpa Webb caught the gist of the conversation and started up 'For he's a jolly good fellow' on the piano, during which my father managed to recover himself, announcing: 'We expect the engagement to last at least a year to give these two children time to change their minds.' I glanced at Bill, who was obviously amused and gave me a wink. We knew there was nothing that could change our minds.

After graduating from secretarial college I got a job with an office of the African Explosives and Chemical Industries Company, a local branch of ICI, where I was paid £30 a month, an excellent salary. Bill duly went off to Tsavo East to begin working with David Sheldrick, a major who had been the youngest company commander within the King's African Rifles during the Second World War years. Having returned from active service in Abyssinia and Burma, David had joined Safariland, the first professional hunting safari operating firm to become established in Nairobi. He was married with two small children, was renowned for his film-star looks and had a reputation as an awe-inspiring leader with a sound knowledge of natural history and the wildlife of Africa – an obvious choice for the job of transforming the unforgiving scrubland of what used to be the Taru Desert into a viable National Park. Tsavo had been a curious choice, but it was devoid of any permanent settlement because it was such inhospitable country, covered in an entanglement of dense scrub vegetation infested with tsetse fly, too arid for cultivation and unsuitable for livestock, a parched semi-arid desert that could expect little more than ten inches of rain a year. Although there was not an abundance of wildlife in Tsavo, it was known for its diversity of indigenous species, including fearsome lions, breeding herds of elephants and thousands of black rhinos, and it just happened to be where the northern and southern forms of fauna met, doubling up on the races of giraffe, ostrich and Grant's gazelle (although this was not known at the time). David and his team of workers, Bill included, were there to make something out of nothing, much as the Aggetts had done further up-country nearly fifty years earlier, but in this case they had to transform useless scrubland into a National Park.

Bill's letters kept me going. While I enjoyed my work and the company of my colleagues, the restrictions of an office did not suit me. I yearned for the outdoors, to be among animals and trees again, so I lived for Bill's letters. He described to me how he and David had to hack through the scrubland to carve out a road, and how they needed to walk the land to decide where to establish the Park's headquarters. Their base camp was at Ndololo, on the Voi River, not far from Voi town at the foot of the towering Taita Hills, where fresh vegetables and even strawberries were grown. Voi town consisted of a few Asian-owned dukas that carried an eclectic assortment of dry goods. Also situated there was an historic First World War cemetery where an array of interesting people lay buried, including two First World War veteran Victoria Cross holders, the boots of a man devoured by a lion (all that was left to bury) and several people squashed by elephants. The newly built Voi Hotel, which had been designed on the back of a Clipper cigarette packet, was where he and David seemed to get up to all sorts of mischief. I absorbed all the details of Bill's letters – after all, Tsavo East was to be my future home.

In 1952 a state of emergency was declared in Kenya. Jomo Kenyatta – the man destined to become independent Kenya's first President – was imprisoned, accused of masterminding the Mau Mau. Bands of Kikuyu tribesmen had taken to the Aberdare mountain range, armed and dangerous, and attacks against the establishment and the farmsteads of white settlers became almost daily events. There was one

night when eleven murders took place, an entire family brutally
butchered on the Kinangop, not far from where the Aggetts lived.
Terror stalked the country. The loyalist faction of the Kikuyu tribe,
of whom there were many, bore the brunt of the carnage, culminat-
ing in the Lari massacre, in which almost an entire village was wiped
out – over 100 men, women and children decapitated and mutilated,
left as a sinister warning to other Government supporters. The Government introduced a 'villagization' programme to protect those of
the Kikuyu tribe who were loyal, ringing their villages with dry
moats that bristled with sharpened panjies, or stakes, in an attempt at
making an attack by the Mau Mau more difficult. Soon young white
men of Bill's age were being mobilized for active emergency service
in the Kenya Regiment, and troops from the Lancashire Fusiliers
were sent from England to bolster the local forces. The Mau Mau
insurgents were proving difficult to counter, particularly as the forest
gangs were being well provisioned with food by the women, who
remained behind in their tribal area. Having been sent to Rhodesia
for six months' special training, Bill and Peter were selected for
Officer Cadre. Now a new narrative emerged in Bill's letters, for
while he was not able to disclose operational details, I knew he was
engaged in highly dangerous, clandestine sorties deep in the forest.
Later, he was awarded the Military Cross for his bravery.

The British troops shipped over to help quell the Mau Mau were
viewed with deep scepticism by the settler community, including
Grandpa Webb and Granny Chart, for once in unison. Unlike the
Kenya Regiment, the 'Poms', as they were known, were not seen as a
match for the Mau Mau in the dense, game-infested forests of the
Aberdares and Mount Kenya. They were unfamiliar with the local
people and terrain, not to mention the wildlife. There was resentment at the overtly sympathetic views of many of the British
servicemen towards the Mau Mau cause and their condemnation of
us settlers as a privileged elite who had no real right to be in Kenya in
the first place. I was deeply affected by this. I knew that I was British
through and through and loyal to the Crown, yet here I was being
stigmatized by my so-called countrymen. Of course, our community was becoming something else without us even knowing it.

Labelled the White Tribe of Africa, we were rapidly losing our stake in the country we viewed as home and could never be truly British again, due to long isolation in Africa. Nor could we be truly African either, because of colour and culture. The family embarked on lengthy discussions about this, my father in particular, and I felt troubled and unsettled, so sure in myself that I belonged here in Kenya. I had been born here and I wanted to live my life here. I was part of this land and this land was part of me.

I wanted to be with Bill, for us to be married, living in Tsavo, working to create this new National Park, in the bush, among the natural world that meant so much to us both. It turned out I had to wait just a little while longer.

4. Married Life

'These wretched Colonies are a millstone round our neck,
and will all be independent one day.'

– Benjamin Disraeli, 1852

My wedding dress of lace and tulle was the first shop-bought dress I ever owned. Bill and I had finally named the date, and because I was the first of my generation to get married, the reception was to be a grand affair, on the farm, in the garden, with a huge number of guests. Most of the planning fell to my mother and she set about it with her usual artistic flair, even making lilac bridesmaids' dresses the exact colour of my favourite flowers, Cape chestnuts, which grew wild in the forest behind our farm. We went together to Nairobi to buy my wedding dress – until then I had worn only hand-made or handed-down clothes – and we spent an entire day choosing the dress of my dreams.

The time leading up to the wedding should have been a very happy period, full of excitement and bustle. However, in the weeks before, two tragedies struck at the heart of my family. The first was a barbaric Mau Mau raid on my Great-Aunt Ethel's farm in Nanyuki. Her house was set alight and, unable to escape, her foreman, his wife and their three children were burnt alive. Every single farmworker was brutally butchered outside – the farm a scene of carnage and devastation. Aunt Ethel was staying with Granny Chart at the time of the attack and the loss of her staff was almost too much for her to bear. I found it impossible to find any words of comfort, as she sat ashen-faced, trembling, quite literally stricken with grief.

And then, a few days later, a telegram arrived from Malindi bearing the shattering news that Grandpa Webb had died in his sleep. He had been on the moonlit beach teaching football to the local children before returning home to enjoy a hearty meal with Granny Webb. He had woken once in the night complaining of indigestion, but after a dose of bicarbonate of soda had gone back to sleep.

I loved my grandfather deeply and I was rooted to the spot on hearing of his death, my mind turning over as the impending impact of life without him hit me. I thought: he will not see me marry Bill; he will not dance in his funny way with me at my wedding and I will never again hear his infectious laugh. Grandpa Webb's wicked sense of humour was irreplaceable, and I knew in those brief moments that I would miss him for the rest of my life. Even Granny Chart was upset – secretly I think she had thrived on the many years of matching him in banter.

My mother and Sheila went down to Malindi to be with Granny Webb, who was her usual serene self, convinced that she would soon be reunited with her partner of some fifty years. Granny Webb had always been a deeply spiritual person with an unshakeable faith in the hereafter, not something shared by Grandpa. Later that night, as my mother sat on the verandah sofa, listening to the thunder of the surf, she is sure that her father, Grandpa Webb, appeared before her and said, 'Peg, look after Mother. It won't be for very long.' My mother was adamant that she had not been dreaming and that he had really been in the room with her. Granny Webb was not at all surprised, as she had also had a chat with him that night. Nor did she linger long. She stayed just long enough to attend my wedding and six months later – quietly and with dignity – slipped away to join him, just as she had known she would. My grandfather was laid to rest in a tiny hallowed cemetery on the coral cliffs overlooking the ocean, sleeping to the sound of the sea, but since she died in Nakuru, Granny Webb rests in the cemetery there.

It was difficult to imagine celebrating anything, but we knew that Grandpa Webb would not want us to postpone my wedding on his account. My mother and sister packed up Granny Webb's possessions and brought her to live with us, and as the wedding date drew nearer, she took an active part in all the frenetic activity. Sheila and I made a hurried dash down to Voi to post the marriage banns in the District

Commissioner's office, spending one night in the notorious Voi Hotel. Returning home, I had a busy time attending 'kitchen teas' organized by my friends from the office and the YWCA, who showered me with all the essentials needed for a new kitchen. Then, just before I left my job to move back home, my friends and I decided we needed a real party to see me on my way. A real party meant one with plenty of alcohol, something that was new to me, since my parents never touched it.

I pleaded with the supervisor for just one night of innocent revelry and she very sportingly conceded. When I think back at our naivety, how unworldly we were, it makes me both amused and alarmed. Each of us – and there were about twenty girls – purchased a bottle of liquor, and the impressive array of whisky, gin, brandy, wine and sherry would have daunted even the most hardy of drinkers. The night started well but rapidly deteriorated into an uncontrolled disorderly gaggle of giggling drunken females. Games such as 'Cardinal Puff', which involved sinking the contents of your drink without taking a breath, made us so drunk that pretty soon many of us couldn't even stand. I have a vague recollection of Sheila doing a Florence Nightingale, ministering to the sick and then dragging them off by their heels to bed. I was incredulous that she was still in control when I was so totally undone.

Even the passage of so many years has not dimmed the memory of the hangover. Most of us were laid low for three full days, feeling very sorry for ourselves, puzzled at how anyone could enjoy being drunk. I haven't ever been that drunk again, nor would I want to be. When Bill appeared a couple of days later, he was concerned to find me moaning and groaning in a darkened room. He thought I must have been struck down with some dreadful disease, but having sworn him to secrecy – my parents would have been horrified at the real story – we set off for the farm to help with the final preparations.

On 27 June 1953, three weeks after my nineteenth birthday, I woke up early, unsure whether I was ready for what lay ahead. Granny Webb helped me dress, sewing a piece of lace into my petticoat that had belonged to her mother for the traditional 'something old'; she gave me one of her handkerchiefs, which I tucked into my bra, for the 'something borrowed', and a blue garter – 'something blue' – that she had made especially for my wedding day. 'Something new' was no problem and I felt good in my wedding dress, my hair and make-up for once done carefully. Arriving way too early at the church in Naivasha, I became increasingly nervous, eventually breaking out in a rather unattractive rash all over my neck and chest. My father suggested a stiff drink at the local pub and soon I was calmer, able to appreciate the beauty of the church. It was set among a cluster of pepper trees overlooking Naivasha town, the place where my father had lived in his youth and where Great-Granny Aggett had come by wagon to shop. This little rural centre in the heart of the highlands had long been a focal point for my family, and at that moment I would not have chosen to be married anywhere else. Below, Lake Naivasha lay like a shawl of blue on the green floor of the Rift, with the surrounding hills and volcano clearly mirrored in its surface. It was a perfect afternoon – the sun shone from a clear blue sky, making it warm even at this high altitude, wild flowers blossomed on the road verges and the air was humming with sound.

I don't remember too much about the service, only that the church was filled with the fragrance of flowers whose colours blended beautifully with the lilac of the bridesmaids' dresses. At the altar, I remember thinking how immaculate Bill looked in his full Kenya Regiment dress uniform, with his Military Cross on its purple and white ribbon pinned to his chest. I was relieved that Bill managed to keep a straight face during the solemnity of the vows, for he was well known for bursting into fits of uncontrollable laughter in formal situations. Walking back down the aisle on his arm, I thought: I am now Mrs Frank William Woodley.

Back at the farm, friends and family gathered to toast us, catch up with each other, exchange views on farming and political matters and exhibit growing children, especially those of marriageable age. My mother had pulled out all the stops when it came to the food, and the free flow of sparkling wine ensured that the guests were well fed and watered. Bill and my brother Peter made typically accomplished speeches and we cut the stunning cake, which was topped by an icing replica of Mount Kenya. There were over 375 guests in our garden, and Bill and I did the rounds, talking with as many as possible, but it was Granny Chart who socialized most. Primed with wine, she was having the time of her life, busy hoovering up all the family gossip.

Before dark, I slipped away to prepare myself for leaving. Because of the Mau Mau attacks it wasn't safe to travel at night, and we were heading for the Brown Trout, a country retreat on the Kinangop Plateau, before our honeymoon in England. As I changed into my going-away two-piece, the colour of crushed strawberries, I reflected on the many changes to my life that the thin gold ring on my finger was going to bring. I was about to leave this beautiful home that had always been my anchorage, and it began to dawn on me just how much I was going to miss the warmth, security and love of my close-knit and caring family, as well as the animals that had been so much a part of my life. To be honest, I was a bit scared about what lay ahead – both immediately that night and into the future as Bill's wife. I had only just turned nineteen, and from the distance of today, I can see just how young and naive I was. When I think back to that night, when the anticipated passion fell a bit flat, I realize how inexperienced I was.

Our honeymoon in England was hugely memorable. This was the first time I had travelled overseas and I was looking forward to seeing the country of my ancestors. We sailed on the SS *Kenya*, and during the voyage I bought a string of cultured pearls with the money that my father had so generously given me for the holiday. From the earliest times of sitting on Granny Webb's bed encased in all her necklaces and bracelets, I have been passionate about jewellery, and I still treasure those pearls. Once in England we visited many of the famous sights of London and then travelled up through England to Scotland, meeting a vast number of Bill's elderly aunts and their offspring. On the way, we made a detour to Lincolnshire to see Sleaford, Grandpa Webb's family home, and in York we encountered a ghost – not one of Bill's relatives, but a replica of Robin Hood seated on a stool in a library. He was clad in old-fashioned green leggings and a soft tall cap with a large feather protruding from one side, and he looked so authentic that we assumed he had been planted as a tourist gimmick. Only when we read in the paper the next day about the ghost that habitually haunts the library on that day each year, matching the description of Robin Hood, did we wonder what we had actually seen.

Returning refreshed and animated, feeling as though we had seen a bit of the world, we moved into a small rented bungalow not far from the Kenya Regiment's Field Headquarters at Maguga, just outside Nairobi. Kenya was still in the grips of the national state of emergency, the Mau Mau even more militant since the arrest and imprisonment of Jomo Kenyatta. Despite the British deploying forces to quell the uprising, the Mau Mau insurrection and the guerrilla tactics of its militants continued, armed members of the Kikuyu tribe emerging to carry out gruesome murders, hold oathing ceremonies and generate unrest. Bill and his colleagues continued their secretive and highly dangerous missions, penetrating deep into the forest and actually into Mau Mau hideouts. They were familiar with the terrain, the people, and how to move in the dense forest, and were very successful in penetrating the enemy ranks.

Bill brought many of the captured insurgents back to the rented house we shared with another young officer, Francis Erskine. Bill's role meant that we were at risk from the Mau Mau, so we had to get used to living with armed guards outside our front and back door. As darkness fell, Bill and Francis would dress in moth-eaten greatcoats or skins, pull balaclavas low over their heads, rub charcoal on their skin and daub themselves with a light coating of cow-dung to conceal the scent of soap. The smell of soap was a dead give-away, easily detected by the Mau Mau, whose senses and instincts had been sharpened by their wild existence.

Bill and Francis operated with a team of specially chosen men, some drawn from the Waliangulu elephant-poaching fraternity, whom Bill had recruited as trackers from areas bordering Tsavo. Bill had great respect for these expert bushmen, as proficient at tracking humans through the forest as they were at following a dikdik under desert conditions. Mau Mau converts who had turned informer were also a crucial part of Bill's team. They knew the forest intimately – every path, every glade, every ravine, the location of the hideouts, the clandestine ceremonial meeting places, the hollow forest trees in which communications passed between the rebel commanders. Above all, they knew the secret signals and calls used by the Mau Mau: a stick tossed on a path at a certain angle; the leaf of a particular plant left on the ground; a twisted stem, a pebble or two – all conveyed a specific message, as did various sounds, which no outsider could decipher as anything other than the call of a bird or animal. It was these Mau Mau defectors who were best qualified to bring about the downfall of the hardcore within the forests.

Much of Bill's work entailed short nocturnal sorties into the neighbouring tribal lands, but there were also more prolonged absences when the operations took him and his team deep into the Aberdare forests and up into the moorlands. It was here that the Mau Mau gangs were most elusive, and here that Bill and his men spent a good deal of their time in pursuit, often crawling about blindly on all fours, drenched to the skin, scratched and bleeding, nerves taut as they anticipated a Mau Mau ambush or an attack from a wild animal. As the bombing of suspected hideouts – using Lancaster bombers from the Second World War – by the security forces gained momentum, the unfortunate animals of the Aberdares became increasingly crazed with fear, many of them wounded by flying shrapnel, charging at anything that moved and becoming even more dangerous. At the mere drone of a Lancaster bomber, the smaller forest dwellers such as bushbuck and suni dashed around aimlessly through the undergrowth, not knowing where to hide for safety, and the monkeys leapt terrified from tree to tree, huddling together for comfort.

The Mau Mau gangs based themselves in cleverly hidden hideouts, some of which were elaborate constructions of bamboo, furnished with log stools and beds of animal hide, usually with several exits for a quick getaway. Many even had piped water flowing from springs and streams through chains of hollowed bamboo stems. Other hideouts were simply dug-out bushes covered with hide, and yet others, known as dakkis, were built underground, with entrances so well hidden from the inside that they were almost invisible from outside – just a tiny tell-tale hole the size of a penny left for air. Finding the hideouts required expertise that took some practice for Bill to master. He told me how he disguised his tracks by putting all his weight on one side of his foot so that no toe or heel mark showed, and how, as he tracked through the forest, he could use a stick to thread together disturbed vegetation.

It was often possible to detect the presence of a hideout by the smell of animal hide. The Mau Mau wore skins: hats for a general, armbands and pelts for his lieutenants. Under-jackets were usually made from the soft pelts of small forest animals such as tree hyrax, squirrel or tiny suni antelope, the fur worn near the skin for warmth, while the hides of larger animals such as elands and bushbuck provided the outer clothing. I was appalled by the toll taken on these animals – a single under-jacket was made up of thirty to forty hyrax or suni pelts, not to mention the huge karosses – skins with the hair left on – that were used in place of blankets at night and which entailed over 100 pelts.

Infiltrating these gangs was highly dangerous work and I had no illusions about the threat to Bill's life. It didn't help that he and Francis were absolutely determined to be the ones to capture the most famous of the Mau Mau generals, one of whom was Dedan Kimathi. His was a household name, symbolic of the Mau Mau struggle for freedom, determined to deal with loyalists whom he regarded as traitors to the Mau Mau cause. He was cunning and elusive, endowed with an amazing capacity to remain at large in spite of everything pitted against him. I was hugely relieved every time Bill returned home safely.

Just after our first wedding anniversary, I realized I was pregnant. I was twenty. The thought of having a child of my own seemed so surreal that at first I could hardly believe it. And while morning sickness and an increasing girth brought the reality home to me, I was terrified not only at the thought of going through the agony of labour but at the daunting prospect of becoming a mother myself before my twenty-first birthday. At times, I wished I could turn the clock back and revert to the carefree and independent life of all my friends. Instead, I reflected grimly, I was this generation's pioneer – the first to get married and the first to have a baby. Secretly, too, I was worried about the fact that my marriage, and sex in particular, fell far short of my girlhood expectations, that all the love stories I had read hinted at an ecstasy which seemed to have escaped me and which I had yet to experience.

In January 1955, towards the end of my pregnancy, Bill took me back to the farm for a break. I longed for the reassurance of my mother as my time approached. On the way to Gilgil, Bill had to call on a splinter group of his unit in Ol Kalou to report on some operational activities. Bill was always late and typically it had taken all day to get going. I was already edgy, for this particular area was a hotbed of Mau Mau activity, particularly at night, when forest gangs left their stronghold under cover of darkness to strike terror. Night falls rapidly in the tropics, and soon Bill had to switch on the headlights of the car. Uncharacteristically, I was overcome by an acute sense of foreboding, barely able to speak, staring at the road verges to detect any hint of danger. After several miles that appeared endless, the rutted murram track curved sharply towards a small stream, so Bill had to slow right down in order to negotiate the rickety wooden bridge. It was just as we were accelerating up the other side that we could detect dark shadows on the embankment.

And then terror struck. A terrifyingly loud sound erupted and in the arc of the headlamps we could see crazed, menacing figures, clad in skins, coming towards us in a great swirl of anger and noise. Some were wielding pangas, some were hurling enormous boulders and others were firing at us from point blank range, barrels vomiting flashes of fire, bullets – and boulders – hitting the car with alarming force. At the time the noise felt remote, as if coming from a faraway place, and even the torrent of missiles seemed unreal. It was as if time stood still and I was watching from afar. Oddly, I felt no sense of panic, although I knew of course that we were facing very grave danger. Something shut down in me and I was unmoving. Bill, however, was used to this. He shoved my head down below the dashboard, snatched his Luger pistol, revved the car into full throttle, and, in an incredible feat of driving, hurled the car headlong at the barricade ahead, firing at our assailants out of the car windows. The car bounced and lurched and crunched over the obstacles in its path, hesitating for a heart-stopping moment against a huge boulder, wheels spinning without traction, and then, thankfully, toppling off to hurtle on through, carried clear of the road block by sheer momentum.

At this moment, to me Bill was like a hero in a Western movie, shooting as he drove, remaining calm and collected, courage coming to the fore to save our lives and that of our unborn child. The baby stirred inside me, shaking me out of my paralysis, adrenalin now pumping through my body. Bill took my hand and held it tight, driving to report the incident at the Ol Kalou police station. There the police pointed out a bullet in the top of the car window frame, a fraction of an inch from where Bill's head would have been, making me realize just how close to death we had come. I thanked God for Bill's courage and later, in the warmth of my parents' home, my mother wrapped my trembling frame in a blanket as I collapsed in a flood of tears back in the room that smelled of roses. These were tears of profound relief that we were all safe.

Our daughter, Gillian Sala Ellen, was born on 26 January 1955, two weeks late and in perfect health. I remember longing to be left alone – like the animals – to get on with it, free of distraction, interruption and instruction. We chose her name with a great deal of thought – Gillian because we liked it, as well as its shortened form Jill, by which she quickly became known; Sala because it was the name of a small conical hill within Tsavo as well as the Mliangulu word for the oryx antelope, and Ellen after both Granny Webb and Granny Chart. My sister Sheila was none too pleased because apparently she had earmarked the name Jill for her firstborn. She had finally married Jim Wren, her boyfriend of our YWCA days, and I had been too pregnant to be a bridesmaid at her wedding. Actually her first child turned out to be a boy, so she couldn't have used the name Jill anyway.

I found it difficult to adapt to motherhood: breasts swollen, sore and tight with milk, despair at my flabby tummy, endless sleepless nights, and envy at the freedom of everyone else around me. Trying to feed Jill was a relentless struggle, for she seemed to lack the ability to suckle, which convinced me that there must be something wrong with her. It was my mother who talked gently to me, emphasizing the rich blessing of children and how lucky Jill and I were to be here at all, and she pointed out that it had been my choice to get married young. Chastened and contrite at my selfish immaturity and having been reassured by a doctor that there was nothing at all wrong with Jill, I worked through my anguish. 'Children bring love with them,' said my mother and I soon found this to be true. The bond that emerged was strong and enduring, with us both for life.

By the mid 1950s, the state of emergency was drawing to an end. It was estimated that only about 1,500 hardcore Mau Mau activists were still at large in the Aberdare forests, and since the 'mopping up' operations would be the responsibility of the police, Bill was able to return to civilian life. He was disappointed not to have been able to capture the elusive Dedan Kimathi, but the skills he had honed in the forest would stay with him, useful in hunting down the wildlife poachers who were rife in what was now Tsavo National Park. His boss, David Sheldrick, was eagerly anticipating Bill's return to the Park. I was apprehensive at the thought of my baby having to grow up in an area teeming with malaria, scorpions, hairy bird-eating spiders, deadly snakes and scores of other biting and stinging hazards. I knew also that the logistics of running a home would be challenging; I would have to order many fresh provisions not available at the Indian dukas in Voi from Nairobi, which would have to come by train and be collected from the 'local' station on a weekly basis.

How I would fit into the rather wild local community of which I had heard so much from Bill was another consideration – not least Bill's rather intimidating boss. I had only met David Sheldrick once, four years earlier when I was seventeen, and had not exactly made a good impression. It was my first time in Tsavo East and Bill had taken me to Mudanda Rock, a magnificent vantage point from where we could see herds of elephants drinking, socializing and playing in the pool beneath a huge outcropping of basement rock. On that particular day, not only were there literally hundreds of elephants to entertain us but there was also a film crew, busy shooting scenes for the movie *Where No Vultures Fly*. David was with the stars, Anthony Steele and Dinah Sheridan, and as our party clambered up the rock, he signalled to us that filming was in progress and we must be as silent as possible. We crept up, settled ourselves at a discreet distance and soon became engrossed in the scenes below. Bill, who could never get through an afternoon without a cup of tea, had brought a saucepan and, without me noticing, had plonked it down beside me. Swinging round to point out something of interest, I inadvertently sent the pan clattering noisily down the rock face; as it gained momentum, the sound could be heard for miles around until, with a final splash, it plopped into the pool below.

There was an immediate and deafening hush as every single elephant froze, fanned out its ears in alarm and then, en masse, fled in panic. So rapidly did they disappear that it was difficult to believe that their presence merely seconds before had not been an illusion; that so many elephants could vanish so silently, leaving just a soft cloud of red dust hanging in the air. The crew stopped filming, the actors stopped acting and time seemed to stand still as everyone looked up at me in disbelief. I was mortified.

David made his way over to us and Bill introduced our party to him, finally muttering in a guilty tone, 'And, er, this is Daphne.' I looked up in embarrassed confusion as David held his hand out in greeting. He was tall, and in his eyes of deepest blue there was a mixture of interest and amusement; eyes that were fringed by long thick lashes that would be the envy of any girl. His handshake was strong and his legs shapely, the shoes he wore, chupli bush sandals. His bush jacket was tailored to fit his figure, and around him there was an unmistakable air of authority that was invisible but powerful.

And now here I was aged twenty-one, married and a mother. I had matured in many ways, and yet on arrival at the newly completed Park Headquarters at the foot of Mazinga Hill I found myself tongue-tied and awkward as David emerged to greet me. Taking charge of Jill in her carrycot, he escorted me into his new home, saying that we were to be his guests until our own house had been redecorated. This had not been done in advance because he felt that the colour choice and finishing touches should be mine. As I went to unpack and settle Jill in the guest wing at the end of a long open verandah, he took Bill off to show him the many changes to the Headquarters during his four-year absence. I was surprised that David's wife, Diana, was nowhere to be seen because I was interested to meet her, but later Bill told me that not all the changes were to do with the infrastructure of the Park. David and his wife had apparently recently separated and she had taken with her their two young children.

At dinner that evening, David and Bill mulled over the problems facing Tsavo. I had not really considered the daunting logistics of trying to gain control of such vast and unchartered territory, of creating the necessary infrastructure for a park covering 8,000 square miles, an area the size of Wales, Israel or Michigan State. Tsavo was by far the largest Park in Kenya, the most remote, the most unknown, the most untouched − uninhabited, shunned by all except the ruthless bands of professional poachers in pursuit of ivory and rhino horn. No other Park in the country was as fraught with such obstacles, and yet, David told us, he had to fight furiously for a reasonable portion of funds for its development. In essence, Tsavo was the only sizeable chunk of country that the colonial Government could afford to set aside for wildlife without conflicting with human land claims, and yet it was being treated as the Cinderella of the system. He was firm and passionate as he spoke of the urgent need to strike at the heart of the poachers, to eradicate the terrible toll taken of the breeding herds of elephants for their ivory, and of the rhinos for their horn. He catalogued the appalling loss of wildlife he and his colleagues had uncovered. 'If we do not put an end to this menace, there will be nothing left worth preserving,' he said.

The next morning, I awoke to the dawn chorus of the little francolins, so reminiscent of the camp at Selengai, and looking out of the window I watched a young bushbuck feasting on the flowers in David's terraced garden. Two little elephants, their ears out like dinner plates, trunk-wrestled in play, and I was instantly uplifted, ready to embrace my new life. Later, I learned that the bushbuck was a wild orphan whom David had named Bushey and that the elephants were the famous Samson and Fatuma, the first orphaned calves we in Kenya knew of outside those held in far-off zoos. These two featured in a weekly column of the *East African Standard* and were already household names. At breakfast I asked David about their rescue and how he had set about 'taming' them. Samson, a two-year-old bull, had presented the greatest challenge. David had actually got into the stable with him, and every time Samson charged, David punched him on the trunk, forcing him to retreat into the far corner. David then talked to him gently, holding out a peace offering before warding off another charge. Eventually, having been chastised so often for aggression, Samson began to recognize that it did not pay and that the odd creature facing him could not be easily intimidated. By that same afternoon he had calmed down completely, to the extent that he could be easily handled, and from that moment on a special affinity existed between David and this elephant. Fatuma, the female, had recently been attacked by a lion and she had allowed him to clean and treat her wounds, bravely enduring the discomfort because she understood that he was helping her.

Listening to David talk with such compassion and depth of understanding about his two elephants impressed me greatly. I could not help being surprised by such sensitivity in so forceful a character, for this was a rare quality in men of his time, who tended to view wild animals dispassionately. During David's professional hunting days he had obviously done his fair share of killing, but I sensed that he derived no pleasure from taking an animal's life. He had an unusual reverence for life as well as a deep empathy for animals. I also sensed that there was much I could learn from this man, particularly about elephants, and the way he spoke about Samson and Fatuma made me decide that I wanted to begin right away.

More immediately, however, I was eager to see our new home and tour the Headquarters, which was a hive of activity: carpenters turning out rustic cedar signposts and furniture for the houses; a huge hydraulic press which David sometimes diverted from its normal purpose to produce 'pilipili hoho' – the fiery chilli sauce that accompanied every meal in his home and would soon set my tongue on fire; a mechanical workshop equipped with everything needed to repair the Park's fleet of vehicles and heavy machinery; an enormous lathe which only he could operate, with which he transformed bits of scrap iron into bolts, shafts and spares. David had trained up the Park's artisans and its entire workforce himself, most importantly the rangers, whose duty it was to bring the illegal poaching of elephant and rhino under control and provide security for the animals.

At first sight, my new home was alarming – immediately below the front doorstep was a towering red-earth anthill, providing an ideal refuge for snakes and other creepy-crawlers and surrounded by impenetrable sanseveria, the wild sisal. Behind that grew interminable commiphoras, deciduous arid, shallow-rooted trees with contorted boughs and sharp spikes and thickets that no doubt sheltered buffalo, elephants and the dreaded Tsavo man-eating lions. The house itself was simple and stark, but it was the absence of any semblance of a garden that distressed me most. I turned away, not wanting to embarrass our host, but David said quietly: 'Don't worry, Daphne. This can all be transformed.'

And he was as good as his word – the next day a tractor was sent to level the anthill and clear the bush, the masons began to stone-wall newly created terraces, the carpenters installed shelving and the painters put the finishing touches to the walls in the cream colour I had chosen. Over the next few weeks, in between tending to an unusually fractious Jill, who was getting used to the heat, I made curtains and unpacked. David sent round a gardener to plant up the lawn on the top terrace and he himself came to supervise the installation of a birdbath, which became one of the beautiful features of my new garden. When I felt everything was ship-shape, Bill and I invited David for supper. He looked around the living room and smiled: 'Happier now?' I assured him that I was, adding, 'I am going to love living in Tsavo.' He looked at me searchingly and then said, very quietly, 'I certainly hope so. My wife hated it with a passion.'

Ominous words. But from those very early days, I really did come to love Tsavo. Every dawn gently wove a subtle spell on me as the sun rose in a fiery crimson ball, shedding a warm glow over the immense and mysterious landscape. I fell in love with Tsavo's wilderness and its space and with the natural world it sheltered.

And as the years ahead unfolded, it would not be just the landscape with which I would find myself in love.

5. Falling in Love

'There are no words that can tell the hidden spirit of the wilderness,
that can reveal its mystery, its melancholy, and its charm. There is
delight in the hardy life of the open ... Apart from this, yet mingled
with it, is the strong attraction of the silent places, of the large tropic
moons, and the splendor of the new stars; where the wanderer sees
the awe-full glory of sunrise and sunset in the wide waste spaces of the
earth, unworn of man, and changed only by the slow changes of the
ages through time everlasting.'

– Theodore Roosevelt, *African Game Trails*

Since I was a trained shorthand typist and book-keeper, I offered to
help David out in the office. In between looking after Jill, running
our home and planting up our garden with seeds and cuttings sent by
my mother, I soon became immersed in the day-to-day workings of
the Park. I loved being a part of the thrum and vibrancy of all that
was going on. I shared David's office – it was the only one in the
Headquarters – and it was a hub of activity: the radio network
buzzed constantly, reports from the rangers coming in from afar. As
David's anti-poaching campaign gained momentum, I took on
responsibility for the upkeep of the 'rogues' gallery', detailed,
exhaustive files on every known poacher. I came to understand the
severity of the poaching crisis, for during patrols Bill came across the
sickening signs of slaughter at almost every waterhole – tusk butts,
vacated hideouts, ashes from poachers' fires, bones and broken cala-
bashes. Carnage on a huge scale was going on.

David's brief was to develop the eastern 5,000 square miles of
Tsavo and turn this vast, unexplored and inhospitable region into an
accessible National Park that would attract and accommodate paying

visitors – Tsavo East, lying to the east of the railway line from Nairobi to Mombasa. The remaining 3,000 square miles of Tsavo, the other side of the line, would become Tsavo West. David's task was not easy. Carving out roads and paths in this hostile land of interminable scrub and barbed entangled undergrowth was back-breaking work. In the early days there was no earth-moving equipment, so huge stumps and boulders had to be levered laboriously by hand out of earth baked as hard as concrete. So intense was the heat that David had to allow all work to be routinely discontinued between ten in the morning and three in the afternoon so that the exhausted workforce could flop flat out under what shade they could find. Water, more precious than gold, had to be rationed, every drop carted from base. It was a very scarce commodity, since the 5,000 square miles of Tsavo East had just two permanent rivers. Both Bill and David suffered constant bouts of malaria, not to mention minor hazards such as scorpions, snakes, and charging rhinos and elephants that resented the intrusion of humans into their world.

The northern section of the Park was very remote, with just one means of access, since the Galana River dissected the Park into two distinct halves, isolating the north. During the dry seasons, when the river was at low ebb, one could, of course, brave the crocodiles and hippos to wade the shallows and swim deeper channels – which the rangers did regularly during their routine patrolling. Nevertheless they were then confronted by a huge stretch of waterless country forming yet another effective barrier, with the next likely source of water the seasonal Tiva sand river some sixty miles away. During the two wet seasons of the year, both the Galana and the Tiva flooded, leaving an area of country in virtual isolation for several months on end. David recognized the urgency of establishing better access to the north and early on began work on a giant causeway to span the Galana River at one of its narrowest points. This entailed tramping up and down searching for a suitable rock seam that could form the foundation, and eventually he found a place just above Lugard's Falls, where the Galana River was channelled into a narrow rock chasm of turbulent waters. The construction took a full year, with months spent breaking up the tons of ballast needed and frustrating delays every time the river swelled. But once it was done and the first vehicles were able to cross, the 3,000 square miles of the northern area became more easily accessible. Fifty years later, this original structure, made entirely by hand, remains a lifeline across the Galana, a living testimony to the skill and endurance of those pioneer wardens.

While developing the Park, David also had the preservation of its natural habitat at heart. Tsavo was renowned for its elephants and black rhinos – in fact there were more black rhinos in the Park than anywhere else in the whole of Africa, as well as some of the largest tusked elephants in the world, giants that carried over 100lb of ivory on each side. It was these magnificent creatures that had, for countless years, been the target of both White Hunters and poachers. It was estimated that in the mid 1950s over 1,200 elephants and hundreds of rhinos were being poached each year, both ivory and rhino horn being valuable commodities, sold by the poaching fraternity to corrupt Asian and Arabic middlemen dealers at the coast before being smuggled to Far Eastern countries, where they fetched large sums of money.

Ivory has long been coveted, fashioned by stone-age men into crude implements or used to prop up dwellings; as adornments to the palaces of Biblical princes and kings or carved into objects used by the ancient Greeks, the Romans and the Chinese. It saddened me that it should be no less prized in the twentieth century, when we had discovered so many alternatives. Elephant tusks were fashioned for modern-day Western markets into piano keys, billiard balls, carvings and chessmen, and in the East into chopsticks, marriage bangles and signature seals – hardly essential items. There was evidence too that it was used as a 'white gold' hedge against inflation and the vulnerability of paper money. Rhino horn was valued in the East for supposedly medicinal properties alleged to have mythical powers that cured a host of human ailments, such as impotence, rheumatism, fevers and poor eyesight. In truth, rhino horn is comprised of nothing more than keratin, the substance of a fingernail, so consumers could get the same thing simply through biting their nails.

Poaching was taking an enormous toll of the Park's wildlife, and David was determined to get it under control. The newly appointed rangers were not drawn from the fighting tribes and were reluctant to confront poachers armed with deadly poisoned arrows and also unwilling to apprehend members of their own tribe for fear of reprisals. David made impassioned pleas to the National Park Headquarters in Nairobi for the right sort of men and equipment so that he could at least begin to cope with the crisis, but Tsavo East was of low priority compared to other more attractive areas, so he had to make do with limited resources and foot patrols of inexperienced, under-resourced and reluctant men.

Beyond the eastern Park boundary south of the Galana River was the home of the Waliangulu people, who were the professional elephant poachers, with elephants interwoven into their tribal culture. By the time we arrived at the Park, the monetary value of ivory had eroded their hitherto strict code of ethics and commercialism had taken hold. Now the very animal upon which their tribal structure and livelihood was based was being ruthlessly killed for gain. An even more sinister threat came from the Wakamba tribe, which hailed from the Park's extreme northern boundary. Although not as skilled or fearless as their Waliangulu counterparts, they were proficient killers, hunting in gangs of up to fifty men. The two tribes seldom trespassed on each other's hunting preserves, mutually observing an unwritten law reinforced by the threat of reprisals through witchcraft. In fact the Waliangulu despised the Wakamba, scorning them as inferior in hunting prowess, courage and bushcraft.

Both tribes used poison to kill elephants and rhinos. Poison-making was a highly specialized profession, and a closely guarded secret of the Giriama tribe – the people of Bantu Swahili origin from the Mombasa coastal belt – who brewed and sold it. Ingredients included bark and leaves taken from the particularly toxic acokanthera trees, which were boiled in water for about seven hours with a few other ingredients added to the potion as it was rendered down to a sticky tar-like substance. The poison was deadly, active as soon as it entered the bloodstream, and could kill an elephant within a couple of hours and humans within minutes, disrupting the muscular rhythm of the arteries and heart. Before sale, its potency and effectiveness was tested on a frog or lizard jabbed by a thorn dipped in poison or injected into an egg that apparently exploded. In the absence of a live specimen or an egg, the seller would prick his own arm to make the blood flow, place a little poison in its path and see how quickly the blood turned dark. There was no known antidote to acokanthera arrow poison. Poison-making was a lucrative trade.

The poison was applied to the arrowhead and its steel attachment and bound with cloth or hide as a protective measure. Upon impact, the arrowhead and its attachment separated from the wooden shaft, which was embedded with vulture feathers at the end as an aid to flight. Once detached, the poisoned arrowhead and steel attachment travelled on deep into the body, so that the poison entered the blood-stream while the wooden shaft could be retrieved by the owner and used again. The arrowhead was always marked with the owner's special insignia, showing who owned the carcass, irrespective of who came across it first. Poachers usually waylaid their quarry by waiting in ambush at a strategic vantage point overlooking either a drinking place or a well-used elephant path, and when a suitable target presented itself, an arrow was fired into any part of the anatomy, avoiding the stomach. The stomach was not a good target, since stomach contents could neutralize the effects of the poison. A second arrow directed to the foot of an elephant ensured lameness, so that the animal would not be able to travel too far before dying.

Meat from an animal that had died of acokanthera poisoning was in no way contaminated and could be safely eaten, usually being sun-dried in long strips back at a bush hideout. Tusks were hacked out of the skull with an axe if the carcass was fresh, or else drawn with ease once putrefaction had set in. They were then sawn into manageable lengths or buried in caches for collection at some future date, usually at the onset of the rains, when there was less chance of being apprehended. Occasionally, if the haul warranted the expense, porters were hired to carry the booty back to a base or to a rendezvous with a middleman buyer. He would then pass it on at a handsome profit to some unscrupulous dealer at the coast and from there it would be smuggled out aboard a dhow, ending up in the Far East where it fetched its true market value.

Dying from the effects of acokanthera poison, particularly if the poison is not fresh, is cruel and agonizing, and some images still

haunt me to this day: the torment of a dying cow elephant, surrounded by her distraught loved ones, frantic in their attempts to try
to keep her on her feet, her tiny newborn calf already doomed by her
impending death, but still desperately suckling a shrivelled udder
that would yield no milk; a wounded bull drawing water from his
stomach by inserting his trunk deep down his throat in order to suck
it out and spray it over his fevered body, standing helpless in the baking sun, stress 'tears' pouring from his temporal glands, anchored by
a foot too painful to put to the ground, five times its normal size;
emaciated victims with festering wounds oozing black poisoned
blood surrounded by flies, crippled giants in agony, hobbling along,
every footfall torment. David voiced my thoughts graphically, saying: 'I wish those responsible for this could suffer just a little of the
pain that has been paid for their ivory trinkets.' Difficult as it was for
me to witness animals in such pain, I could see the anguish and strain
felt by Bill and David, as they had to end the lives of those animals
found beyond hope. The bodies of many were so poisoned that they
simply exploded when a merciful bullet ended their agony.

It wasn't just poisoned arrows that killed the Park's wildlife. Sinister double-ended hooks, baited with meat and welded to stout steel
cables tethered to trees, were uncovered in the Galana River, set to
poach the crocodiles so that they could be pulled clear of the water
and clobbered to death. On another boundary of the Park, game pits
dug into the ground by the Wateita tribe also took a heavy toll of
wildlife. Cunningly camouflaged, these pits were often up to twelve
feet long, three feet wide and nine feet deep and were positioned in
long lines along well-used game trails, brush barriers several miles
long laid at an angle of forty-five degrees to funnel unsuspecting animals towards the deadly traps. Sometimes beaters were employed to
actively drive the animals in the desired direction. Normally the
Wateita poachers visited the pits only sporadically, being mainly
agricultural people, and any victim that had not already died of thirst
was speared from above. One such fence-line discovered by Bill
extended over 100 miles. Snaring through the use of wire nooses was
another indiscriminate form of poaching, the nooses anchored to
trees and shrubs, some positioned high up to trap taller animals such

as giraffe by the neck. When an animal either stepped in, or put its head into a noose and tugged to free itself, the wire tightened to hold it fast, cutting deeper into the flesh as the animal struggled. Larger species such as elephants and rhinos usually managed to break free, but faced an excruciatingly painful death from horrific suppurating leg or neck injuries.

Early on, the method of combating poaching had been to operate from a series of outposts situated at strategic points, but this system had proved ineffectual due to tribal affinities; many rangers were discovered to be actually colluding with poachers of the same tribe. When David found two elephant carcasses near the Sala Road – seventy miles from the Voi Park Headquarters – and the resident rangers based close by pleaded ignorance, he knew things had to change. Drawing on his army experience, he decided to train a mobile force on paramilitary lines and recruited an ex King's African Rifles Somali sergeant-major, along with a seasoned soldier who had served under him in Abyssinia and Burma. Meanwhile Bill was dispatched to the remoter regions of Kenya to recruit the new force – instinctive, fearless men from the Turkana, Samburu, Somali and Orma tribes who were skilled in bushcraft. On arrival they looked a pretty unlikely bunch – not one of them spoke a single word of Swahili, and from the way they stared wide-eyed at their new surroundings it was clear that this was their first contact with the outside world. And, from the way they stared wide-eyed at me, it was also clear that I was probably the first white woman they had ever seen. Astonishingly, however, within three months, after being put through intense military training, drill and target practice, these same wild tribesmen metamorphosed into a smart, disciplined unit which David named the Field Force. Now they were ready to go out into the field, as the embryo of what would become an extremely effective anti-poaching unit that would prove the blueprint for all the other National Park forces in East Africa.

Over time, the new Field Force brought poaching under control within the Park, but this did not provide the lasting solution needed. The long arm of the law needed to be able to follow the poachers beyond the Park borders when they managed to escape with the loot, and, of course, there was an urgent need to tackle the sinister octopus of middlemen traders both at field level and at the coast. After endless discussions and reams of red tape, it was agreed in Nairobi that the same powers of search and arrest vested in the Government Game Department scouts and police should be extended to the Field Force rangers, thereby empowering them to arrest poachers in their home villages whenever there was sufficient evidence for a conviction. Anti-poaching patrols usually spent many weeks out in the bush before returning to base, so invariably captors and captives came to know each other quite well by the end of it all, even establishing friendships based on mutual respect and a common interest. Bill would spend unhurried hours happily chatting to prisoners over a campfire when out on patrol. Any discussion usually involved big tuskers and this always broke the ice, the poachers recounting tales of such encounters and other exciting bush incidents. As time went on they invariably became more relaxed and ever more talkative, and in this way Bill was able to gather much useful information for the 'rogues' gallery'. Sometimes, if a prisoner proved very cooperative and volunteered information that led to the arrest of others, he was released against a promise not to transgress again or possibly even enlisted as a paid informer.

The Waliangulu village of Kisiki-cha-Mzungu, some twenty miles from the Park's eastern boundary, was known to harbour a host of wanted poachers. So, fortified by these new powers, members of the Field Force launched a series of night raids on this and neigh-bouring settlements. During one particular sortie, while his men rounded up known suspects, David came across a cluster of huts at the far end of the village and there, quietly contemplating the moon-light, sat a man who rose politely at his approach. 'What is your name?' asked David. 'I am Galogalo – Galogalo Kafonde,' was the reply.

Galogalo Kafonde was the most famous of all the Waliangulu poachers – revered among his people for having killed hundreds of elephants – and for a moment David was rendered speechless, he was so taken aback. Having asked to search the huts and plot, he came across two enormous tusks hidden in undergrowth nearby, so

Galogalo was duly arrested. During subsequent questioning he revealed that his four sons were operating in the Park from a hideout on the Yatta and he readily agreed to lead a patrol to them. Under the dim light of the moon and handcuffed to one of the rangers, he led the party along a narrow elephant trail, but when they were about two hours into the long walk he managed to slip out of the handcuffs and sped off into the night. David knew at once that it would be hopeless to try to follow; bitterly disappointed that one of the most notorious poachers had managed to escape, he ordered his men back to base. I had never seen David so crestfallen.

We all shared his frustration, but a few days later pulses were once again racing, for a signal from the Game Department at Kilifi, on the coast, informed us that another infamous poacher, Wambua Makula, had been arrested. He turned out to be a very valuable informant. As well as knowing partners in crime from his own tribe, the Wakamba, he could also tell us a lot about the Waliangulu poaching fraternity, having been associated with them and having no liking for them. Consequently, my 'rogues' gallery' swelled with information. All charges were dropped against him and he became an official informer and interpreter and a vital member of the anti-poaching team, leading the patrols to hidden hideouts near hitherto unknown water seepages along the walls of the Yatta. Wambua was a real character: wiry, slightly built, and short on teeth, he had a hollow-cheeked, cadaverous appearance and when he spoke, his nose bounced up and down against his chin, which mesmerized me. His encounters with animals were legendary and certainly livened up the office. He'd been tossed by buffaloes, gored by rhinos, mauled by lions, grabbed by a crocodile, caught by a python, and had narrowly escaped death on many occasions from elephants. With his help many poachers were eventually rounded up and brought to justice.

Of course one informant, however informative, could not put an end to poaching, any more than one Field Force could. So it was with enormous relief that soon David got formal recognition from Nairobi that poaching was indeed reaching crisis proportions and needed to be dealt with more forcefully. Noel Simon, the executive head of the newly established East African Wildlife Society, was a far-sighted

and practical man who took up David's cause and lobbied the great
and the good with amazing effectiveness. The Army Commander-
in-Chief, the Commissioner of Police and the Chief Game Warden
of Kenya all ended up convinced, pledging support to the creation of
an enlarged unit that would be capable of covering the entire south-
eastern region of Kenya. In addition to radio field sets, a police
Airwing plane and pilot and a police prosecuting officer were seconded to David. The Governor of Kenya, Sir Evelyn Baring, gave the
campaign his blessing, with a directive to all magistrates to issue
deterrent sentencing to those found guilty of wildlife offences and to
be especially tough on the dealers. This entire operation came under
David's overall command from Park Headquarters near Voi, now
named 'Poacher Control'. The Park's Field Force was expanded and
became known as Voi Force, and two additional Game Department
anti-poaching units were also created – 'Makindu' force, which
would operate between Voi and Nairobi, and 'Hola' force in the
north, near the Tana River.

David and Bill were elated. This was exactly what they needed to
manage a truly effective anti-poaching campaign, and while a lot of
developmental work around Tsavo had to go on hold, our HQ now
became a hive of fevered activity. Several new officers joined us:
Hugh Massey, an ex-army major, as well as three Game Department
personnel, Ian 'Chickweed' Parker, David 'Makebi' McCabe and
David Brown. The Prosecution Officer who shared the office with
David and me was Alan 'Chillicracker' Childs. All the nicknames
were mine. I have always had a tendency to attach appropriate nicknames that stuck to acquaintances, something that used to amuse my
mother and the rest of the family. For me, a welcome addition to our
staff was my brother Peter, who had been serving as an assistant warden in Tsavo West and was sent to join Bill in Tsavo East for the
anti-poaching campaign. It was a busy time as the new forces were
trained up and new staff accommodated. I was more than happy to be
playing even a small part in support of wildlife, and happier still to
have been given a brand new manual Remington typewriter.

Jill was a calm and contented child and I liked to think she had
inherited these traits from my mother and Granny Webb. She could

amuse herself for hours, playing with whatever Nature could provide – sticks, pebbles or, better still, a beetle or ant that could be gently manoeuvred about in a make-believe game all of her own, steered along her various 'roads' and into a 'house' beneath a little stone or bush. As she became older, we settled into a routine: at 8 a.m. we ambled over to the Headquarters together, where she would play with her 'Ayah' while I worked. She was a great favourite at the office and particularly loved it when her father and uncle stopped to play with her. I, on the other hand, was becoming less enamoured with her father. His casual time-keeping had long been a source of frustration, even before we were married, for he would think nothing of turning up at any hour for a meal and expect me to produce something, or even not turning up at all after I had gone to a great deal of trouble. He was essentially laid back and happy-go-lucky in his attitude to life, and as we settled into marriage it became clear that I was expected to shoulder all responsibility for running our everyday affairs. In addition to bringing up Jill without much input from him, I was expected to handle our finances, settle the bills and cope with income returns and bureaucracy solo, ensure that the car was licensed and manage all domestic staff matters. I was the opposite of Bill. Like my father, punctuality was a priority for me and I liked to be organized and orderly. There were times when I yearned for a more assertive partner, someone who would share the load and at times take the lead. The seeds of incompatibility were sown early on in our relationship, and as married life progressed they became ever more pronounced, raising ever-louder alarm bells within me.

One thing that Bill was not laid back about was hunting, and the hunting of elephants in particular. I had known this of course from the day I met him, for he purchased an annual elephant-hunting licence from the moment he was eligible. Although this disturbed me, while the stars were in my eyes I had overlooked it; however, here in Tsavo I found it difficult to reconcile the obvious pleasure he derived from it with his role as the custodian of the elephants' safety. Furthermore, this passion of his was impacting on our life together, for whenever his annual leave came round, and I expected the two of us to take Jill on holiday to my parents, who were now living at

Malindi, Bill would have an elephant-hunting expedition as a priority. Since in the course of his anti-poaching duties he was away a great deal, this meant that I hardly saw him and we were gradually drifting apart.

The professional hunting fraternity – of which Bill was a part – was a vexing part of the Park's fabric. Areas adjacent to Tsavo were classified as hunting blocks under the jurisdiction of the Government Game Department, where licensed professional hunters and their clients were allowed to shoot whatever animals appeared on their licence, for which they paid a fee. This was irrespective of the fact that the Game Department had no idea what stocks of game the hunting blocks held. It was feasible that a licensed hunter might shoot the last living lion in the area for all they knew, so their supposed 'control' of these areas was a myth. Furthermore, poaching was rife in these areas, since the Game Department personnel were thin on the ground and were usually fully occupied with dealing with wild animals that had intruded into settlements and were in conflict with the interests of humans. Discipline within the Game Department was lax, with a great deal of shooting 'for the pot' condoned and even practised among the officers, many of whom had joined more because they enjoyed the hunt than because they held any ideals on conservation. David was particularly intolerant of the professional hunters who skulked around the periphery of the Park hoping that one of its magnificent giants would put a foot across the border. I felt a sense of embarrassment that Bill derived so much pleasure from shooting an elephant, and even the National Parks' director, Colonel Mervyn Cowie, frowned upon that fact, and voiced it to David. There had been a time when David had also hunted elephants during his professional hunting days, but since acquiring Samson and Fatuma, and as Warden of Tsavo learning so much about them, nothing was further from his mind.

Having now been married to Bill for some six years, I found myself in a state of inner turmoil. In truth I could not blame this entirely on Bill's inadequacies as a husband, for my initial feelings of respect and admiration for David were turning into something confusing and troubling. Every time I set eyes on him, something shifted inside me.

I could not avoid seeing him because he was part of my everyday life and I worked alongside him in the office. I realized, not without some guilt, that we had also been spending a lot of time together – time that was not strictly work-related. When Bill was away in remoter parts of the Park or on one of his hunting expeditions, rather than leave me on my own, David would take me along on game drives and sometimes to the Voi Hotel Saturday night gatherings.

Saturday-Night-at-the-Voi-Hotel were words that fitted together as one, since it was almost an institution, mandatory for everyone in the district who happened to be around at the time to gravitate there after a week of hard labour and, for many, isolation. Voi was, after all, quite a social place during colonial times, for in addition to the Frenchmen brought over to install the new water pipeline from Mzima to Mombasa in the mid-fifties, there were about seventy other local expatriate European government officials as well as several managers on neighbouring ranches.

It was at these parties that I saw the wilder side of David. Disciplined, focused and hard-working throughout the week, he certainly let his hair down at the Voi Hotel, renowned for his 'paraffin trick', which entailed blowing out a mouthful of paraffin and igniting it so that a long jet of flame shot across the bar. He enjoyed playing mischievous and amusing tricks on visiting revellers and winding up the rather long-suffering manager, Henry Hayes, a large genial Yorkshireman.

I found my heart stirring with jealousy when I saw how attractive David was to other women. He was by far the most attractive man in the district and I soon noticed that he was the perpetual target of female admirers. There was one hot-blooded woman in particular who was an outrageous flirt, capable of drinking any man under the table, and she would home in on David the moment he set foot in the hotel. Shaking her dark curls and draping her arms around his neck, she would come on to him in a shameless manner. Although she was married, she had no qualms about seducing other men, even when her husband was present. David handled her masterfully, with a quiet amusement that simply enhanced the attraction, for he managed to retain an air of unassailability, even though her pursuit of him was relentless. It was interesting to observe David in the company of other women. They were invariably drawn to him, vying for his attention, even though he made no secret of the fact that he was relieved to be free of his matrimonial shackles, and repeated over and over again that he would never be tempted to fall into the same trap again. 'I'm a loner,' he told me, 'far too selfish ever to make a girl happy.' But when I danced with him and he held me in his arms, my knees went weak and my heart raced. I told myself over and over again that David was thirty-seven, way beyond my reach, and that I had a husband and daughter to consider, so I was careful to keep my feelings well hidden, happy to enjoy what I could of him while it was possible.

David made the rugged aspect of Tsavo come alive for me, opening my eyes to the spell of space and the contrasts that transformed the semi-desert of brick red earth and grim leafless trees in the dry season to a vibrant painted paradise after the first rains. The first precious drops of rain had an intoxicating effect on us all, much as they had in Gilgil when my father had stood on the verandah with his arms outstretched, watching a curtain of rain approach. In Tsavo, when rainwater ran in red torrents down the roads and luggas, and the seasonal, normally dry Voi River ran in response to rain from the Taita Hills, we would pile into David's little rubber dinghy and launch it into the flooding river, wobbling precariously as we battled to keep afloat amid all the debris being carried midstream.

David and I sometimes went for a walk, times that were for me an enthralling nature study. No two walks were ever alike. David was a fount of knowledge, pointing out all sorts of things that most people would not even notice – the silken-lined hole of a trapdoor spider with its little lid neatly attached; a gallant dung beetle battling to roll his enormous ball before burying it deep in the ground; the frothy white baubles of the tree-frogs attached to the branches that held the spawn until the little hatchlings plopped into the puddles and pools beneath; the water beetles that could torpedo in any direction. As we went along, he would tell me how everything we saw fitted together. For him every living organism, however humble, was an integral and vital cog in the complex wheel of life, each with its own function, important to the wellbeing of the whole. He taught me to trust my instinct and common sense rather than seek complicated explanations to Nature's riddles. He said: 'You can always count on one thing and that is that Nature usually knows best and can provide the best solution under any set of circumstances, for Nature is adaptable. Don't ever be fooled into believing that man must be obliged to play God, because when he does, he usually messes things up and triggers another set of problems.'

Sometimes Jill and I would accompany David on expeditions to remoter parts of the Park when he had to visit various works-in-progress. As it could take all day to get to our destination, we would set up camp in the bush, sometimes for several days at a time, before heading home. Travelling to and from these sites provided an ideal opportunity to catch up on a backlog of paperwork, and I would take down dictation in shorthand as we went along and type it all up on our return. These excursions afforded me an opportunity to see places I had not visited before, for instance the 6,000-gallon water tank on Kiasa Hill – midway between the Galana and Tiva Rivers – established so that the anti-poaching patrols could operate in the north during the dry season, when there was no permanent water for over seventy miles. Over time, I came to know and love many of the remoter parts of Tsavo that I might never have otherwise seen. At Lugard's Falls the force of water moulded the rocks into sculptural formations bejewelled with red garnet chippings; the Yatta Plateau, Tsavo East's most striking feature, ran like a thin spine the entire length of the Park and beyond, the longest lava flow in the entire world; the Mopea Gap, one of two natural passes in the plateau, was worn down by the passage of millions of elephant feet over the ages, where we always apologized to 'Rudolf', an old bull rhino who had lived there in seclusion until the road disturbed his peace. Thabangunji was the second natural pass in the Yatta, where a lone boulder stood sentinel to graves of the forgotten braves killed in fierce fighting during ancient battles as they defended stolen livestock. David explained that warlike nomads had used this route long ago, preying on others less powerful, and in passing each warrior had tossed a pebble on to the rock, a ritual that was deemed to bring luck. I found it a moving experience to sit quietly by this huge rock, with the whisper of the wind sweeping down the pass, and contemplate ancient battles and fallen men buried under mounds of stone on the shoulders of the pass.

There were many species in Tsavo that were new to me: little Peter's gazelles; the graceful fringe-eared oryx; Somali ostriches, the males of which had blue legs and necks, and cerise shins and beaks in breeding plumage; the gerenuk, a graceful rust-coloured antelope that had abandoned its dependence on water entirely and which stood on its back legs to browse at a higher level. The black leaf-like patterning of their ears captivated me. Even under conditions of extreme aridity, gerenuk shunned water, resorting when hard-pressed to drinking one another's urine, the moisture extracted from the vegetation they ate apparently adequate for their needs. David could talk about the habits of any animal we came across, but it was his insight into the elephants and their role in Nature that impressed me most and that made me realize just how knowledgeable he really was. He had told me of his interest in wildlife since his childhood, how his father had instilled a foundation that David had continued to build upon during his schooldays in England, his job as a professional hunter after the war and his time living in Nyeri. Yet listening to him, I could sense that this was his passion, something that came from knowledge but also from deep within his soul. Long before any studies of elephants had ever been undertaken, he said to me: 'In order to interpret elephant behaviour, you must simply analyse it from a human point of view and that way, you will usually end up close to the truth, something the scientists have yet to learn. They seem to have an arrogant mental block about attributing to animals human aspects of behaviour, particularly in terms of emotion.' Later, I would recall these conversational foundations upon which my own work rested.

David called the northern area and its Tiva River 'the jewel in the crown of Tsavo East'. Whenever duty called in the north, we tried to engineer a night at Tundani around the full moon, erecting our low Hounsfield camp beds in a row on top of a large outcropping of rock from where we could watch the nocturnal action. When the moonlight played on the pale sand, elephants emerged silently, as though from nowhere, dark galleons moving sedately, ivory trapping the moonbeams and gleaming silvery white. Then the rhinos arrived from the shadows on the riverbanks, each one intent on gaining possession of water in a hole in the sand dug by the elephants and, having got one, modifying it to accommodate head and horn. And after night-long activity the theatre opened for the diurnal cast – monkeys and baboons came down from the trees; mongooses scampered about, followed by giraffe, zebras, elands, flocks of sand grouse; doves, weavers, starlings, vulturine guinea fowl and then the raptors, falcons, hawks and eagles, in search of easy pickings. Gradually more and more creatures stepped into the riverbed to slake their thirst at the elephant holes, a symbiotic mass of coexistence, until an alarm sounded at the approach of a predator – a leopard, the lions, hyenas or large packs of hunting dogs. At this point the stage was rapidly vacated in a thundering of hooves and a flurry of flapping wings.

I remember one occasion when, as humans, we experienced a magical moment, accepted as 'belonging' within the animal kingdom. We were in the riverbed, inspecting footprints in the sand, when a shy kudu appeared on the opposite bank. 'Crouch down and pretend to drink,' whispered David urgently. Then, with infinite grace, this beautiful animal with ivory-tipped spiral horns picked its way down the slope, walked straight up alongside us and began to drink from the neighbouring hole just a pace or two away. It was a special thrill to be trusted and accepted as a harmless member of the natural world and I shall never forget that moment as long as I live.

For me these trips were heavenly, providing David with a brief respite from the intensity of the anti-poaching campaign and the day-to-day running of the Park. But it was soon back to business, and while conviction of the dealers who managed to slip through the net eluded us, there was every reason to be pleased with progress. By the end of 1957 almost the entire population of the Waliangulu tribe had either served, or were serving prison sentences – except of course Galogalo Kafonde, who still managed to keep one step ahead. At the end of their prison terms, David and Bill always tried to find employment for the ex-poachers that would keep them otherwise occupied.

They were much in demand by safari operators in the country for work as spotters and trackers.

Up-country, events were unfolding that would have a direct effect on the white settlers. Deep in the Aberdare forest, Operation 'Hot Scrum' had finally closed the net on the last of the Mau Mau insurgents, including the legendary Dedan Kimathi. Just prior to capture, this famous Mau Mau general seemed to have an inkling that his time was up. He had been seen dashing daringly across open spaces, something no seasoned Mau Mau fugitive would normally ever do, and having been on the run for twenty-eight consecutive hours, covering a distance of eighty miles, he collapsed and spent a lonely night on the edge of the forest. The next day he crept along the fringe of trees until he came to a point from where he could see the place where much of his childhood had been spent, and there he sat quietly all day gazing down at the sprawling patchwork of smallholdings and thatched huts. That night, driven by hunger, for the first time in more than forty months he set foot back in the Kikuyu reserve to snatch some sugarcane and unripe bananas before darting back into the shelter of the forest, and three days later, it was all over. He was captured by tribal policemen, who halted him with a shot in the thigh, and although he managed to drag himself back into the forest, he was found some time later. Once his wounds had healed, he was tried in the Supreme Court of Kenya, his charisma evident throughout the trial, the courtroom packed with people who had come from miles around to see this legendary figure. He was found guilty by a jury of African assessors and was hanged in February 1957; in the years ahead an independent Kenya would come to view Dedan Kimathi as a freedom fighter who epitomized the struggle to break free from colonial rule.

With Kimathi's capture, the last of the Mau Mau resistance crumbled and the five-year-long state of emergency officially ended. This was cause for celebration among the white community, of course, and we hoped that life would return to normal. But it was not to be. The winds of change were gathering in far-off Whitehall, blowing in towards the White Highlands, of which Cedar Park, my family's farm, was a part. The strain of the Emergency years had taken a toll on my father and he began to talk of selling up, something we all found inconceivable. I had many sleepless nights thinking about how catastrophic it would be for him and my mother to give up thirty years of hard work and investment. The farm was our anchorage, our homeport in any storm. My father and his farmhands had laboured without rest, without bank mortgages, loans or help from anyone. I was relieved when I learned that he was putting the sale on hold and instead was leasing the farm while he and my mother took a long rest in Malindi.

Malindi is only three hours away from Voi, on the direct route through the Park's Sala entrance gate on the eastern boundary, and it was comforting to know that my parents would now be much more accessible. En route, they stopped to stay with us and catch up with Peter. We could see at once that my father was far from well. Disconcertingly, my mother noticed that things between Bill and me were not quite as they should be. She questioned me closely about David, and although I vehemently denied anything more than a close friendship, she knew me far too well to be fooled. 'I can see the attraction myself,' she said quietly. But thankfully she did not probe me any deeper.

If she had done so, she would have intuitively realized within seconds how deeply in love I was with David. I had seen the fire of desire sometimes burn fleetingly in his eyes when he looked at me, but he was always quick to turn away and envelope himself in aloofness, leaving me confused. I was desperate to know how he felt towards me, but didn't dare ask.

6. Decisions

'Man requires three things in Life: Identity, Stimulation
and Security and the most important of these is Identity.'

– David Sheldrick

David filled my dreams as well as my days, thoughts of him flickering
constantly in my mind. Knowing that our paths would inevitably
separate at some point and I would have to live a lifetime without
him, I made a conscious decision to make the most of the time we
spent together. I had been getting to know him slowly over the years,
storing away the thrilling biographical fragments he shared with me.
I didn't discover for quite some time that he had actually been born
in Egypt, where his father had been serving in Alexandria during the
First World War. He had come to Kenya as a child when his father
took up a Soldier Settler Scheme to become a coffee farmer at
Mweiga. However, while he would tell me things about himself, it
was not easy to penetrate his reserve and get beyond the facts of his
life, and I doubt that I would have become close to him had I not had
the opportunity to work and sometimes party with him. I was sensitive to his inner quietness and soon learned not to pry and enquire
too deeply. Of course, in my heart, I wanted to know everything
there was to know about him.

David kept his innermost thoughts to himself, no doubt the legacy
of being sent to boarding school in England from the age of seven to
seventeen. When I asked him if he had found it difficult being away
from his parents for so long, he said, 'I missed them and our home
sorely to begin with, crying quietly into my pillow at night for
months. But that passed and by the time I came home, I could hardly
remember them. In fact, at the end of my time at school, I walked

straight past my mother at Nyeri station.' Actually David was the pride and joy of his parents, an only child, whom they adored. At school he excelled in sport, as a lightweight boxer and a fine horseman. When I met his mother, I could sense the fierce love she felt for her son and it made me realize the inconceivable sacrifices his parents had made in sending him abroad for his education. They must have been overjoyed when he came back to Kenya in 1930, after which he worked as a farm manager on the Kinangop. Never one to boast of his achievements, I had heard from many people that his outstanding ability as a polo player would have qualified him for the Kenyan national team had not the Second World War intervened. While David served in Abyssinia, Somalia and Burma, his parents once again waited stoically for him to return. They were rewarded when he was among those chosen to represent the East African contingent of King's African Rifles at the victory parade in London.

While he kept his thoughts strictly under wraps, I could sense that David was not entirely indifferent to me. When we danced together at the Voi Hotel and he held me close, I could feel his heart racing in unison with mine. On the rare occasions that I saw the fire of desire in his eyes when off guard, my heart sang, only to become disillusioned again when he became detached and apparently indifferent, too preoccupied by other things to even notice my presence. When one day he murmured, 'Bill is a really lucky bloke,' I was euphoric for days. Bill was not 'lucky', for our marriage had long been devoid of any passion. Now we were more like brother and sister than husband and wife, and when Bill confessed that he had made contact with Eugene, an old flame, I was surprised to find that I cared less about this than I did when David was pursued by other women.

Jill was my greatest source of comfort and happiness, her childlike innocence so refreshing, her inquisitive and adventurous spirit blossoming. She adored David's baby orphaned elephants Samson and Fatuma, and in the early evening we would sit together and watch them with a running commentary between us about what they were up to, what we thought they were thinking and what we thought they were 'saying' to each other. Jill already knew Fatuma very well. Even at the tender age of five Fatuma was showing a strong motherly instinct; she would often make a point of seeking Jill out and with her trunk would gently try to steer my little daughter between her forelegs, as a mother elephant would her calf. Jill, of course, had been brought up with the baby elephants and viewed them just as another child would a tame dog or cat. When Fatuma's displays of affection happened to interrupt a special game, it was amusing to watch Jill fearlessly try to push the elephant aside. Fatuma was endlessly patient and gentle but she was also determined in her protectiveness, so it usually ended in a compromise, with Jill merely incorporating the elephant's four column-like legs as she carried on with her game beneath Fatuma's expansive belly. I knew enough to know that elephants never unwittingly step on anything they don't intend to, and I could see that Jill's every move was monitored by Fatuma's highly sensitive trunk, as her soft brown eyes fringed with lashes as long as my hand gazed downwards shining with a calm intelligence, the eyes of an animal that thinks and understands.

These were special times, of great consolation to me. Watching the tame orphaned elephants also took me outside of myself and I began to build a good understanding of their behaviour and habits, becoming absorbed in their routines and emotions. When you begin to look, you see things you did not notice before, or you look beneath the surface and ask yourself questions. I watched the myriad ways in which Samson and Fatuma used their trunks, marvelling at their dexterity. The trunk was an ultra-sensitive nose that could be raised like a periscope to test scent on the wind, or a hugely flexible and powerful arm, its tip divided into two nimble fingers to pluck or pick up food and water and carry it to their mouths. The trunk also added the loud 'trumpet' tone to an elephant's voice that at first had startled Jill, although she was now completely used to it. We knew, of course, that the trunk could also be dangerous, capable of extinguishing life with just one swipe. A few years before, a young soldier stationed at the local army camp had walked jauntily up to an elephant and offered it a bun, just as he would an elephant in his English zoo, and with just one quick flick of the trunk the elephant had hurled him into the air, instantly crushing every bone in his body as though it were matchwood.

I could spend hours watching the ways in which Samson and Fatuma browsed, deftly using their trunks to carefully search out one tiny shoot or strip an entire branch of its leaves in one swift operation. We marvelled at the ingenious way in which they removed bark, using their trunks to swivel a branch round their mouths, chomping a neat circle with their massive molars and then taking hold of a loose end with a finger of the trunk, allowing the branch to fall so that the bark peeled off in a long sliver. Alternatively, if they wanted a plant where nourishment was stored in the roots, they would uproot it, and with their trunks flap it against their forelegs to shake off the earth before eating it. And if a plant was difficult to grip because it grew too low, they used a front foot in conjunction with the trunk to lever it up from the ground.

Both Samson and Fatuma knew how to turn on a tap with a twist of the trunk and would often pick up the hosepipe to place it directly in their mouths, thereby sparing themselves the trouble of first having to fill their trunks with water. However, not even David could convince them of the necessity of turning off a tap once they had quenched their thirst, which, to me, was perfectly logical from the elephant point of view. If, by a twist of the trunk, water could be made to flow in a parched land, why on earth would they want to stop it? Samson also had a flair for manipulating gates and early on had mastered the art of opening the door to his stable, stretching his trunk through the bars at the top to lift the latch, at the same time pushing against the door with his body to open it. And, ever the gentleman, having let himself out, he would then go round to Fatuma's stable and open her door as well, this time reversing the procedure, pulling the door open instead of pushing it. David had been forced to devise an elaborate system of bars, locks and wires in order to keep Samson confined and out of his garden at night.

I was constantly amazed at the sensitivity of their skin, for although it was thick and covered in rigid hairs, it was spongy and they could feel the touch of even a feather. Segmented like a giant patchwork quilt, the hide hung loosely over the hindlegs like baggy harem pants. The hairs of the tail were long and pliable and much sought after by the rangers, who plucked them from the bodies of the dead they came across in the Park to fashion beautiful, adjustable bracelets – that is, if the poachers hadn't got there first. These bracelets were very popular and everyone, regardless of sex, in those days wore them with pride, for they were the stamp of a bush-loving person.

The great ears, as soft and as smooth as silk on the hind side, were also accurate mood indicators that played a significant role in the subtle body language of the elephants. Sometimes we would see Samson and Fatuma spread their ears as though listening to far-off sounds, and when Jill and I were hot and bothered, we wished we could use our ears like fans as they did.

I illustrated to Jill the role of elephants in ancient times by telling her about Hannibal's legendary crossing of the Alps, and their service to men during war. They were depicted in early African rock paintings, and on ancient coinage. Of course I knew all too grimly how elephants were sought after for the ivory of their tusks and about the exquisitely carved objects dating from the past to the present day. However, in spite of long historical interest, by the mid 1950s there was a noticeable absence of scientific data about elephants, no detailed observational studies about their habits or the pattern and movements of herds. And while scientists often visited Tsavo, generally David's opinion of them was not altogether favourable. I had seen him at his most frustrated once, when trying to persuade one group that in times of extremity, elephants were capable of drawing on reserves of stomach water by inserting their trunk down the back of the throat and drawing it out to spray over a fevered body, something he had witnessed many times – as had I – but astoundingly the scientists remained sceptical. He said, 'I suppose it won't be "scientific" until one of them writes it up as his own discovery in one of those scientific rigmaroles that no layman can interpret.' Actually, in this case it was the camera that settled the matter once and for all.

David had long set about gathering data in order to solve some of the unanswered questions about elephants himself. Having noticed my interest, he asked me if I had the time and inclination to help document the various experiments he was planning. Little did I know at the time how my involvement would come to shape my life.

To begin with David believed it was crucial to ascertain the movements of the herds in the Park as accurately as possible, so as to assess the extent of their range. There were no such things as radio transmitters on collars then, so we had to find a way of marking as many elephants as we could. David constructed a rather primitive marking gun consisting of a container filled with paint, with a nozzle at one end and connected to a compressed air cylinder at the other. We decided to test it on Samson, in order to test its range, so one afternoon, as he was browsing just below the workshops, David squirted him with water. Looking puzzled and a little put out, Samson removed himself to more peaceful surroundings, eyeing David most suspiciously first over one shoulder and then the other, with his ears slightly raised. We couldn't help laughing at his wounded ego, but David was satisfied with the result.

We then took the marking contraption to a popular waterhole on the road to Mudanda Rock. From the top of a small rocky promontory my job was to signal when a herd was approaching; David and a ranger meanwhile crouched hidden behind a spindly little sapling that I considered was barely adequate protection against an elephant. We were rewarded when a group of eight elephants turned up, led by a cantankerous old cow known to us as Flop Ears. She waded into the water ahead of the others, thirstily sucking up trunkfuls of water while I signalled to David. Anxiously awaiting the moment when a jet of white paint would hit Flop Ears, instead all I could hear was a faint hissing noise as a dribble of white paint oozed out of the end of the nozzle, dripping on to David's shoes! Attempts to remedy the device immediately attracted the attention of old Flop Ears, who let out a blood-curdling trumpet, turned and hurled herself at the sapling, sending both David and his assistant into full-blown retreat. By the time David had been able to deal with the blocked nozzle and the next herd arrived, it was already getting dark, but fortunately this time the experiment was successful, marking a matriarch's rump with a large splodge of white. As soon as she felt the spray, however, she too spun round and put on a furious demonstration that sent the men scrambling once more up the rock, while the rest of the herd stampeded. Obviously the rather limited range of David's marking device was a handicap, but in spite of this, over the following weeks, we managed to successfully mark eighteen wild elephants.

Keeping tabs on these elephants was another matter, for this was long before the days of any aerial surveillance capability. However, we chanced upon the marked individuals intermittently during our travels around the Park, one spotted close on seventy miles from where it had been marked, way out in the middle of the northern area. Coupled with regular sightings of elephants with distinctive tusk configurations, this meant that David now knew that Tsavo's elephant herds were not restricted in their movements, but instead utilized the entire Park and beyond, depending on where rain had brought on a green flush of vegetation and been sufficient to replenish dried-out waterholes. They could be in the southern section of the Park one day and in the far north the next, for 100 miles was just a little stroll for an elephant. Although our paint experiment lasted only until the onset of rain, when the elephants plastered their bodies in red mud, it had served its purpose.

We were soon on to the next experiment, which involved assembling a collection of elephant food plants. Specimens of each were pressed and sent for analysis to the Scientific Research Centre in Kabete, outside Nairobi, where Dr Phil Glover, a botanist who was incredibly encouraging of David's research, set up a file for each plant species. Samson and Fatuma were an invaluable resource for this research. During the course of one full day David walked with them, monitoring and collecting everything they selected to eat from the moment they left their night stockades, until dusk when they returned. We were astounded that Samson browsed sixty-four different plant species during the course of that one day, and only devoted four hours and twenty-two minutes to purposes other than feeding! To finish off the experiment, we also collected and weighed the output of Samson's eating, and it took me some time to shake off the smell of the rather fruity paper bags containing all the elephant 'balls'.

David was interested to know how long food took to pass through an elephant's gut, so for that experiment we fed Samson a large quantity of oranges. Oranges were his favourite titbit and he gobbled them up greedily, one after the other. We had not anticipated quite such a long vigil, for the first orange took eleven hours to appear in Samson's droppings, expelled in a very neat half, and the last one did not appear until a full nineteen hours later! This, combined with an analysis of the protein passed in elephant dung, prompted a discussion on the surprising inefficiency of an elephant's digestive tract.

One of the qualities I admired most in David was that he never expected anyone to do anything that he could not do himself, and his proficiency and competence in every aspect of his work was awe-inspiring, his research findings contributing to reliable and valuable data about Tsavo's biodiversity. In between gathering evidence from the elephant population, he also managed to find time to compile a checklist of all the birds of the Park, before adding rodents. This entailed night sorties to capture rare nocturnal species for documentation, so exciting mouse hunts after dark became the norm. Unusual specimens were kept alive in boxes of earth on the back verandah of his house, where they could establish their underground tunnels and nests and become the subject of more prolonged scrutiny. Looking after the rodents was added to my list of tasks until such time as they were set free again. Jill and I would do the rounds of the boxes daily to tend to them, giving each a story. Her growing imagination was very attuned to the inner working of the lives of animals.

Nor did David stop there. The office was becoming crowded with frogs, snakes and insects, of which my police prosecutor colleague, 'Chillicracker' Childs, was outspokenly disapproving: 'Things are crowded enough around here without boxes of bloody rats, jars of frogs, bags of puff adders and flies stuck on pins in the drawers!' he moaned. Meanwhile, David was making new discoveries. He found a soft tick known to carry relapsing fever in a warthog burrow far from any human settlement; a rare species of free-tailed bat with a dead flat head, never before recorded in East Africa but known in Egypt; and a small tree-frog, new to science, which was named *Hyperolius sheldricki* in his honour, as was a red mite. Such was David's passion for chronicling the life of the Park that we were often visited by experts who came to share his research expeditions. Alex Duff-Mackay of the Coryndon Museum (now the National Museum of Kenya) was a regular visitor as the first tropical rainstorm heralded the end of another long dry season. As he came up the path to the office in his signature long green wading boots, 'Chillicracker' would mutter disparagingly, 'Oh my God, here comes the frog man!'

Rain – and we had two rainy seasons a year, the unpredictable long rains in April/May and the more reliable short rains in October/ November – literally woke up Tsavo's rich diversity of frog-life, which rejoiced with a vigorous cacophony that filled the night with croaks, squeaks, chirrups and chirps. My favourite were the tree-frogs, whose voices sounded like a thousand tinkling bells. Alex's arrival meant nights sloshing around in waterholes and puddles trying to catch some of the more interesting species and record their specific calls. Giant bullfrogs emerged only occasionally, in response to exceptionally and unusually heavy rain. They plopped around inundated stretches of land with a loud splash, frenzied in their feeding as their cavernous mouths barbed with ferocious teeth voraciously gobbled up whatever was in their path, be it other frogs, small rodents, snakes, or even huge scorpions which protested with repeated stings from their lashing tails as they were on their way down. When David presented me with 'Edward' and asked me to oversee his feeding in an elaborate custom-built enclosure with a pond and everything else a bullfrog could wish for, I declined, backed up by 'Chillicracker', who simply enquired of David: 'Are you bonkers?'

A very interesting visitor was the famous herpetologist C. J. P. Ionides, who made David's collection of snakes look like those of an inexperienced amateur. 'Iodine', as he was affectionately called, was a colourful eccentric, utterly fearless and remarkable in the pursuit of his beloved snakes. In fact he was so passionate about them that he would allow himself to be bitten, sit down to record how he felt, and, when it looked as though he was going under, give himself a shot of snake serum and continue the notes about his recovery. He could whittle out a snake from the most unlikely places, often uncomfortably close at hand. Within half an hour of arriving at the Park, he would be off at a brisk pace with his snake-catching gear – his conical felt hat tipped at a jaunty angle, a cigarette hanging from his mouth – poking about in the bushes outside the office, popping boomslangs and spitting cobras into bags. He unnerved 'Chillicracker' more than any other visitor we hosted, much to my amusement.

It was just after David found a rare and beautiful pinkish snake of the ramphiophis family, which Iodine deemed unusual enough to be sent off to the museum in Nairobi, that the anti-poaching campaign entered its final phase. It had come to light that there was a large cache of ivory at Ushingu, north-east of the Park boundary, and under Bill's command the Voi Force was sent to the area to take a closer look. The country was waterless and featureless, and the heat stifling, so finding elephant skeletons in the endless clumps of thickets was no easy matter. However, from experience Bill knew what to tell his men: 'Look under any broken candelabra trees,' he said. The weight of the vultures waiting atop for other predators to disperse having taken their share invariably flattened the soft top of these euphorbias.

After days of searching in difficult and dangerous conditions, involving aggressive elephants and lions confronted at close quarters, the grisly remains of a poacher's corpse were found, in addition to uncovering over fifty old hideouts, the carcasses of 381 dead elephants and recovering ninety-two tusks.

Following this, David decided to deploy all three anti-poaching units in an area known as Dadimabule, halfway between the Galana and Tana rivers. Once more conditions were hazardous, but again the results of the search were staggering: 352 tusks, totalling 6,604lb of ivory, plus a further 1,589lb of butts and other bits and pieces strewn around in the bush. In all 1,280 elephant carcasses were found, with close on 200 tiny corpses lying beside their slain mothers. It was disturbing to reflect on them, grief-stricken and orphaned, their soft petal ears frazzling painfully to wafer-thin parchment in the scorching Tsavo sun, crying helplessly for a mother who in her dying moments knew all too well the fate that awaited her calf – the terror of lonely isolation and eventual death by dehydration and starvation, or a violent end as a meal for a lion.

In all, an overwhelming 25,719lb of ivory was recovered during the anti-poaching campaign, all of which would be sold at the annual ivory auction in Mombasa to more than cover the costs of the three-year operation. For David this huge amount of ivory served to justify the stern measures he had masterminded to combat the illegal poaching, for a slaughter on this scale could not be left unchecked. There was, however, a negative spin-off from the campaign, for having made the Park more secure for elephants, many more were coming in from outlying areas, especially from places where the human population was expanding. It was becoming obvious from our travels around the Park that the elephants were responsible for large-scale destruction of vegetation through their feeding habits and travel patterns. I had seen stretches of the Park near sources of permanent water that were beginning to resemble a battlefield, with twisted debris – mainly of the commiphora myrrh tree – littering the ground and only a few unscathed trees left standing. We had even witnessed Samson and Fatuma making their own contribution, especially after rain, when they became positively exuberant, trumpeting excitedly as they raced around downing every commiphora in sight below the office, a sort of off-Broadway enactment of what was happening on a grander scale out in the Park. Broken and mutilated trees were fast becoming the hallmark of Tsavo East and calls for action were starting to appear in the press: 'Too many elephants! Something must be done!' The press had covered the anti-poaching campaign in largely sympathetic tones, so talk now of over-population and irreversible habitat degradation as a result was an acute embarrassment. We were terrified that we would be made to follow the pattern of the South Africans, who 'culled' their elephants on an annual basis in order to keep the population at a fixed level and, so as not to waste the resource, processed them in meat factories for sale as pet food. Should this happen in Kenya, how could we possibly explain to the poachers a sudden necessity for having to kill large numbers of elephants when they themselves had been denied doing so?

The anti-poaching campaign closed on a fitting accolade for David, who was awarded the MBE in the Queen's Birthday Honours of 13 June 1959. Even more significant than this, however, was the sudden surrender of none other than the legendary poacher Galogalo Kafonde himself, who strode into the Malindi police station and asked to be taken to Bwana Saa Nane. He arrived at Park Headquarters handcuffed and under police guard, and yet I could see at once that he had about him the same tangible aura of authority that characterized David. It seemed he was disillusioned, tired of being constantly hounded, and wanted to pay his penalty and live in peace. And as he answered David's questions simply and with quiet truth, I was struck by his inner conviction. At the end of one session he fixed his steadfast gaze on David and said, 'The elephants are finished. Rich people wanting more and more are responsible. Like you, I fear the demise of the elephants, for they are at the core of our culture and our daily lives. Always the Waliangulu have lived among elephants and have hunted them honourably as true men, only targeting large bulls and never killing cow elephants or their babies. Now "others" who do not care about them kill them clumsily for mere gain. I want no part of that and I swear I will never hunt an elephant again.' David replied simply, 'I believe you.' From that day to this, no Waliangulu tribesman has ever been found poaching in the Tsavo National Park.

Towards the end of 1959, with poaching within the Park and its immediate environs now under control, it was time for the two Game Department units, Makindu and Hola forces, to be disbanded and for colleagues to return to normal duties. The farewell party at the Voi Hotel was the usual riotous event, but despite the revelry there was a thread of sadness running through the evening. We had forged unlikely friendships and strong bonds during the campaign, overcoming adversities, experiencing highs and lows together, and it was with deep regret that we parted. I was especially fond of 'Chillicracker', with whom I had shared an office for so long and who, as the recipient of many practical jokes, had been such a good sport. He returned to police duties only briefly before leaving for England and regretfully our paths never crossed again. I have thought of him down the years and wondered if he knew of the legacy of his work, the tangible contribution he had made to the conservation of the elephant population of Tsavo that lives on today.

Now that the campaign was over, David had to decide how best to employ senior members of the anti-poaching team. David requested that my brother Peter now be officially put in charge of the northern area, where a rustic but very attractive cottage was being erected on the slopes of Ithumba Hill. Here, a crystal-clear spring provided a good source of permanent water, and the view across to Kimathena Massif, which marked the Park's northernmost boundary, was spectacular. Peter would be in control of the ongoing development of the northern area, the custodian of some of my most favourite corners of Tsavo, as well as the giant elephants of the Tiva sand river. Like David, he had the challenge of taming the region yet keeping it wild, and I knew Peter would apply the meticulous standards of perfection that he had inherited from our father. I was very fond of my brother and was pleased he had been given this opportunity. While he was popular and outgoing on the surface, inside he was more unsure and introverted and I felt proud that he had achieved this promotion.

That was Peter taken care of, but what of Bill – and by extension Jill and myself? One clear-skied morning David came into the office and handed me a note. He asked me to type it up and send it to the National Park's director, Mervyn Cowie. This is what it said:

I have been given a lot of credit for the anti-poaching work in the National Parks Annual Report and I feel very much of it is undeserved. I would like to point out that any successes we have so far achieved in the field have been mainly due to the efforts of Bill Woodley. He has been quite tireless in his efforts to break the poaching racket and has infected everyone in the field with his enthusiasm. He has gone to endless trouble to obtain information and to get to know the country in which the poachers operate. The methods used by Bill and the forces under his command were adopted without question by the two other forces engaged in anti-poaching with spectacular results. His knowledge of the Waliangulu people is unrivalled and his advice invariably sought by the other Force Commanders when dealing with the Waliangulu. In view of this, I should be grateful if tribute could be paid to his work as I am anxious that his part in the campaign should be duly recognized.

It was. When Colonel Cowie came to Tsavo East to congratulate all who had contributed to the success of the campaign, he singled

Bill out and offered him promotion – the job of Warden in charge of the Aberdare and Mount Kenya National Parks. As Bill shook his hand and people around us smiled, I felt the blood drain from my face. Nyeri was some 300 miles away. Living there would mean leaving Tsavo and David and my mind was in turmoil, even though I was proud that Bill's contribution to the success of the anti-poaching campaign had been recognized. But at that moment, I felt as though my heart would break. I slipped quietly from the room and, once outside, fled in disarray.

I needed to be entirely alone to martial my thoughts in the solitude of a wild place. I only had to walk a short distance before the nyika engulfed me. Sitting at the foot of a gnarled old commiphora tree, I wrestled with the dilemma that now confronted me until I ran out of tears and my jumbled thoughts began to cohere. I knew that it would not be fair to Bill to live a lie, for I would never be able to erase David from either my heart or my mind, but at the same time I was deeply aware of the stigma attached to divorce at that point in time, for it turned one into a social pariah and impacted on all who were close. David had always made it clear that he would never contemplate marriage again, so I could not expect a future with him, however passionately I felt. But at the same time guilt assailed me, for were I to leave Bill, Jill would be deprived of her father. Moreover, she and I would have to move to Nairobi so that I could take on secretarial work to cover our expenses. I knew that I would not be able to depend on Bill for help in this connection.

The thought of having to go back to work in Nairobi terrified me, for I could not imagine either Jill or myself in a city environment. Tsavo was our spiritual balm and I longed to live here for ever alongside the man who was undoubtedly my soulmate. How could I bring myself – even for the sake of my precious daughter – to turn my back on Tsavo and David in order to endure a union that had grown as cold as the mists of the high altitude where we would now be expected to live?

And then, with a clarity that startled me, I knew that I had to make a break, whatever the cost. I would return to my family, find a job in Nairobi, settle Jill into school and get on with life, returning to

Tsavo from time to time whenever I could. By now darkness had fallen without me even being aware of the passage of time, and I knew I must get back to Jill. I heard a soft footfall beside me and instinctively I knew that it was David. Confused and embarrassed, I buried my face in my hands and began to sob all over again. His voice was gentle: 'Daphne,' he said, 'it's for the best. Your future is with Bill and Jill, not here in Tsavo with me. In time you'll forget that I ever existed and I know you will grow to love the mountains, just as you did Tsavo.'

I was aghast, my dreams shattered: 'How did you know I was here?' I spluttered through the onslaught of tears. 'Go away! I hate you!' But David took me in his arms, holding me against his chest, and as he stroked my hair, he murmured: 'It would be easier for us both if you did.' His bush jacket smelled of tobacco and soap. Desperately I clung to him, but he untangled my arms and took me back to his house, where he handed me a brandy. When I felt calmer, he drove me home, apologizing to Bill for keeping me so late.

Back at home, dishevelled and desolate, I sat down on the sofa. Bill sensed at once that I was in some sort of crisis. He said, 'Talk to me, Daphne. We must sort ourselves out,' and somehow I found the courage to tell him what I had in mind – that I would not be coming to Nyeri with him but instead wanted a divorce. For a moment Bill looked away, but then he told me that he had known for some time that my affections lay elsewhere and he blamed himself, as he had been no angel. We talked late into the night, especially about Jill, and then about our plans for the future. We decided we would carry on pretty much as normal until the time came to leave Tsavo and that meanwhile, I would break the news to my family. We spoke without bitterness or recrimination, understanding the bond of friendship that existed between us and how necessary this decision felt. I could only think how lucky I was that Bill was so stoic and dignified. In fact his acceptance of our separation not only lessened the trauma for Jill but also cemented an enduring, lifelong friendship between us. As sleep eluded me later that night, I thought of Granny Webb and how much I missed her – she had predicted this outcome, but I knew she would have counselled me wisely on the uncertain next stage of my life.

The next morning in the office, as David was working at his desk, I told him what Bill and I had decided, hoping against hope that he would reassure me and be happy at the news. Instead, he looked up sharply, and said: 'Are you quite sure you know what you are doing, Daphne? I hope I have not unwittingly influenced your decision or that you might have included me in your future.' At that moment I felt as though I had been punched in the stomach and instantly saw red. 'You should be so lucky,' I retorted, striding from the room. At that moment I hated him, and driving back home I vowed never to set foot in his office again.

Needless to say, that resolve evaporated rapidly, and the next day David apologized for his tactless words. I could sense that he had something to ask me, and over a conciliatory cup of coffee he told me that Sir Julian Huxley, a much-respected scientist, and several other experts were flying down to Tsavo to take a look at the elephants' impact on the habitat. A safari into the northern area was planned, and David asked me if I would be prepared to come along to supervise the catering in camp. Bill agreed that Jill and I would enjoy another safari, since he needed to fill his elephant licence and had planned, while on his hunting expedition, to spend time with Eugene.

The visitors were due to arrive imminently, so an advance party went on ahead to set up camp. There was nothing I enjoyed more than camping out in the bush, and I was well versed in what to do, consulting my reliable 'master list'. Professional and a perfectionist in all he undertook, David's safaris were luxurious compared to those of Bill, for he had, after all, escorted many VIPs, including the Aga Khan and his vast entourage, when working for the early professional hunting firm Safariland. Recalling my father's take on Bill's early camping habits, I couldn't help smiling! David even had a safari fridge, which, in those days, was the height of luxury in a bush camp. It was enclosed in a stout box that opened at the front and back, and it made housekeeping in the bush a great deal easier, since we could take along plenty of fresh provisions. I took great pleasure in packing the smart green numbered chop-boxes with whatever we needed to produce gourmet meals for our VIP visitors. Like my mother and our pioneering ancestors, I was proficient at turning out fresh bread and even cakes while in the bush, something that never failed to impress important guests, and, more importantly, David. The oven was an empty paraffin tin, with a lengthways shelf halfway down and a door in front that closed. By heaping varying quantities of glowing coals around and on top of the tin, the temperature could be easily regulated, the trick being to know how much coal made up a hot, medium or cool oven. There were a few other tricks of the trade that I had up my sleeve, gleaned from my forebears. Carrots and other root vegetables could be kept for longer if 'planted' in damp earth, and poultry when gutted and stuffed with charcoal and leaves would keep for longer if it were left unwashed and hung in an airy place.

So it was that within minutes of arriving at our camping destination the tents sprang up like mushrooms under David's supervision, and Jill and I busily began gathering wood so that a huge bonfire could be lit and the embers scraped aside for the safari kettle and the much-needed cup of tea. The safari kettle was mine, a huge black cast-iron monster weighing a ton that had come with Great-Uncle Will all the way from South Africa. Although water took ages to boil in it, it held the heat like no other, and once it was heated, tea or coffee was readily available at short notice. I knew that Jill was well versed in the do's and don'ts of safari life, instinctively on the lookout for snakes and scorpions that might be sheltering in the nooks and crannies of the fallen logs we collected for the fire, and careful not to wander on her own too far from camp. As the tea brewed, the camp rapidly took shape. Ready-made bedding for each camp bed was unfolded from a rolled-up canvas bedroll; camp tables for the mess tent were draped with brightly coloured kekoy tablecloths, and a basin positioned beside each tent was filled with hot water, with towels secured to the guy ropes by a clothes peg. David's camps were always sited with great attention to pleasing surroundings, with an eye for shade and the view and, where possible, within reach of water. Twelve-volt bulbs connected to a vehicle supplied electric light, and a hot bath or cold shower was always available, with a bamboo mat to keep feet clean as soon as one stepped out. The shower itself consisted of a rose fitted to a drum, which was filled with water to the required temperature, hoisted over a branch and anchored by a stout rope. Such luxury and detail in terms of camping was unusual and impressive in the 50s, even though today it is expected.

The night before the guests arrived, when Jill and the safari staff were asleep, David and I found ourselves alone by the campfire. We sat long into the night talking of many things and sharing memories, as the embers of the fire slowly dimmed to the music of the night – the plaintive piping of a pearl-spotted owlet, the roar of a distant lion, the splashing of elephants drinking downstream. As the embers were reduced to just a soft glow, inhibitions evaporated and our souls opened to the mutual longing in our eyes. David put his arm loosely around me as he walked me towards my tent. At the entrance, he turned as though to move away, but within a heartbeat he was back, crushing me to him as he kissed my lips, my hair, my eyes, my neck, murmuring that perhaps we should share a camp bed, just this once.

That night remains with me, indelibly etched in my soul. It was a night of wonder, igniting an all-consuming love that has not faltered since. It was a magical night, unleashing a passion and tenderness in David that I had hardly dared to allow myself even to dream of. Today I would give the rest of my life to simply experience that time again. I hold it deep within my heart, along with an image of him that never fades. As the cool yellow light of the Tsavo moon framed the entrance of the tent, I knew that I would love this man for ever.

With daylight came the guilt, of course – and with the guilt, the guests. From then on neither he nor I could deny ourselves the stolen opportunities that came our way in all sorts of wild and unlikely places. Now I knew David's body as well as his mind, and both were strong and beautiful.

7. New Beginnings

'I have a very handsome man, who is honey to a bee; he fluttered
every female heart, and that included me. And some were coy, and
others bold, and some had hair of shining gold. But of the many
in the game, just one would live to bear his name.'

– Anon

At the end of 1958 Jill and I left the wild spaces of Tsavo and headed
for Nairobi. We moved in with my sister Sheila and her family and I
found work as a secretary in a finance office. While I mostly felt as if
I were suffocating, Jill adapted to our new life, enjoying the company
of her young cousins, Alistair and Valerie, and attending a nearby
nursery school. Sheila and her husband, Jim, kindly welcomed us
into their home, the sound of children's voices and lively piano-
playing filling the house each evening after work. Nights were my
worst time: I was haunted by the decisions I had made, racked by
insecurity and anxiety. It was not as if David had even hinted at a life
together with him, and on the evening of my departure from Tsavo,
as the night train left the platform at Voi station, I tearfully watched
his tall figure diminish until the station was just a glow of yellow
lights beyond the curve of the horizon. I knew that I could not live
without this man. But David had continued to make it clear that he
was too scarred by the experience of his first marriage ever to contemplate it again, so I had no idea what lay ahead. It was the love and
support of my family, together with Jill's sunny disposition, that got
me through those dark-blue days.

By this time, my younger sister Betty was also working in Nairobi
and it was she who secured me a job, working in the same office but
for a different boss. Her fiancé, Graham Bales, was extremely helpful

and supportive of our family and was already a great favourite with us all. Betty and I had not spent much time together as we grew up, the four years between us separating our paths through school. I had left home when she was just fifteen, so this was a welcome opportunity to get to know her and Graham, whom she had met at their Baptist chapel. It was a surprise to find that Betty had become so religious, but she was never judgemental about my situation, already very fond of David as well as Bill. Graham was a truly good man who I could see was going to be a devoted husband, and I was happy for Betty – happy, too, that Jill now had the opportunity to spend time with her cousins and aunts.

Like me, Jill missed being in the open air of the bush country. Bill was soon settled at Nyeri, with the Aberdare Mountains, with which he was so familiar, just a stone's throw away, so Jill enjoyed visiting him whenever opportunity permitted. The sordid process of initiating divorce proceedings of course fell to me and it turned out that there were two avenues I could pursue – proving cruelty, which certainly was not an option, or adultery. The lawyer advised me that the charge of adultery would be easy to prove but would require Bill's cooperation, along with a considerable loan from my father, for it would entail employing a detective who would have to witness Bill and a hired lady 'partner' signing in at the hotel as Mr and Mrs. They then had to be seen leaving the hotel together the next morning, having ostensibly shared the same bed. The detective's testimony together with the hotel register would suffice for the court proceedings, and this, said the lawyer, was how most incompatible couples managed to untie the marriage knot. Bill was willing to follow this option and so duly signed into the Avenue Hotel, though he remarked later that he would rather have taken Eugene along than the woman he found himself with in the hotel room. Following presentation of the 'evidence', the court then issued the decree nisi, but we had to wait a full year for the decree absolute to come through and officially dissolve our marriage. Bill was amusingly supportive throughout this process and we remained good friends, something that seemed to amaze everyone. From our perspective, we had merely made a simple mistake when young – no reason at all now to become arch-enemies.

However, every day my mind was 300 miles away in Tsavo with David. I missed him and Tsavo sorely and lived for his letters, unsettled whenever he alluded to a Saturday night party at the Voi Hotel. I longed to meet Kanderi and Aruba, two newly orphaned elephants that had been welcomed joyously into the fold by Samson and Fatuma. By now Samson was well over six feet tall and the self-appointed 'prefect' of the group, basking in the admiration of the other little bull, Kanderi, while Fatuma as the matriarch was the leader, focused on mothering both Kanderi and Aruba. She and Samson often met up with wild elephants during sorties along the Voi River, where they went to enjoy a wallow during the heat of the day. David wrote that Fatuma had played truant one day, opting to go off with a wild herd and taking Kanderi and Aruba with her. By nightfall they had not yet returned and David wondered whether this was the parting of the ways. Samson was restless that night, bellowing and trumpeting, obviously missing his three friends, and the next morning he was even more forlorn, refusing to accompany the keepers out into the bush as usual and even uncharacteristically disinterested in food, fluid running from his temporal glands an indication of emotional distress.

At the time, wrote David, he had guests in residence, and that evening, returning from a trip to Mudanda, they came across a herd of twenty-five or so elephants feeding on an open plain. At the approach of the vehicle the herd moved off, but three familiar figures remained behind, clearly puzzled by the nervousness of their wild friends. 'I recognized Fatuma at once,' wrote David, 'so I got out of the car to call her. She immediately came hurrying over to me, little Kanderi and Aruba trailing behind. She wanted me to join her in following the herd, after a few paces turning round to see if I was coming. When she saw I hadn't moved, she came back to me, rumbled softly and wrapped her trunk around me, so I stood there with her beside me until the herd had moved off. I decided to let the guests drive the car back while I walked Fatuma, Kanderi and Aruba home.'

David then recounted his walk with the elephants back across country and I could visualize every step as though I were there myself. The night was pitch black, the indistinct outline of Mazinga Hill just a distant beacon, so he could see only a couple of paces in front of him. However, the elephants knew the way unerringly, never faltering for a moment. What touched him the most was the fact that they seemed to understand that he was disadvantaged in the dark and knew he needed guidance. As it became darker, they pressed closer to him, until he found himself sandwiched between Fatuma and Kanderi, walking with a hand resting lightly against a foreleg, the pace of their walk adjusted to match his own. He knew that they passed other groups of elephants in the dark, as he could hear them and even smell them, and it surprised him that the orphans avoided contact, presumably because they instinctively knew that David's presence would be unwelcome. 'It was such a humbling and stirring experience,' he continued. 'I felt at one with them in their world, entirely dependent on them for my safety, sheltered and protected as if I were one of their own. How I wish we humans could interpret what was going on beyond our field of vision by smell or hearing like they can. It took about four hours to get back, and you should have seen the welcome Samson gave us. He was beside himself with joy.'

This account made me yearn to return to Tsavo, and I was elated when a week or so later, with the Easter weekend break approaching, David invited me to visit the newly completed 'game blind' on the banks of the Tiva River. He added that he would invite my parents as well, sure that they would enjoy seeing Peter, and I would be respectably chaperoned. In those days it was not proper for a single girl to be alone in a house with an eligible man, so my parents agreed to meet me in Tsavo while Sheila offered to look after Jill, who was more than happy to stay with her cousins. I will never forget this first journey back to Tsavo from Nairobi – boarding the overnight Mombasa train straight from work, dozing to the rhythm of the rocking carriage and waking in the moonlight as the nyika began to unfold in the early hours of the morning. As the train passed slowly through the eerie little station of Tsavo and shadows danced on the windows, my thoughts turned to the infamous Tsavo lions, which were known to patrol the platform at night and in the past had dragged people out of the carriages and had devoured hundreds of Indian workers building the railway. When the train rattled on towards the home stretch and the hands of my watch approached 4 a.m., my heart began to race with nervous excitement. Soon I could detect the glow of Voi station and make out David's tall silhouette on the platform. It took all my self-control to walk sedately down the steps, kiss him lightly on the cheek in front of the throng of people also waiting on the platform, hand him my bag and walk to the waiting car. But once we were clear of the town, David stopped the car and took me into his arms, holding me tight and kissing me passionately.

The next morning, I was overjoyed to be reunited with my parents, warmly welcomed by all the team at Park HQ and delighted to see Samson and Fatuma, who proudly showed off their two new friends. Over breakfast, David spoke vividly about the 'elephant problem', about which he was clearly deeply concerned, explaining that Sir Julian Huxley had concluded that one third of the elephant population of Tsavo would have to go if the Park were not to be reduced to a desert. This was a shocking recommendation. The prospect of an indiscriminate cull of Tsavo's elephants seemed like the ultimate betrayal, but no alternative solution had so far presented itself. The Galana Game Management Scheme, in which a large chunk of land between the eastern boundary of the Park and the coast had been set aside for the Waliangulu to be able to harvest a specified number of elephants and other animals annually on a sustained yield basis, marketing the ivory, meat and hides legally as a cooperative game ranch, had failed. All the elephants had left for the sanctity of the Park, and others had become so wild that it was impossible to get at them. In any case, for David the concept of 'sustainable yield' was flawed, as it was quite impossible to try and 'farm' wild free-ranging animals as one would the domestic species. The only solution would appear to be in targeting breeding female age groups throughout the entire population to reduce recruitment and numbers, but the practicality of this was non-existent. The conventional method of annihilating intact families, as in southern Africa, merely relieved the pressure on the land, made life easier for the elephant population, and the breeding rate went up. Female elephant units remain bonded for life, their love and support of family members strong and enduring, so wading into the female herds would result in a dangerously berserk elephant population that would pose a threat to visiting tourists.

But something had to be done, for sure, and public pressure was mounting through the media. As we set off for Ithumba and David's new game blind, I couldn't help noticing the scale of devastation bordering Tsavo's main watercourses, far worse now than when I had last been there. Tree debris lay in tangled heaps on bare baked soil; baobabs were actually gouged out, with some even felled entirely. The elephant problem obviously dominated David's mind and kept him awake at night, but here, on our first reunion – albeit with my parents in tow – he put it briefly aside and enjoyed the moments we could share.

Once we reached Ithumba we could see that Peter had done a fantastic job opening up the northern area, and we enjoyed a tour of his charming living area and offices as well as going through some of the new tracks he had opened up, formerly hidden places now made accessible. It was dusk by the time we reached the new Kathamulla bunker, having stopped short of it to pitch camp underneath some shady trees on the riverbank, everybody speaking in hushed voices to cause as little disturbance as possible. Needless to say, under David's guidance, the blind was meticulous. A flight of neat steps led down to a palm-logged room sunk below the level of the bank, large enough to house six camp beds with the floor slightly raised in order to give a clear view of the river while reclining in bed. More steps led down to a row of chairs from which, when seated, you had a ground-level view. Enchantingly, the blind was open to the stars. We took our seats in this theatre of David's dreams, not without wondering what would happen if a lion jumped in, despite the ditch dug round the sides and back of the hide. David's rifle was beside him and I relaxed.

And so, as a little Scops owl began its monotone call, the large orange moon rose above the palm trees and the sand below us gleamed yellow-white. David reached for my hand, sending electric thrills through me, and I couldn't help thinking that this would have been the most romantic of nights had it not been for the inhibiting presence of my parents and brother. However, I reminded myself that we were here for another reason and the quiet beauty of the scene was in itself sheer magic.

Three dark shadows – bull elephants – moved along the sand and like stately phantoms approached the blind, stopping opposite us. They inspected the holes that had already been tunnelled in the sand of the riverbed and began extracting the loose sand, so that they could insert their trunks to draw up the water. Every time the largest one raised his head to put his trunk in his mouth, I found myself surreptitiously calculating his reach to make sure that we were beyond trunk range. More shadows appeared, and as they moved towards us we could see fifty or so elephants and their young. Soon the splashing of water, happy trumpeting, rumbling, and the odd squeak of a calf being tossed aside filled the night, and it was possible to observe the automatic privilege of rank: how the biggest tusker always had right of way, how as he approached the others would stand aside, leaving his path clear. At the holes, smaller elephants would give way to the high-ranking bulls, but they in turn would always share their holes with the tiniest calves. They were such polite animals, a rigid code of ethics reinforced in their society down the ages.

It felt as though we were watching a play, the cast of characters keeping us enthralled. Next on centre stage were the rhinos, one sliding down the bank opposite us, clumsy in comparison to the dexterity of the elephants. He meandered from hole to hole, emitting a plaintive mewing, finding it difficult to select a suitable spot from which to drink. Before he could make up his mind, another rhino approached from downstream; faced with competition, he quickly commandeered the nearest hole and swung round aggressively to defend his rights. Puffing and snorting, the two proceeded to shunt backwards and forwards in a war of nerves, every now and then making short rushes at each other accompanied by an intimidating roar that meant business. Finally, the newcomer reversed away and settled for another hole nearby which he clearly intended to occupy for some time, as he lay down in it, making himself very comfortable. Seeing the threat subside, the first rhino then set about modifying his hole so that it could accommodate his cumbersome head and horn. Scraping his feet in the sand, he wore away a channel, at the same time tossing his head up and down and using his horn to enlarge the opening at the top, careful to keep an eye on his rival, warning him off with periodic puffs and snorts. We were very close to all the action, enthralled at this ritualistic test of status.

The arrival of a small herd of cow elephants and their young increased the tempo instantly, as the two rhinos rose in a barrage of noise. This succeeded in persuading the elephants to turn and walk upstream. All was calm for a while, until another rhino arrived – this time a female – with her calf at foot. She wandered around pleading for one of the two occupied holes, so the tactics of bluff and counter-bluff began all over again, with the incumbents refusing to budge and the female trying to pressurize them into doing so. This meant that no one could take a drink for fear of being horned from the rear, and, confronting one another, they argued on until the female decided to accept defeat and began to modify another drinking hole.

Upstream the elephants had long since drunk their fill and gone about their business elsewhere, while we wondered whether any of the rhinos would actually get a drink at all. Only when one decided to move off could the other risk lowering his head into the hole, but it was not quite over yet. He failed to notice the silent approach of a high-ranking bull elephant, who strode up to the up-ended large brown bottom, lowered his head until his tusks were underneath it and effortlessly heaved the rhino out, sending it head over heels in an undignified somersault. We had difficulty in muffling our laughter once we had ascertained that the rhino was not injured, since it was such a ridiculous sight, but we couldn't help feeling sorry for the poor old fellow, who, having collected himself and protesting vociferously, had to initiate the tedious process of trying to find himself a suitable hole all over again, intent, of course, on those already occupied by someone else.

And so the night passed – other rhinos coming, each one bent on usurping another from its hole – until eventually in the early hours of the morning we left them to it and retired for the night. Only fitful catnaps were possible due to the noisy bouts that went on unabated, until the birds began to sing as dawn blushed the eastern horizon, signalling the end of my first night in the Kathamulla game blind. David had gifted me many new experiences, opened my eyes to so much already, but that spectacular night remains indelibly etched in my mind, the sights and sounds still sharp all these years later. Waiting for the Land Rover to take us back to camp for breakfast, we strolled around the riverbed in the cool hour of dawn, scrutinizing the evidence of the night's activities to the pungent smell of fresh dung and the lingering scent of the animals themselves. As we packed the car, the diurnal cast of animals were beginning to arrive to a dawn curtain-raiser – birds, monkeys and baboons, zebras, buffalo, impalas and shy kudus.

The prospect of returning to my office job left me subdued on the return journey, heavy-hearted at the prospect of being again parted from David. As usual, though, the drive was not without excitement. David had to keep an appointment at Park HQ and did not want to pause on the way back, even to watch a lioness and her cubs who were sitting in the middle of the road. As we approached, the lioness and one of the cubs trotted off, but the two remaining cubs continued to run along the road in front of the car. The country was too broken at this point for us to be able to deviate from the track, so David closed in on the cubs in order to overtake them. 'Watch out!' yelled my father, and I swung around to see the lioness heading for the car at lightning speed, ears flattened and tail straight. David slammed down the accelerator and for one horrific moment it looked as though he might run over the cubs, but by some miracle he managed to narrowly avoid them. As we sped past I saw a mass of sharp teeth and claws as they flung themselves on their backs beside the wheels of the passing car, the lioness meanwhile ranging alongside the open Land Rover almost level with my knee, snarling and growling, the epitome of feline fury. I hurled myself across the seat, almost knocking my mother out, fully expecting the lioness to land in my lap at any moment. Luckily, however, she was not able to muster the additional speed to launch a spring, and as we drew ahead, leaving her and the cubs in a cloud of red dust, David said: 'Never a good idea to get between a lioness and her cubs!' The rest of us were too shaken to reply, and only when my heartbeat had slowed did I understand that David's quick thinking had saved us from disaster.

Later, as David drove me to the station, I averted my face to hide the tears. We found a private moment to hold each other and I sensed that David was just as desolate. As the train drew in, I wondered how I would be able to face the loneliness of the months ahead.

On my return I was plunged straight back into the ferocious debates that were raging through the settler community. We had all been stunned by British Prime Minister Harold Macmillan's 'Wind of Change' speech to the South African parliament in February 1960, in which he outlined his Conservative Government's intentions to grant independence to many of the British colonies in Africa. Now, some months later, this wind appeared to be blowing with a gale force. It was only recently that the British Government had been actively encouraging white settlement through its Soldier Settlement Schemes, and more recently still had been at pains to reassure the settlers that the multi-racial balance would definitely be preserved in any new constitution, and that the white community would always have a voice and an economic future in an independent Kenya. But it was apparent to us now that Britain was going for what my father called an outright sellout – simply 'one man, one vote' – which would in essence mean black majority rule. The settler community was a small minority in the colony and it was obviously unrealistic to expect to have any representation in an independent Kenyan government. Yet for us Kenya was our home, and many of us knew no other.

The recently held Lancaster House Conference, at which Iain Macleod, the Secretary of State for the Colonies, had begun negotiating a new constitutional framework for an independent Kenya, divided our community deeply. Some more liberal settlers, optimistic of being stakeholders in a new Kenya, supported the multi-racial New Kenya Party, founded by Michael Blundell, the classically trained singer-turned-farmer. But the elders of our community and many pioneering families, including mine, were furious at being discarded as mere flotsam and jetsam by the British and allied themselves to the Federal Independent Party. They were impressed by its leader, the straight-talking, fiery war hero Group Captain 'Puck' Briggs, who vowed to fight for a fair deal for the minority settlers. Many of those had come to Kenya as children of pioneering families who had lived through difficult times as their parents struggled to farm the land, and when grown had served Britain with distinction in its World Wars. Britain began to turn its back on those people – even the daily BBC programme previously announced as 'Home News from Britain' became 'News about Britain', a subtle change that did not go unnoticed. So angered were many that when Michael Blundell returned from the Lancaster House discussions, seemingly for handing over the country to African rule, he was showered with thirty small silver coins as befitting the Biblical traitor, a label that was further endorsed when he was awarded a knighthood in the Queen's Birthday Honours List.

The African politicians at the time were mainly from the Kikuyu and Luo tribes and were jubilant at the prospect of a Kenya fully independent of Britain. The Kikuyu faction made no secret of the fact that they had their eyes on the White Highlands, land they viewed as rightfully belonging to them, despite the fact that it had long been occupied by the Masai prior to the white man's arrival. An ambitious and passionate young Luo trade union leader, Tom Mboya, delivered inflammatory speeches that did little to settle our fears. Europeans, he said, would have to go down on their knees to their new African masters, who would take over their land and everything else they owned when independence finally came. But the main focus of African attention was on securing the release of Jomo Kenyatta, the Mau Mau leader who had been imprisoned since 1953 in Lodwar, a remote part of Kenya. Early in 1960, 25,000 Kenyans had held a public meeting in Nairobi demanding his release, followed by a petition of over a million signatures presented to the Governor. Later, he was elected in absentia as President of the Kenyan African National Union and was finally released from prison, to a hero's welcome, the following year.

Knowing that the White Highlands were the 'hot potato', the British Government came up with a proposal for an organized official and mandatory buy-out of all the settlers who occupied land in the most contested parts. Only a few families had the confidence to stay put, and even fewer opted to take up citizenship of a newly independent Kenya, despite assurances that we could retrieve our British nationality should things go wrong. I remember at this time meeting a beautiful young Belgian refugee who had fled from Zaire, the recently independent Belgian Congo, and as she told me of her traumatic escape I had a deep sense that such turmoil could be coming our way. Meanwhile, my father had made up his mind to opt for the buy-out, to offload our beloved Cedar Park farm 'lock, stock and barrel', so that he and my mother could retire to more congenial surroundings at the coast. In theory, selling the farm to the British administration sounded straightforward, but the coming months proved unimaginably frustrating. When it came to evaluating how much the land was worth, compensation seemed to be heavily hinged to the 'Old Boy Network'; and unfortunately for my father, it happened that a friend of the Governor's had recently bought the farm right next door to Cedar Park and rumour had it that he did not fancy an African neighbour. Due to his lofty connections, he managed to arrange that all the farms surrounding his particular patch be excluded from the British buy-out so that he could have a white buffer to his own property.

We did all that we could as a family to get this decision reversed but our pleas fell on deaf ears. It was heartbreaking to watch my father return from meeting after meeting in Nairobi almost broken under the strain. Eventually there seemed no other option than to try and sell the farm independently, something that was not easy due to the prevailing political climate. Buyers with the sort of money that Cedar Park was worth were simply not to be had, so he ended up more or less giving it away to an African buyer. For his life's work my father received a paltry £6,000, the new owner acquiring 6,000 acres of fertile land with its river and pristine cedar forest; our beautiful old home; the 100 or so treasured pedigree cattle imported at such cost from Australia; miles of fencing, the dipping tank, spray race, paddocks, stables, pig-sties, storerooms and milking bales, generators, the hydraulic ram, butter churns and all the farm's assets. My father did keep his most prized possession, a state-of-the-art tractor, gifting this with much gratitude to Wanjehia, his faithful Kikuyu foreman.

My father's half-brothers Harry and Fred Chart fared a little better, though still not getting the proper value of their holdings. Like my parents, Harry decided to retire to the coast, but Fred purchased another property close to Lake Elmenteita in the Rift Valley. Granny Chart was not getting any younger, and with two of her three sons leaving the district it seemed a sensible idea for her to be moved nearer to Fred. The three brothers clubbed together and built her a sweet cottage on Fred's new farm, but she protested mightily until the very last moment as her mountain of possessions was crammed into my father's lorry. I remember the unbelievable amount of stuff she had hoarded over the years and the way in which she stood over it all, like an enraged old tigress guarding its litter, not even allowing us to throw out a pile of newspapers dated 1912. It was only after frustrating negotiations that my father managed to acquire the freehold title for the house at Malindi, giving my parents the sense of security they both sought.

In addition to the turbulent political and social unrest of 1960, we found ourselves in the grip of a severe drought, the driest period on Kenyan records for over forty years. Tsavo East, a semi-desert at the best of times, began to take on the aspect of a desert. Each day the sun rose in a fiery red ball and blazed down with increasing intensity, sapping our strength, leaving us drenched in sweat. The consequences for the wildlife were catastrophic, and on one of my visits camping upstream from Lugard's Falls I witnessed large numbers of rhinos suffering and dying along the banks of the Athi River. Even with help from the mobile pumps and sprinklers that David used to get water from the river to irrigate stretches along the banks, the emaciated rhinos were beyond saving. A tiny rhino orphan we named Lokwan was brought back to camp, and although my mother and I tried to save him, tragically he didn't make it. To our knowledge no one had ever reared a newborn rhino before, so we really didn't know how to begin, and it soon became obvious that the powdered cow's milk on which we fed him was not ideal. We were shocked by his sudden and unexpected death a few days later; we were yet to learn that upset and stress trigger latent tick-borne diseases to which rhinos in good health are normally immune, and that a course of injected antibiotics administered immediately after capture is a prerequisite to success.

I have to admit that it was pretty frustrating to have to spend my precious time with David in the company of my parents, and while they made sure we had some time alone, there were few opportunities for us to do as we really wished. I was too cowardly to probe David about any possible future together, even though he knew my decree absolute had by now come through, and he made no mention of it in conversation. So it came as a complete shock when on the way back to Voi station, David stopped the car and said: 'When shall we get married, Daph?' All I could do was gasp. After all this waiting and wondering, it had all come down to this moment. I was taken aback that he should be so sure of my response, and found myself saying, 'What makes you so sure I want to marry you?' David turned from me and gazed out of the window. 'You're right,' he said. 'I am such a selfish devil and you'd be better off forgetting me altogether.' Panic gripped me – no I wouldn't – but then he looked at me and added softly, 'I would die for you, Daph. Please find it in your heart to give my suggestion a little thought.' Then with great tenderness he reached for me and the long, lingering kiss spoke my answer. This was all I had ever wanted.

I couldn't wait to get back to tell my sisters and break the good news to Jill that she and I would be moving back to Tsavo. I handed in my notice at work and began to make preparations for a quiet wedding. David had gone straight back from the station to ask my father's permission for us to marry, and so for once I smiled throughout the long journey back, pinching myself from time to time to make sure I wasn't dreaming. When I arrived back at Sheila's I was, however, met with sad news. Old Mrs Woodley, Bill's mother, of whom I was very fond, had been admitted to hospital in the last stages of cancer. I found her propped up against her pillows, deathly pale, but she still had spirit and the usual cigarette in her hand. She said: 'I have always been very fond of you, Daphne, and I don't blame you for leaving Bill. He's just like his bloody father.' On the way out I bumped into Bill and his new girlfriend, Ruth Hales, whom I had not yet met. She looked at me through her dark liquid eyes and there was something about her that I warmed to instantly. Bill told me that he and Ruth were planning to marry in three months' time and I beamed my congratulations, relief flooding through me – it wouldn't be difficult now to break my own news to him.

David and I set our wedding date for late October, opting to get married in Mombasa, by the sea. I chose a modest navy and white polka-dot dress with a broad white collar. It fitted very snugly over my eighteen-inch waist, and the frilly stiffened petticoat hid the family bum well. A few days before the wedding, we went to the up-market Oceanic Hotel overlooking Mombasa harbour, where the sea gleamed a mixture of sapphire, viridian and jade and the famous giant baobabs, said to be the largest in the world, stood sentinel to the harbour entrance. This unusual group of baobabs had always fascinated me, as these particular trees did not grow gregariously. It was said that a baobab pod had been buried with every Portuguese soldier that died during the Portuguese occupation between 1500 and 1720, and there was a long-held superstition that djinns from the spirit world inhabited each tree and that during the construction of the railway the workers could not be persuaded to chop any down, something that halted work for months. Finally, a wily Scot devised a solution – the djinn must be given notice to quit in Arabic, since djinns didn't respond to instructions in English. This was duly done, and after a suitable period of time to allow the djinn to arrange alternative accommodation, the Scotsman dealt the first blow to the tree with no sinister repercussions.

On arrival at the hotel it came as an unexpected but very pleasant surprise to find Granny Chart waiting. We had a noisy dinner that evening – David and Peter arriving from Voi to join only my very close family. I had arrived by train from Nairobi that morning, and seeing David set all the butterflies dancing inside me all over again.

We managed to escape to the beach for some brief moments alone. Taking me in his arms, he held me close and as the breeze wafted across the ocean, I breathed in the exotic jasmine-scented ylang-ylang from the garden of the hotel, which also grew in David's garden at home. I knew that the scent of this plant would bring back that moment for the rest of my life. I was intensely happy.

And so it was that at 11 a.m on 20 October 1960 I became Daphne Sheldrick. Over a simple band of platinum ringed with gold, David slipped a beautiful ring of sapphires and diamonds that had been his mother's. Later, at the hotel, the champagne corks popped as Peter — our best man — delivered a witty speech to which David replied, and everyone toasted our future happiness. It was a joyful, private family occasion. My parents had kindly offered to look after Jill for a week while David and I went on honeymoon, but first we had to get back to the Voi Hotel for a Saturday night wedding celebration organized by the regular Saturday night residents. There we were greeted by a crowd of familiar faces, plus a surprise guard of honour mounted by the rangers. The party was pretty raucous, something that I could have done without on my wedding night. We got home in the early hours of the morning, the familiar garden bathed in moonlight as we walked hand in hand towards the front steps of the house. David lifted me into his arms and smothered me in kisses as he climbed the stairs to the verandah. At last we were free of guilt, and what followed will remain with me for ever. I awoke in the morning to sunshine streaming in through the window, to find a red rose plucked from the garden placed beside my head on the pillow. No bride could have had a more romantic introduction to marriage.

I already knew my new home well. It was spacious and lovely, built of concrete blocks painted white, with a red tiled roof, and it reflected all David's careful attention to detail. A long broad front verandah opened through glass doors at each end into the two main bedrooms and in the centre into another large airy room, separated midway by a red curtain into the lounge and dining area. Large windows back and front ensured a cooling through breeze to ease the intense Tsavo heat. At the other end of the house the dining room was linked to a well-equipped kitchen, protected by weld mesh on its open side. It must have been puzzling for Frederick, the cook, and other members of the household to find Bwana Bill's former wife metamorphosed into the lady of the house and David's wife. But on that first morning Frederick, who was tiny and frail, clasped my hand and welcomed me with open friendliness. Together we made David his favourite late breakfast – a hot curry with an egg on top.

As we sat together enjoying our first breakfast as husband and wife, David told me that there were some matters – involving Piglet and some sheep – that needed sorting out before we left for our honeymoon at Lake Manyara, in what was still Tanganyika. I had to laugh when I realized that Piglet – a mischievous orphaned bush pig – was causing such mayhem. He had been left with David by 'Chickweed' Parker, and at first this tiny squeaker appeared wickedly endearing, attaching himself to the legs of anyone who went past him. He had recently ingratiated himself into Fatuma's affections, not in the least bit shared by Samson. Periodically Piglet would dash out from beneath her legs to nip the heels of Samson, then dart back again to shelter beneath Fatuma before Samson could swipe at him with his trunk. Because of Piglet, the elephants were becoming increasingly neurotic and the elephant attendant had come to David early that morning, pleading with him to help sort this out once and for all.

Another hindrance to our departure was the arrival of six fat sheep, sent to us as a wedding present from the Orma pastoralists who lived on Tsavo's north-eastern boundary. The sheep had been housed in the empty stable next door to Samson, who clearly resented the intrusion and late at night had exploded out of his stable, demolishing the door and reducing the stable that housed the sheep to a pile of rubble. Two of the sheep had been eaten by a leopard but the rest had managed to survive the night. Before finally leaving for Lake Manyara, David had to organize the repairs to the stable and give instructions for the sheep to be housed elsewhere. Thankfully we did manage to leave for our honeymoon later that day.

This introduction to married life with David was just a taste of what would become part of every future day, each spiced by the unexpected and the unforeseen, so much so that we were rarely able to enjoy a quiet meal together without some form of interruption, whatever the hour. Notwithstanding, nothing could diminish my sense of inner peace and tranquillity, or the happiness of being married to such an astonishingly wonderful man. Every day married to David was a honeymoon.

8. Love and Orphans

'Our task must be to free ourselves by widening our circle of compassion to embrace all living creatures and the whole of nature in its beauty.'

– Albert Einstein (1870–1955)

Aged twenty-six, I settled into a period of great happiness, married to the man I loved passionately and who was my perfect soulmate. Our honeymoon in Lake Manyara National Park was blissfully romantic. David was such an intuitive interpreter of all that was taking place, and we spent hours watching the animals as they went about their daily lives. He opened my eyes to the body language of the wild animals – the meaning of different stances and nuances. All these years later, I can still feel his presence as we sat close to each other, still and quiet and uninterrupted. Our body language told the story of love throughout our married life.

I did not want the week to end, but the sands of time never stand still and all too soon it was time to go home. I had missed Jill hugely, and was looking forward to picking her up from my parents. As it turned out, I was glad she was not in Tsavo, for there was news that would have upset her – Fatuma and Kanderi had gone. Piglet's recent departure – the Warden of Nairobi National Park had kindly offered to look after him – had plunged Fatuma into inconsolable grief, and soon afterwards she and Kanderi had joined up with a wild herd and had not been seen since. Fatuma was Jill's favourite and Kanderi such an impish elephant, who made us laugh at his antics. At least he was old enough to survive out there in the wild.

Sensing my sadness, David gently reminded me that every wild orphan was 'on loan' and could never 'belong' to us. We were merely custodians for the period that they were dependent and needed our help, but after that their place and quality of life lay not in semi-captivity for the benefit of humans, but with their wild kin. The fact that Fatuma and Kanderi had graduated from our care to become wild elephants again was a cause for celebration, irrespective of how much we humans would miss them. Of course, I knew this from way back when Bushy had left me, but any parting from a loved one is emotional. I thought carefully about how I would tell my little daughter when we were reunited.

At least Jill would be able to find some consolation in 'Rufus', a newly-born rhino calf that Dennis Kearney, the new Assistant Warden, had found one dawn outside my old home. There had been no sign of the mother, but a search party later came across the spot where she had given birth, so it was assumed that she had taken fright and abandoned the calf when people had begun to appear in the morning. For the time being Dennis and his wife were happy to raise this newly orphaned rhino alongside three recently arrived buffalo orphans. When I told Jill about Fatuma, she looked at me gravely, saying: 'That's OK, Mummy. She will help look after other baby elephants now and have lots of new friends.' At five, she was already far more astute than I had been at that age.

I knew too that she would be captivated by a very different orphan that had been brought in by one of the rangers – a bedraggled little mongoose that had clearly suffered a painful head injury. I remembered Ricky-Ticky-Tavey of my childhood days and just how endearing members of the mongoose family were. While this tiny creature could now fit into the palm of my hand, as a banded mongoose he would grow to be about half the size of a cat, a lot larger than Ricky-Ticky-Tavey, who had been no bigger than a large rat. Covered in brown grizzled fur with thin black bands over his back, we named him 'Higglety' because he moved in a 'higglety-pigglety' fashion.

In time, Higglety made a full recovery from his head wound, though it was several weeks before he was able to stand without toppling over and thereafter retained a slightly lopsided look, holding his head at a jaunty angle. He was clever and fearless, with an insatiable curiosity, and when displeased made his feelings known by erecting the hairs on his tail like a bottlebrush. We always knew where he was by the characteristic birdlike 'peep' of mongooses, and the only time he was silent was when he was fast asleep. At mealtimes he bustled up, sat on his hind legs with his little black nose twitching to savour what might be on offer, jumped up on to a lap and for the rest of the meal laid his little paws on the table, every now and then hooking a morsel off a plate. Being mainly carnivorous, insects and meat were his staples but unusually Higglety became obsessed by cheese, so much so that the mere mention of the word brought him scampering along, growling in anticipation.

Higglety quickly became so attached to us – as we to him – that soon after his arrival he came with us to Ndiandaza, on the lower reaches of the Tiva River, in the northern area of the Park where David was supervising the construction of a borehole. It was urgent to provide a source of water that would open up a vast stretch of country during the dry season and also enable the Field Force anti-poaching patrols to operate further afield. A contracted drilling rig had already begun work on this project and now we were set to follow. Along the way, we passed Rudolf, the old rhino who still lived in the Mopea Gap just across the causeway at Lugard's Falls, relieved to find him still alive and in good shape, but a while later we witnessed a pack of African hunting dogs tearing chunks of twitching flesh from the belly of a living impala. Jill and I were distraught because the impala was literally being eaten alive, but David was consoling, telling us that at such times the animal is in deep shock and feels nothing, since the brain releases endomorphins, substances to numb the nerves and extinguish all feeling. He told us how he had seen soldiers suffer terrible injuries during the war and that they sometimes had not even known they had been wounded until they noticed blood. The pain came much later. In the future I would experience this myself and understand the truth and wisdom of his words.

It was surreal to be in the northern region, this time as the legitimate wife of David. It evoked memories of an aching longing for things that then I had believed could never be. I was now able to indulge myself, bringing feminine touches to our camp – a little vase of wild flowers on the dining table, the bedlinen turned back at night – and with the help of Frederick provide the dishes David enjoyed, accompanied by freshly baked bread and cakes. Great-Uncle Will's cast-iron kettle was always on the go for much-needed tea for the team.

Our camp was pitched close to the scene of the drill and the Ra-koub Camel Section of the Field Force, a recent innovation at a point when as yet we had no access to an aircraft. The object was to enable the rangers to become much more mobile and operate further afield, since camels could carry a supply of water. The camels appeared to be a disgruntled and temperamental lot who lay down with bad grace to have their loads strapped on to their backs, groaning and roaring in protest. Apparently this was nothing compared to the noise they made when given their regular injections against the dreaded tsetse disease of trypanosomiasis. When not on patrol, they were kept in a thorn enclosure that Higglety was quick to discover and he instantly became fascinated by these noisy 'ships of the desert'. Every morning he dashed across the open plain to be with them, risking being scooped up by a bird of prey. Thankfully, however, he survived such hazards and was happy to spend the rest of the day scrabbling in the thornbush fence, fascinated by his new friends.

There was much wild activity around the camp to keep Jill and me busy. Every morning at eight, flocks of sand grouse swooped in to drink at a shallow puddle near the rig. Their timing was so precise that we could accurately adjust our watches by their arrival. They came from far and wide, leaving their tiny speckled eggs or fluffy baby chicklets exposed on the bare baking ground, banking entirely on the chicks' camouflage for them to survive. Only the male birds were equipped with the special quill feathers capable of holding the water that had to be carried back to the flightless young, sometimes over great distances. As soon as their father landed the babies would suckle his feathers to get the moisture they needed. Curiously these water quill feathers were absent in the female birds, so if some mishap befell the male, the tiny chicks were doomed to die a miserable death of thirst. This troubled me greatly, knowing full well how sand grouse were slaughtered in droves by shotgun-wielding 'hunters' for sport. I found it shocking that people could derive pleasure from killing a tiny bird, or any living creature for that matter, but the killing of sand grouse was particularly abhorrent in view of the vulnerability of the tiny chicks that had to battle so hard to survive under such harsh and adverse conditions.

We also became intrigued by a female hornbill who, entombed in a tall acacia tree, was wholly dependent on her mate to feed her while she was sealed inside naked until she grew another feathered dress. The proximity of the nest to the drilling rig placed her mate in a quandary. He was understandably frightened of bringing food and could be seen hopping around trying to pluck up the necessary courage to approach his nest, so for the first few days Jill and I relieved him of this responsibility and offered Mrs Hornbill juicy grasshoppers, which she gobbled down with relish. However, her mate soon took over from us, sailing down in spite of the thumping of the rig to push a titbit into the nest for his wife. The Peter's gazelles also plucked up courage to come and feed on the nutritious twisted pods that rained down from the *Acacia tortilis* trees shading our tent. Because of them the antelopes of Tsavo were usually in better condition during the dry season than in the wet, their coats sleek and shiny and their bodies lithe and well-covered. The superb starlings also became tame, enjoying the breadcrumbs we threw down for them each day and splashing about in the hollowed-out stone that served as a birdbath just outside the mess tent. They hopped around screeching rudely at Higglety, trusting and unafraid, and Jill loved looking at the starlings' iridescent breasts, which, in the bright sunlight, took on all the colours of the rainbow.

At last the day came when the rig struck water at a depth of 170 feet, and there was great rejoicing in the whole camp. We all went along to see the first water being heaved up from the bowels of the earth, and sampled it as we waited impatiently for the results of the test pumping that would reveal the quantity the hole could yield. Unfortunately it wasn't quite as much as we had hoped, but we were relieved that a supply had at least now been secured. When the rig hauled up a bucket of dark grey mud, David said, 'How about a celebratory mud pack, Daph?' I laughed: 'Well, it does the elephants no harm, so why not!' and much to the amusement of the workers, David then set about plastering my face with the grey ooze from the depths of Tsavo. Soon it hardened into clay and it occurred to me that rather than easing my wrinkles, it would probably create a few more, but it felt good and after all, here I was – the first woman to have a mud mask from the first borehole in Tsavo East. It took time to peel it all off, and I doubt that anyone has had a Tsavo mudpack since.

The mood was buoyant in the camp that evening but over the noisy chatter came an extraordinary sound of a distant booming, rather like a muffled explosion. We were puzzled, for there were no humans around for hundreds of miles. Within a couple of minutes one of the Samburu rangers came running up to us exclaiming, 'Elgubu, Elgubu!' and announced that this was the sound made by the yellow-legged Kori bustard bird as it predicted exceptionally heavy rain. He told us that when his people heard this sound, they would begin to move their cattle into the area, knowing surely that there would soon be fresh grazing for their herds, and he added that the bird was never wrong. It was difficult to believe that this sound could emanate from a bird, even one as large as a Kori bustard, which was, after all, the largest bird with the ability of flight. Curiosity soon got the better of us and David suggested we went to investigate. Sure enough, some distance away was a Kori bustard, puffing out his grey-white fluffy chest as he thundered his rain song to the heavens.

For two more days the skies remained clear, but around midday on the third day, large brooding black clouds gathered in the sky as if from nowhere and the air turned humid and hot. It was breathlessly still as a hush descended, every living creature seemingly waiting for something to happen. Even Higglety tore himself away from the camels and came dashing back to seek shelter in the tent. And then came great claps of thunder and the first drops of rain fell from the sky – big, heavy droplets, hesitantly at first, sending up tiny puffs of dust as they hit the dry powdery soil of the ground. It wasn't long before we found ourselves in the midst of a monumental tropical downpour, so heavy that the afternoon became as dark as dusk and the roar of the rain on the tent deafened all other sound. The tent began to sag under the strain, and we had to continually heave up the canvas to release a waterfall that gushed down the sides and seeped beneath the groundsheet.

At first, we savoured the refreshing scent of newly dampened earth, our spirits uplifted, but then with rising alarm we watched the parched earth rapidly becoming saturated and turning into a sea of mud. Little rivulets were forming, tentacles spreading out in all directions and racing off to swell the Tiva watercourse. Once this flooded, we could be cut off completely, isolated in this remote corner of the Park for months. Meanwhile, as we were harbouring mixed feelings about this unexpected downpour, the camels, who had probably never experienced anything like this before, were the epitome of misery, as was Higglety, who had curled up into a shivering little ball beneath the blankets at the foot of David's bed.

The fury of the storm abated and the next morning we awoke to a newly wet world – a tinge of green rising from the enlivened vegetation and the air vibrant with the joyous chorus of innumerable birds. The fallen gossamer wings of countless flying ants carpeted the ground outside our tent, and those termite queens that had not fallen prey to birds were scuttling around with their tails in the air, sending their scent out to suitors. I had seen this before, of course; when joined in tandem, the queen and her mate would disappear to a lifetime underground, where her sole role would be the laying of eggs to create and sustain a new colony of termites, while he would be condemned to a life of imprisonment – the proverbial 'drone', seemingly with no other function than keeping the queen company once their union had been consummated.

The sudden appearance after rain of these insects in their billions presented a welcome banquet for all, so on this wet morning the camp was abuzz with activity. Mr Hornbill feverishly embarked on a rapid shuttle service back and forth to his wife with a beak full of wriggling victims, while Higglety stationed himself on the nearby termite mound and crunched up the insects as they emerged. Other birds swooped and dipped, taking them on the wing, while Agama lizards devoured them in pairs before they could dig themselves into the ground. The rangers were busy feasting on the termites, roasting them over the coals, enjoying what they said was their delicious nutty flavour. I knew from my childhood days on the farm that like the locust, flying ants were a delicacy to most African tribes. Indeed, some tribes from the Nile region had even perfected the art of inducing the would-be termite queens to emerge out of season, simulating the sound of falling rain on their nests by the tapping of sticks and pouring of water.

There was so much to watch that Jill and I could have stayed there all day, but David decided it would be unwise to dally at Ndiandaza in case the region flooded, so later that morning we packed up camp. It turned out that the Kori bustard had been correct, for this storm heralded the onset of a pluvial decade of plenty, and in honour of this prophetic bird we named the borehole 'Elgubu'. Now, over fifty years later, a windmill above it draws up the life-giving water for the Field Force rangers who still patrol this sensitive region of Tsavo.

Arriving home, we were presented with a box containing a mate for Higglety. I was getting used to the ongoing appearance of wild baby orphans in my life at Tsavo, gaining in confidence about how to rear each species based on knowledge of their wild habits. It was a steep learning curve, but I enjoyed every moment nurturing the orphaned young. Combined with David's patient tutoring, each one taught me so much, laying the foundation of all I know today. Needless to say Higglety was frantic to investigate the contents of the latest box, chirruping away with his tail in bottlebrush mode. Knowing how fraught the introduction of wild creatures could be, I had doubts about Higglety's good intentions, but David insisted that they had to meet and opened the lid of the box. Instantly the little orphan shot out and tore underneath an armchair, pursued by Higglety, who had a dangerous glint in his eye. Fortunately he had been eating so much cheese that he was now too rotund to follow, so he busied himself prowling ominously around the chair, from which squeaks and angry growls emanated. I couldn't bear the thought of a mongoose fight, so I left David to it, only venturing back about an hour later, expecting to find a mangled corpse. Instead I was amazed to see Higglety and his new companion walking round and round each other, well on the way to establishing an amicable friendship, and by nightfall they were quite obviously delighted with each other and slept curled up together.

Thereafter Pickle and Higglety were inseparable. Higglety was becoming increasingly independent from us and started taking Pickle off with him, sometimes two miles from home each day, to his favourite spot at the main Voi entrance to the Park. At first I doubted Higglety's homing ability and went to retrieve them in the car, but I soon discovered that he knew his way around very well. Nevertheless we were concerned that Pickle was still far too young for such adventures, but Higglety was determined that she should accompany him everywhere he went and was most persistent in his persuasion, running off chattering away, then stopping to look around to see whether she was following, and if not, returning to prod her with his nose, before repeating this strategy all over again.

We decided that since it was company that Higglety craved, we should try to introduce him to his wild cousins down on the Voi River circuit. A resident pack of banded mongooses lived there and it seemed an ideal place – plenty of cover, no shortage of food, water nearby – in fact, a mongoose paradise. That evening, feeling like Judas, we took him to the river and placed him on the ground beside the car. For a few moments he looked rather confused, regarding us with his baleful lopsided look, but soon he set about busying himself with an interesting hole in the grass and while he was so engrossed, we slipped away. Taking one last backward glance, I could see Higglety gazing at the departing car. We drove away in silence, feeling very guilty. 'I feel an absolute cad,' said David. Back at home, we poured ourselves a drink and sat miserably on the front verandah as darkness closed in. Pickle lay in my lap, dejected and still, and as I stroked her I was overcome with remorse, picturing Higglety confused and alone in a strange place, without even the comfort of his nest and the bedclothes he snuggled up to as he fell asleep each evening. Even David looked anxious as he sat contemplating his drink. Jill was already in bed. I had no idea how I was going to tell her the next morning.

All of a sudden Pickle began to chatter, leaping off my lap and heading out of the front door. We followed her and there, hurrying up the stairs, was Higglety, every hair on his tail standing at right angles in mongoosian outrage. With enormous relief, I rushed up to him, intending to pick him up and welcome him home, but he made it clear he wanted none of it and nipped me sharply on the toe. Ignoring David and Pickle, he refused all food – even cheese – plonked himself in his bed, wrapped himself in his cuddle blanket and lay down to sleep in an offended huff. Over the coming days we tried to ingratiate ourselves with him but he remained aloof for ages, obviously not prepared to forgive our treachery, although actually he couldn't stay mad at Jill for too long. Eventually his animosity vanished and life returned to normal.

One evening, a few weeks later, when Higglety and Pickle failed to return from their daily excursion, I drove down to the main gate to see if anyone had seen them. I had only gone a short distance when I caught sight of a large martial eagle sitting on the ground, devouring a small animal. I left the vehicle in order to investigate, and as I approached, the eagle took off into the sky carrying what I recognized as Pickle's little corpse in its talons. Stumbling through the bush, I clapped my hands and shouted in an attempt to make the eagle release its hold, but it was too late and it soared off into the sky with Pickle in its talons. Putting my face in my hands, I sat down in the bush and sobbed. After a while I became aware of something rubbing against my back, and remarkably, there was Higglety. At least he was still alive. I held him tight and carried him back to the car.

I knew that for Pickle it had been a natural end, but her death haunted me for days. I hoped that the endomorphins released by the brain had made it painless and swift. Higglety was terribly subdued, staying close to home for a few days, keeping one eye directed skywards. Inevitably, though, the call of the wild returned and once again he took to disappearing, sometimes spending a night out and then days on end until he disappeared entirely, and we never saw him again.

When caring for animals, whether domestic or wild, one experiences a whole range of emotions from love to grief. I had known both many times. Parting was always painful and never became easier. Of course, Higglety had returned to where he rightfully belonged, and as David reminded me, this was cause for celebration, not self-pity. It was the quality of life that counted, he said, not the duration, and our orphans, irrespective of their end, had enjoyed a second chance of life that would otherwise have been denied them.

David loved me to massage his scalp and in the evenings, when Jill was asleep and the day had settled, he would sit at my feet as I rubbed his head, mulling over the events of the day. These were precious moments and we discussed a great deal – David's philosophy playing a very important part in my understanding and interpretation of animal behaviour. He believed that wild animals were, in many ways, more sophisticated than us humans, more perfect in terms of Nature, honed by natural selection over millennia and specially adapted for the environmental slot they occupied, contributing to the wellbeing of the whole. He was intolerant of those who viewed animal 'intelligence' as inferior to that of the human animal, for in his view, each species had evolved along a different branch of life in a way that suited its purpose; there were bound to be things that we humans would never fully understand about animal 'intelligence', and those who claimed that they did merely illustrated ignorance. 'The more you know, the more you know you don't know,' he said. We should never be so arrogant as to believe that we had all the answers.

David was of the firm belief that all animals possessed powers of communication, mysterious and hidden to human ears – for example, telepathy and the infrasound of the elephants and also probably the language of giraffes, animals that were believed to be mute. He had already taught me how to observe the body language of many animals, and that chemistry played an extremely important part in daily rituals – the footprints that left more than a mark on the ground, a whiff of scent on the wind that gave advance warning of impending danger. He understood that identity was a subconscious quest of all male mammals, mankind included, and inherent to a lesser degree in the females as well. How one was rated among one's peers had a bearing on self-esteem, and the confidence that brought peace of mind. 'Mammals require three essentials in life,' he said, 'identity, stimulation and security, and by far the most important of these three psychological cornerstones is identity.' No doubt he was right, but during these tender moments, I was secretly convinced that love was the source of all wellbeing.

David was openly contemptuous of those who viewed animals as a mere commodity placed on earth for the benefit of mankind, as well as of those who had the 'anthropomorphic block' which prevented them from accepting that animals were endowed with the same emotions as humans. After all, we humans in terms of Nature were also 'animals', and since Nature often repeats certain basic blueprints for mammals, such as warm blood and mammary glands, why not psychological and emotional parallels as well? Like us, each animal is individually unique. They can be happy and joyful, or depressed and sad. Furthermore, he often voiced the opinion that in terms of Nature we humans were arguably the most endangered species of all, having become so alienated from the natural world. We ran the risk of imploding, said David. And this was in the 1960s!

Life in Tsavo was becoming hectic. David and I were rarely at home for very long, for the distances involved in supervising development work in remote areas of the Park usually involved camping out, sometimes for extended periods, often accompanied by Jill if she was not spending time with Bill and Ruth. When Jill turned six, Bill and I decided to send her to the Government Primary School north of Nairobi in Nyeri, a well-respected boarding school not far from Bill and Ruth's Mweiga home at the foot of the Aberdares. Boarding school in those days was the only option for parents who lived far from suitable schools, and since my siblings and I had always been boarders, I thought nothing of it, knowing that when the time came Jill would have to do the same. As usual, it was the parting that was the difficult and always tearful part. Jill accepted her lot stoically, and during term time Bill and Ruth visited her regularly, keeping me updated on her progress. David and I would join her at the half-term breaks, taking the opportunity to also visit his mother and see Bill and Ruth, and I consoled myself that the terms were relatively short.

David was always eager to head out into the field. There was an urgent need to utilize the Water for Wild Animals grant – allocated to us to produce watering points for wildlife in arid areas such as

Tsavo – before up-country rains rendered the causeway at Lugard's Falls impassable and cut off the northern area entirely. Following the 1960 drought, a new pumping station was being installed at the Athi section of the Galana River near the Thabangunji Pass in the Yatta Plateau, along with a huge holding tank on top of the plateau itself, the idea being that water from the river would be pumped to the Yatta holding tank and then gravity-fed to a series of natural water-holes in the arid country beyond, thereby avoiding another rhino catastrophe. This entailed complex engineering that necessitated David's presence, so we established our camp at a place called Kitani ya Ndundu, higher upstream.

I had a new, rather unusual, orphan to nurture on this safari – a civet cat that we named Old Spice. He was a kitten-sized nocturnal creature, who when brought to me looked more dog than cat, since he lacked retractile claws, but as an adult would be about the size of a small bull terrier and resemble a raccoon. His body was covered in coarse grey hair with black blotches and his long sturdy tail was marked with prominent black bars. His most striking feature, however, was a crest of long black hairs along his back, which were the barometer by which you could gauge his mood. When angry or alarmed, he would erect this crest and suddenly appear twice his normal size.

He acquired the name Old Spice because just a whiff of David's Old Spice aftershave lotion sent him into a rubbing and jumping frenzy. My own precious perfume had an even more electrifying effect, but since it was an expensive luxury that did not come along too often, I was reluctant to let him have any. David wasn't all that keen to share his aftershave either, but when Old Spice began to return from nights out reeking of a rotting carcass or worse, we decided it saved a lot of trouble if we gave him the scent of our choice rather than leaving the selection to him. After only a brief altercation, it was decided that it was David's Old Spice that had to be sacrificed.

Because Old Spice was a nocturnal animal, he found us rather dull company. Invariably, just as he was beginning to wake up, we were about to go to bed. Thereafter, throughout the night in an attempt to make us play with him, he would jump on our bed and nuzzle our arms with his rubbery nose while kneading us strongly with his front paws, until our arms felt as though they had been pulped. When he realized we were falling asleep, he would jump off the bed and pad his way out into the night, crunching up the beetles attracted by the verandah light and pouncing on any hapless millipede, which was obviously a civet delicacy.

I didn't know much about civets, having never had contact with them before. David told me that they were battery farmed in Ethiopia and North Africa, where they were cruelly confined in small hutches stacked one on top of the other for the perfume industry, their anal scent gland 'milked' and the pungent contents collected for use as a base to make perfume linger longer on the wearer. It troubled me greatly knowing that these wild, gentle creatures should have to suffer so for the vanity of women. Jill was so upset when she learned of this practice that to this day, some fifty years later, she refuses to wear expensive perfumes that might include a product derived from the suffering of an animal, choosing instead the essence of flowers and essential oils.

Old Spice was secretive and reclusive. Whenever there was a stranger in the house, he would not appear until the dead of night. He underwent a marked mood change at the first hint of daylight, becoming tense and eager to retreat into hiding, seeking out the densest thicket around. We learned that this secluded spot had to be his secret alone, for if he so much as suspected that anyone had seen him entering it, he would become agitated and instantly move house. I always felt more comfortable knowing where he was during the day, but in order to do so I had to resort to subterfuge methods, spying on him with my back turned, using a mirror to monitor his movements.

The water project, both planned and designed by David, was important to bring a large stretch of once waterless country into production, the aim being to relieve the impact of the elephants' browsing on the river's vegetation so that the rhinos in the area had more food and water. The recent death of over 300 black rhinos had been attributed by many to 'elephant damage', but as sizeable numbers remained, David concluded that the recent catastrophe might simply be due to an over-population of territorial black rhino along this particular stretch of the river. The engineering was challenging, since it entailed diverting the river at a point near Thabangunji where it was swift-flowing and took a sharp bend. There, a concrete wall had to be built against a bank to which the pumps could be anchored. The construction of the large circular holding tank at the very top of the Yatta Plateau – the idea being that the pumps would feed water to the tank, which would in turn feed the water out to waterholes or depressions on the other side of the river that had no surface water but good pasture – was also no easy matter, for all the building materials had to be manually hauled up the rugged steep sides of the escarpment in punishing temperatures of over 35 degrees, and since work was happening at both sites, David underwent a good deal of enforced exercise going up and down in order to be present at both. I supervised the cooking for the team back in camp, where I had an opportunity to observe the curious symbiosis between birds and crocodiles, the birds picking the crocodiles' teeth clean, sometimes even venturing right inside open jaws that could have swallowed them whole with just one snap.

As the onset of the rains became more imminent, it became a race against time to get the work at the pumping station done before the river flooded. Generators that would eventually power the pumps were wired up to provide floodlighting so that the men could work in shifts around the clock, David leading by example and working long into the night. Meanwhile, my work was cut out for me, having to ferry meals from the camp to the construction site several miles away. Arriving at the site, I would rest beneath the shade of a huge baobab festooned with the untidy nests of a noisy flock of buffalo weavers. The tree was a hub of constant activity and chatter, the nests buzzing with life. Clustered along the branches, the birds had carefully laid barricades of thorns to deter arboreal snakes. It was easy to become absorbed in the hustle and bustle of buffalo weaver life, watching the little black males with their bright white shoulder flecks reinforcing the nests by jabbing in twigs and grass stems, while others popped in and out with offerings of food for the young.

1. Sheila, me on Mother's lap and Peter.

2. Cedar Park – our Gilgil home.

3. Betty and me at Malindi.

4. Bill and me at our reception at Cedar Park after our wedding.

5. With Jill, aged six months.

6. Bill, Jill and Fatuma.

7. Bill on a foot patrol.

8. Carving out the roads by hand in the 1940s and 1950s.

9. David in the Second World War.

10. Bill, David and me in the flooded Voi River.

11. David in the ivory room.

12. Tiva River anti-poaching
patrol, 1958.

13. David, a friend,
Jill and me camp at
Ndiandaza, 1957.

14. Jill with recovered trophies, 1958.

15. Samson, Fatuma, Higglety (in foreground), me and a friend, with Jill sitting on the boat, 1961.

16. Jill and Huppety, 1963.

17. David with Old Spice.

18. Myself and David with newborn Angela, 1963.

19. Four generations – family group with Granny Chart in the middle, 1963.

20. Kitani ya Ndundu campsite on the Athi River.

21. Angela in her safari chair.

22. David with orphans Eleanor and Rufus.

23. Hugging Wiffle, 1968.

24. Rains in Tsavo, always a most welcome sight.

25. On the Tiva with my parents, Angela and Peter.

26. David with Angela on Rufus.

27. Tsavo's big elephant
herds, 1970.

28. Tsavo, big
bull elephant.

29. Angela, me, Eleanor and keeper, 1968.

30. Myself and Angela at feeding time, with Stub and Lollipa.

31. The ostriches and rangers, 1976.

32. Angela feeding Stub, 1968.

33. Myself and Angela with Bias, our orphaned duiker.

34. Our house at Voi.

35. Angela and me with Lollipa and Stroppy.

36. Jill, aged twelve.

37. Evening walk to the river with the orphans.

38. The translocation of Grévy's zebra to Tsavo East.

39. David, my soulmate.

40. The rangers return with an arrested poacher and recovered rhino horn and ivory.

41. David helped by rangers and keepers at the rescue of Sobo.

42. Punda, the rascal, persecuting Sobo, with Raru looking on.

43. Bukanesi, Raru, Eleanor and Sobo.

44. Stroppy with Raru.

45. Stroppy and Punda,
inseparable friends.

46. Angela, me
and David with
the orphaned
elephants, 1973.

47. At midday Bunty
gives birth to Bouncer
with me by her side.

48. Jill, me, Bunty and David in our front garden.

49. Bunty in the garden with her sons.

50. Bunty, vulturine guinea fowl and me in the garden.

51. Pop in the Land Rover, crossing the river at Lugard's Falls causeway.

52. David helps rescue an elephant stuck in a drying mud wallow.

53. Jill with her father, Bill, on her wedding day.

54. Mixing the milk for Aisha.

One morning, I spotted two tiny bald chicks covered in a few prickly feather buds, all head and gape, squeaking feebly. They had fallen out of their nests and as I stroked them tenderly in my palm, one of them went limp and died. I knew the other would follow if I didn't do something about it, so I consulted David, who immediately asked one of his workmen, a proficient baobab climber, to take the chick back up. Cutting each foothold with an axe as he went, in no time at all he managed to pop the chick back in the nest, but as he began his descent, the chick rolled out and fluttered down again. Fortunately, I managed to break its fall by catching it in the folds of my dress.

'You've got your work cut out now,' laughed David, and I soon found out that he was right. 'Hopgrogging', as it became known, instantly became a full-time preoccupation for me in between the meal runs. From dawn to dusk I was at it, armed with a long whippy stick, stalking every grasshopper in sight and then decapitating it before stuffing it into a jam jar. We named the tiny chick 'Gregory Peck' and he thrived, growing quickly and soon recognizing his name, answering the Peck part with a loud squawk.

Eventually the day arrived when the concrete wall in the river was keyed to the rock of the riverbank and the pumps could be installed at the Thabangunji site. This was not a moment too soon, as two days later the river became noisier and began to rise, swelled by rain up-country. Tsavo remained parched and unspeakably hot, as though it would never ever rain here again, but the expression on the faces around me became increasingly anxious as the river level rose to the point where the newly laid concrete was no longer visible. The fear was that weeks of hard work might be lost should the cement not have time to harden and simply get washed away.

And then, one night, the wind dropped and the air was still. The stars disappeared behind a dark black curtain lit by flashes of forked lightning, thunder boomed, and we could hear the hiss of the coals as the rain began to fall, dousing the flames and sending up wisps of smoke. The whole camp remained seated round the dying embers of the campfire, enjoying the cool luxury of the rain and the refreshing scent of the newly dampened earth, but as the raindrops gathered momentum and turned into a steady downpour, we were forced to retreat to the mess tent. David turned on the radio and against the backdrop of thunder we picked out the news that the main railway bridge across the Athi upstream had been swept away and that there was every indication that more torrential rain was on the way.

'I think we should move the camp to higher ground,' said David, 'right now, before the river rises.' So, in the midst of a blinding rainstorm, we set about dismantling the camp, hurling drenched canvas that weighed a ton on to the back of the Land Rover and ferrying it to higher ground just below the Yatta escarpment. There we took shelter in the hurriedly erected mess tent, chaos prevailing as everyone groped around in the light of a feeble torch trying to locate their belongings and heaving up the sagging canvas of the roof to release a cascade of watery mud down the sides. Finally, having excavated a clearing in the midst of all the kit, we curled up in the middle, wet and weary, but elated that substantial rain was falling in Tsavo, which was always cause for celebration, even though the timing could have been better! I cradled a shivering Gregory Peck to my chest, anxious about Old Spice, who had sequestered himself that morning somewhere on the banks of the river, where he would be very much at risk of being swept away. The roar of the river grew louder as the night progressed, and when I finally fell into a fitful sleep I dreamed of Malindi and the sound of the surf at high tide. By the time a watery dawn lit the sky, the rain had stopped and we stepped out to view a transformed landscape. The river was a chocolate torrent swirling angrily over where our tents had stood just hours before, already lapping halfway up the palm-fruited duoms and acacias, many of which had been uprooted and swept away. Fortunately the men discovered that their wall had withstood the might of the flooded river.

When David came back from the construction site in the late afternoon we went off in search of Old Spice. Our old campsite was now just part of the river itself, but we walked along the water's edge calling out for him as loudly as we could over the noise of the water, imitating his clucking sounds. Darkness set in and by torchlight we picked up plenty of pairs of eyes glowing like embers in the dark, some red – predators – and some green – herbivores – but none that belonged to Old Spice.

As we made our way back to camp, I heard the pattering of feet behind us and lo and behold, there he was. The joy of this reunion was mutual – he purred and nuzzled and we took it in turns to carry him to our new home. There, I rummaged around to find the all-important aftershave, and from then on, he returned at dusk as usual to be anointed and have a cuddle before hurrying off into the night. Now that the rains had come, there were interesting puddles to inspect and a regular nocturnal banquet of insects that crash-landed around the light we had erected outside the mess tent.

Meanwhile, the rain continued unabated up-country, making 1961 a truly memorable year. Wild flowers sprang up as if from nowhere – delicately scented snowdrops, tiny blue and white African violets and the pure white convolvulus creeper. Butterflies fluttered around the flowers and gathered at moist elephant dung-balls. During the daily 'hopgrogging' chore I would pick a pretty bunch of wild flowers for the mess tent, and often when I went to bed I would find a beautiful orchid-like delonix blossom on my pillow, as a token of David's love.

We were sandwiched between two flooded rivers, the Galana and the Tiva, responsible for sixty workmen and cut off from base. A runway was cleared nearby so that supplies could be ferried in by air and sick men taken out if necessary. In many places the river had widened its course by 100 yards or more, and the roar of the water was punctuated by loud crashes as huge trees fell, adding to the unbelievable amount of debris that was already being carried down the swollen torrent. Many of the baboons roosting in trees along the riverbanks at night were being swept away when the trees went down, and we also saw the carcasses of livestock that must have come from beyond the boundaries of the Park.

It was essential to maintain contact with the south bank of the river so that supplies of food and fuel could be ferried across to us. Eventually a cable was dragged and anchored across the river, providing a lifeline to civilization and enabling supplies to be winched across. It wasn't exactly a safe means of transport while the river remained in spate; it was far too risky to ferry the workmen across, many of whom could not even swim, so there was nothing for it but to sit it out and wait for the river to subside. However, now that cement and supplies could reach us, work was able to continue, and for three more months, while the Lugard's Fall causeway was flooded, we lived in our little camp beneath the Yatta Plateau. David kept in radio communication with both the Nairobi Headquarters and Park HQ at Voi and I must admit that I rather enjoyed being away from the usual demands on his time. I wrote long letters to Jill, the musings of a marooned mother!

Old Spice had pretty much grown up in camp and by now was spending more time away from us, ever more secretive and increasingly independent. Sometimes we didn't see him for days at a time, and then he would reappear in our tent in the dead of night. Gregory Peck had, by contrast, turned out to be gregarious and outgoing, sitting on my shoulder as I went about my daily chores. He even participated in the grasshopper hunts, hopping alongside me and quivering with excitement whenever we nailed the quarry. One morning I was carrying him on my hand when he started exercising his wings, flapping them frantically, and the next moment he was airborne, swooping downwards at first and then gaining height and fluttering unsteadily to the top of a tall acacia where I could just make him out at the very top, a long way up for a maiden flight. I called him and he replied with his usual cheep after the Peck, but he appeared to lack the confidence to come down. Just as I was steeling myself to accept that this could be the parting of the ways, he fluttered from his perch and landed squarely on my shoulder, to be rewarded by the fattest grasshopper in the tin.

Gregory Peck was happiest when embroiled in a great deal of activity, so we decided that it was time to introduce him to the car, a trip north to the Tiva having been planned to assess the damage caused by floods there. Rain had transformed the northern area of the Park. Grass was now waist high, the road barely visible. It was as though we were driving through a field of wheat, and every now and then we had to stop to remove the grass seeds that choked the radiator grille and caused the temperature gauge to reach boiling point.

We passed several healthy-looking rhinos who trotted off with a spring in their step, tails held high – a treat to see them thus, after the die-off of the previous drought year. When we reached the Tiva, we could see that the devastation was severe – great trees uprooted, lying amid piles of driftwood on both banks of the river, the crossing at Makoka blocked by enormous sand bars as high as a house. One look told us that the blind at Kathamulla must surely have been demolished.

Gregory became a seasoned traveller, accompanying us everywhere we went, perched on David's shoulder. Occasionally he would be blown off and out of the window, so we would have to pull up and wait for him to catch up with us. On one occasion we inadvertently chose to take a break beneath a noisy colony of buffalo weavers, and I was interested to see how Gregory would react to his own kind. Surprisingly he merely ignored them, and David explained that birds raised by humans tended to imprint to such an extent that they might never recognize their own kind again. Certainly Gregory's rendering of a buffalo weaver's sound was not quite as it should be, more just a raucous squawk. However, he seemed happy enough with it, announcing each new dawn with that lusty screech.

Back down south, the Athi River eventually abated. I was by now anxious to get back for Jill, who would be returning from school for the Christmas holidays. However, at the causeway the approaches had been completely swept away, with just a yawning chasm between the concrete and the bank, the river having extended its width by some 300 yards. David waded in to assess whether there was any chance of getting a vehicle across but decided that it was out of the question. There was no alternative but to risk a crossing in the Aruba dinghy before more rain up-country swelled the river again. I packed an angry Old Spice and a flustered Gregory Peck into their boxes, said goodbye to the people with whom I had shared this peculiar time, strapped myself into a lifejacket and headed for the river. We set off in the dinghy, not without trepidation, for I was very aware that should the boat tip up, I would not be able to save either Gregory or Old Spice in their respective boxes. I was relieved when we all landed safely on the other side without mishap. David remained behind to repair the Galana causeway so that the bulk of the equipment and staff could follow by road. I couldn't wait to see Jill along with the rest of my family, who planned to spend Christmas with us.

The three months stranded in camp had been an adventure, time suspended from the hustle and bustle of Park HQ. Little did I know how busy it was all going to get on our return.

9. Settled

'The monstrous sophism that beasts are pure unfeeling machines,
and do not reason, scarcely requires a confutation.'

– Percy Bysshe Shelley (1792–1822)

During our three months away, our elephants, rhinos and buffalo calves had grown in numbers and become unlikely companions. Back at home David had recently constructed a lion-proof stockade for all the orphans, and at first Samson and Aruba had been dubious about the newcomers, mock-charging the little buffaloes with alarming regularity. Rufus the rhino was indifferent to their demonstrations, and oddly this seemed to reassure the elephants as they began to bond with their new cohabitants. Within a week or two, our little herd of assorted animals – now known as the big orphan group – became remarkably close, travelling everywhere together, delighting any visitors that came across them in the Park.

In no time at all Gregory Peck mastered the geography of the Headquarters. He slept in our bedroom, and each morning, on hearing the dawn chorus, his little eyes popped wide open. Shaking out his feathers, which were gradually becoming mottled with black, he walked to the entrance of his box, looked around for David and me and fluttered straight down on to our bed, making sure that we woke up by pecking our eyelids. When satisfied, he squeezed through the grid on our window, disappearing outside to join in the singing. He never went far. As soon as we sat down to breakfast, he would reappear, inspect the contents of our plates, grab whatever he fancied and fly off. Having eaten his stolen token, he then flew back into our room, eternally hopeful that I had left my powder puff on the dressing table. Ever since arriving at the house, he had been hell-bent on adding it to one of his interminable nests, messy entanglements under construction all over the place. At least I didn't have a beehive hairdo, fashionable at the time, as did one visitor who had to endure twigs and sticks being stuck into her lacquered mop.

I was extremely proud of my new home and appreciated it all the more after living in a tent for three months. Before breakfast, I liked to spend a few quiet moments cutting flowers from the garden, eager to emulate my mother, who had always filled our home with sweet-smelling floral scents. So, it seemed, did Gregory. As soon as my secateurs were out, he would interrupt whatever he was doing, balance himself on my shoulder and chirp away as I cut the blossoms. Never one to just watch, he would make a determined effort to join in, gripping a stem firmly in his beak and hurling himself backwards with all his might. Invariably the stem sprang back but Gregory refused to let go, hanging on for dear life, usually ending up hoisted clean off the ground. With each attempt, his mounting frustration – furious squawking and ruffled feathers – meant I had to lend him a hand, but Gregory was an independent little buffalo weaver, preferring to do things for himself. It wasn't long before he realized that once the flowers had been carefully arranged in a vase and placed in the living room, they were there for the taking. He also understood that disruption to my flower arrangement was not popular, so he would wait until my back was turned, dart in, pull them out one by one and scatter them all over the floor, only absconding with one in his beak when I chased him away.

Gregory was an amazing little bird, my companion at virtually all times of the day. He was the first to report for duty as the day's working activities gathered momentum. After mischievously disrupting my flower arrangement, he headed straight for the office, where he set about picking up the letters and pencils from David's desk, his eyes shining in delight as he dropped each one on to the floor. Next, with a document or two in his beak, he flew off to the workshop to see if the concrete mixer was in operation. This was one of his priority nest sites, so he dropped off any twigs or documents he had on him and then hopped over to the tool shed, where he busied himself with nest-building, shrieking happily at the top of his voice in competition with the giant diesel engine that powered the electrical appliances. Being a buffalo weaver, I suppose he equated noise with nest-building, the most important activity to a colony of his kin, who would all chatter away together as they made their homes in the same tree.

Gregory quickly became a favourite with the workforce, squawking happily as people waved at him or shouted hello as he flew overhead. If you hadn't seen him in the week, you could be sure to catch him on Friday afternoons as the workmen and rangers gathered at the office to collect their wages. Pay day was his favourite time of the week, and trying to outwit him proved especially challenging. In order to prevent him getting in to wreak havoc on the notes and coins as they were being neatly laid out for distribution, the doors and windows had to remain firmly shut. But this didn't deter Gregory one bit. He just waited patiently with the long queue that gathered outside, fluttering down on people's heads and shoulders in the hope they would carry him in. Although everyone had instructions to open the door just enough to be able to squeeze through and immediately close it behind them, at some point in the procedure Gregory usually managed to slip in, swoop down, grab a note or two in his beak and fly round and round the office in great triumph. This always triggered an amused ground stampede, with everyone watching where the note might land, so that it could be recovered.

I was aware that Gregory had missed out on picking up essential skills, despite the great pains that he took in the manufacture of his architecturally sophisticated nests. He needed to learn by example, so having found an old weaver nest in a deserted colony, we placed it in a jacaranda tree on our lawn. When Gregory spotted it, he was beside himself with excitement, cackling delightedly, flying around it, sitting inside it to test it for comfort and rearranging its outer edges. We felt sure he was going to pick up some tips as to how a nest should look, but it soon became apparent that his imagination had been fired not by the construction of the nest, but by the materials that had been used to make it. Within a few minutes, he took to dismantling it, extracting thorns and twigs to carry off to one of his own contraptions.

I was always aware that I could not guarantee Gregory's safety, and during his first few weeks in Voi he had had some valuable lessons in survival, twice narrowly escaping the claws of a raptor by diving into a bush in the nick of time. When I went to retrieve him, he was trembling violently; soon after he began to take note of the alarm calls of other birds, and at the first hint of danger sought shelter in the house or thick vegetation. I knew he was safe at night because he slept in the box on our windowsill. However, I was alarmed when from one day to the next he took to sleeping outside on the ground in a clump of dried grass at the back of the house, tucking his head into his wing, totally exposed to passing snakes, genets, even Old Spice, who was still paying us periodic nocturnal visits. We decided the only thing to do was to carry him back to his box in the bedroom, and as he didn't seem to mind, it became a daily ritual to actually physically put him to bed, to bring him in from the ground to his box. It puzzled us why he behaved in this eccentric un-birdlike way, but then Gregory Peck was no ordinary buffalo weaver and perhaps we were to blame, as we had not provided a twig for him to perch on, which meant he slept on the bottom of his box.

Undoubtedly, Gregory's greatest charm lay in his curiosity for the world around him. He did not, though, like being laughed at by humans, most of whom would indeed laugh the moment they saw him. Gregory was on to this, and whenever we were greeting a visitor at the verandah steps – and there were several each week – he would arrive to give them the once-over, positioning himself opposite with his head held high, looking down his beak, fixing them with a supercilious stare. As – on cue – they laughed, he would give an outraged squawk, rumple his feathers and fly on to the visitor's head. The harder they tried to dislodge him, the more determined he was to stay and let them know just who was boss.

I will never forget the day when the concrete mixer – home then to one of Gregory's all-time favourite nests – had to move from the workshop area to the construction site of the new ranger quarters down near the main entrance gate. As he watched it being transported, you could almost hear his brain ticking and I wondered what he was going to do about it. As soon as it was cranked up at its new location, Gregory cocked his head to one side, listened carefully and flew off to find it. And later that afternoon, just as I was packing up after a day in the office, he returned on the lorry bringing the workmen back, sitting cheerfully on the cab, fluttering to keep his balance as it bounced over bumps in the road. Incredibly, he soon learned that if he arrived at the workshop promptly by seven in the morning, he could hitch a ride on the truck that took the staff to the site; if he arrived late and missed the lift, he simply took to the air and got there himself. Usually he returned with the workers for the lunch break, covered in cement dust and looking thoroughly exhausted, but at the sound of the two o'clock bell, he would be off again. I was astounded at how much understanding went on in his bird brain, and I well remember a visiting scientist scoffing at me when I remarked on this. 'But, Daphne,' he said, 'how can a brain the size of a pea be capable of any thought at all? Where do you think the phrase "bird brain" comes from, eh?' Like David, I was rapidly losing confidence with the supposed infallibility of science.

Now that Gregory was living with us, word soon got around and I seemed to acquire a strange assortment of other little feathered orphans: Oliver Twist, a baby swift who had fallen out of his nest at the railway station, was reared successfully and launched from the roof of the house never to be seen again; Abdul, a baby bulbul whose end was not so fortunate, for on his maiden flight he was intercepted by a goshawk; Puffin, a sweet little puff-backed shrike who in his early life would only take food from me; and not forgetting Red Head, a red-headed weaver who had been a garden resident since 1959. He had a series of nests in the large melia tree on the lawn, the newest and best always reserved for himself, an inferior one for his wife and many in disrepair that were occupied by pairs of chattering sparrows. Mrs Red Head was a dainty greyish bird with an attractive red bar on each wing and appeared to be ruled with a rod of iron by her husband. Although she took a keen interest in each new home, she was forbidden to interfere with the construction in any way, and if, in her enthusiasm, she happened to approach too close while Mr Red Head was busy working on it, he angrily chased her off. However, as soon as his back was turned, she never missed an opportunity to dart in and take a quick look around. She was allowed to lay eggs in the more up-market of the nests, and as soon as their young hatchlings appeared, both parents had their work cut out. Several little gaping mouths appeared expectantly, several times a day, and if we tapped the side of the nest, we could induce the same result. Surprisingly, throughout the years, we never saw a Red Head offspring in the garden once they left the nest. One day they simply vanished and Mr and Mrs Red Head began all over again.

It was no wonder we shared our garden with so many different feathered and furred wild animals. Over time, David had transformed it into a colourful tropical paradise, with paths of lawn winding through a profusion of flowerbeds; a lilac-mauve jacaranda tree towered over the rustic birdbath surrounded by blossoms, and a carefully constructed tiny artificial stream meandered down a slope, tumbling into a beautiful lily pond where veil-tailed goldfish darted beneath blue and pink water-lilies. Rustic benches bordered the lily pond and speakers in a nearby tree provided music as we relaxed outdoors in the cool of the evening. The heady, sweet scent of the ylang-ylang, with its yellow and green star-shaped flowers, permeated the night and the bright red brilliance of the lipstick shrub, bixa, added yet more colour. Our garden was unexpectedly cool in a setting that was harsh, arid and hot. Here, there seemed to be a truce between man and animal, many wild creatures shedding their inherent fear of humans to venture into our garden. During the day you could see wild dikdiks strolling around the flowerbeds, and a flock of powder-blue-and-white-striped breasted vulturine guinea fowl that had multiplied to number over 100 and were as tame as domestic chickens. Ground squirrels, tree squirrels and magnificent orange-headed agama lizards were all diurnal garden residents. Then in the darkness a host of larger animals ventured in, including an old bull giraffe who came regularly to prune the tree on our lawn with loud chomping sounds that interrupted our sleep, as well as several old buffaloes who came to crop the grass. Daylight hours were filled with birdsong, while the nights were punctuated by the roaring of lions, the guttural 'sawing' of a leopard and the eerie howl of hyenas. There were times when Jill's sleepy voice piped up from her bedroom, saying, 'Please chase those lions away, I can't get to sleep.' The music of an African night was as commonplace to my daughter as the sound of traffic to a city-dweller.

After the dry season of 1962, when rain had come and relieved us from the debilitating heat of the previous months, Old Spice and Gregory Peck finally left us for good. I was confident that Old Spice, now grown, would fend for himself, but I have been haunted ever since about what might have happened to Gregory. He was seen by one of the rangers, leaving the Park at dusk on the shoulder of a visitor on a day when David and I had been delayed in Mombasa. Returning after dark, I had gone to collect him from his usual sitting place in the grass at the back of the house, but he was nowhere to be found, and nor did the days that followed bring any sign of his return. Eventually, after tears and real anguish, we accepted that he was gone, and then gone for good, grateful for the pure joy he had brought us during his one year of life and the lessons he taught us about 'bird brains' the size of a pea. I will always remember fondly his antics and quite dazzling abilities.

Towards the end of 1962 I fell pregnant and I knew at once exactly where and when my baby had been conceived – during a safari on the southern side of the Galana River, one stormy evening as thunder rolled across the sky and flashes of forked lightning lit up the inside of our tent. I was initially surprised to feel nauseous and tired, but as soon as my pregnancy was confirmed, I was delighted. I had longed to have David's child for some time, but when I had broached the subject he had not been keen – we already had three children between us and he told me candidly that he didn't want to 'share me' with anyone else. When David and his ex-wife Diana had separated, their daughter Valerie had been only six and their son Kenneth just three. When she remarried, Diana, her new husband and the children had moved from Kenya to South Africa and this had been very painful for David. Unlike Bill and me, the divorce of David and Diana had been acrimonious and he found it uncomfortable even to speak about it. I knew that he was not eager to start another family, so I had to pick my moment carefully to tell him our news.

This was, for the white settler community, a particularly unstable time. As 1962 drew to a close, we knew that Kenya would be granted self-government from Britain in June 1963, followed by full independence in December. Not only did we fear Jomo Kenyatta, the man who was bound to head an independent new African government, but we also worried that Tsavo would be taken over both in terms of the land and the running of the Park. No one doubted that all over Africa, posts held by 'foreigners' would be subjected to rapid 'Africanization'. The Nairobi British High Commission made it crystal-clear to us that should we ever relinquish our British passports to take on Kenyan identity, we would never be considered British again. Still proud of our English ancestry, we were not prepared to change our identity simply for reasons of expediency. I had always had a British passport, having had grandparents born in Britain. It all seemed grossly unfair: anyone living in Kenya who had been born in Britain, or who had parents born in Britain, could retain their British nationality, and although no blood other than English, Scottish and Welsh flowed through my veins, since neither my parents nor myself had been born in Britain, we – the people who had the deepest roots in Africa and had sacrificed so much to support the famous British Empire – suddenly found ourselves in danger of being cast as aliens.

David had recently experienced huge difficulty in renewing his British passport. Despite having been born in Alexandria because his father had been dispatched there by the British during the First World War; despite being the product of two very English parents only born in India because in those days India was British and the jewel in the crown of Britain's far-flung Empire; despite his birth having been registered at the British Consulate in Egypt to establish the fact that he was British, nothing he presented was enough to satisfy the British High Commission that he was, indeed, British. In fact, the official there suggested that David should instead be seeking a passport at the Indian High Commission, but stopped short when David said quietly, 'There was no question about me not being British when the Second World War broke out and I was called up to fight for your bloody country.' Eventually David had to provide documentary proof – at great cost, from the archives at Somerset House in London – not only that his parents were legally married in order to produce him but that his English-born grandparents had also been legally married in order to produce them!

With the Mau Mau insurgency of the mid 1950s still fresh in our minds, many people we knew felt it unwise to remain in Kenya on the cusp of independence and moved to Rhodesia, South Africa, Australia, Canada or back to Britain. All Government servants, including our colleagues serving with the Game Department, could expect generous compensation from the British Government for any loss of career should they find themselves 'Africanized', and were to enjoy an indexed pension as well. But the same benefits were not extended to those of us serving with what was by then the Royal National Parks Service, because the institution did not fall under the Government's remit but instead under an Independent Board of Trustees. It had been set up in this way to safeguard the country's wild heritage from the plunder of political expediency, and so it happened that those few dedicated men who had transformed the National Parks from virgin bush into what, at this point in time, were acknowledged as the finest Parks in Africa, found themselves penalized.

Understandably, David was feeling pretty insecure, and a poaching incident that took place around this time served to highlight just how unsettled things were becoming. A Field Force patrol came across a gang of poachers hunting with dogs in the Park near Maktau in Tsavo West, and in an ambush succeeded in arresting one man. Two others escaped towards a railway encampment, pursued by the rangers, who had left one of their men to guard the prisoner. Emboldened, the captured poacher attempted to wrest the rifle from the ranger, who, fearing himself being over-powered during the ensuing struggle, pulled the trigger in self-defence and shot his assailant dead. Almost at once, a hostile crowd of railway workers armed with sticks, clubs and metal bars surrounded the ranger. Thinking quickly, he fired shots into the air, a signal to his colleagues, who came hurrying back to contain the angry crowd, and soon David, accompanied by a police officer, arrived on the scene, having received a call for help from the patrol. As they drew up in David's car, the crowd surged forward, hostile and angry. David stepped out of the car and walked through the crowd to the dead poacher. At cries of 'Bwana Saa Nane' – the affectionate nickname of 'Mr Two O'Clock' that David had acquired among the locals, since he took his lunch break every day at that time – the people fell silent, David's name and reputation by now respected among all the tribes that bordered Tsavo. But then a chilling voice penetrated the silence – 'Wait until Uhuru – we will kill them all!' 'Freedom' or independence was not that far off, and following the events of the Mau Mau insurgency, those words did not go unheeded.

This incident shook me as I remembered how lucky I had been to survive the ambush by the Mau Mau when I was pregnant with Jill. Now, I was about to announce my pregnancy at a time of imminent upheaval, news that I knew would not be received lightly. When I eventually plucked up the courage to tell him, I was mightily relieved that, having recovered from the shock, David held me close, murmuring, not with a great deal of conviction, that he was delighted! Coincidentally, another baby had come into our lives during the safari on which I had conceived – a tiny newborn zebra foal whose mother had been killed by a lion and who in her distress had attached herself to the car as we passed by. This new zebra orphan became known as 'Huppety' and was a beautiful little creature with perfect markings, a soft bushy tail and the face of a thoroughbred. She loved being groomed as well as taking evening exercises, galloping, bucking and kicking joyfully around the garden. When she tired, I would lead her back to the new nursery stables at the side of the house and try to entice her into bed. This demanded a lot of time and patience, for just as success seemed within reach, she would break back and gallop off down the hill again, so that I was usually the more exhausted of us, something exacerbated by my condition.

Like Gregory, Huppety became attached to me from the moment we found her. Back at home, she would often try to follow me around the house, leaping wildly and lashing out in terror when her hooves slid on the polished concrete floor. When it was becoming increasingly impossible to get on with my daily routine, I came up with the ingenious idea of hanging one of my dresses across a branch of our jacaranda tree and covering Huppety's head with it while I made off.

As long as I was hidden from view by the time she freed herself from the dress, she settled down next to it quite happily. As time went on, she became more problematic, especially when, having been weaned from the bottle, she took to sampling other things, particularly the washing on the line at the back of the house. As soon as it was pegged out, she would gallop over and start working her way through the garments and sheets, chewing them until they were reduced to mangled rags. Many smaller articles of clothing disappeared entirely, remnants turning up in her droppings some time later! We hoisted up the washing line with a bamboo pole, but this seemed to make her even more determined to outwit us and she took to creeping up behind us – ears back and teeth bared – dashing in to snatch an article before the washing line was up and out of reach. She also took to chewing the putty off windows and sneaking into David's office to hoover up all the correspondence lying on his desk; even drinking sludge oil in the workshop with no apparent ill effect. But I forgave all this – most of the time – because when she nudged me with her nose and pressed her head against me in an affectionate embrace, my heart would melt and I enjoyed her all over again.

In 1961, Peter had come back from the northern area to Tsavo East to work with David and moved into the house further round the hill where Bill and I had lived when we were first married. Huppety struck up an immediate friendship with his tame bushbuck, Mr Koo, so much so that Huppety refused to return home, preferring instead to spend nights out with Mr Koo. Having already eaten Peter's unopened correspondence, containing a letter from his fiancée in which meticulous wedding plans were outlined, Huppety made herself even more unpopular by chewing up more of my brother's possessions, including the paintwork of his precious red sports car. This last misdemeanour turned Peter positively apoplectic, with much of his fury directed my way for 'not being able to control that blasted zebra'. Before he left Tsavo for his wedding, he put his car in the workshop garage and fortified the entrance to his house with a barricade of barbed wire and drums.

Peter's wedding to his English-born fiancée, Sarah Woodall, took place in Nanyuki, just beyond Nyeri, north of Nairobi, the 17,000-foot snow-clad peaks of Mount Kenya providing a stunning backdrop. David was anxious throughout the proceedings, fearing that our baby would make its appearance at any minute. Knowing that this was a distinct possibility, I was glad of my mother's calming presence. Jill loved her pale yellow bridesmaid's dress and being able to run around with her cousins at the reception in the beautiful grounds of the Burguret Estate. Afterwards we returned to Nairobi, where we were staying with my younger sister Betty and her husband, Graham, until the baby was born. David seized the opportunity to undergo training for his private pilot's licence, so that he could fly Tsavo East's newly acquired Supercub aircraft. In typical David fashion, he was sufficiently proficient to go solo after only eight hours. Having a plane at Tsavo would be transformative, enabling us to conduct aerial surveillance over the entire Park, track the movements and patterns of different species more easily, ferry supplies to the Field Force rangers operating in remote corners, and observe changes to the habitat.

During the evening of 30 June, five days after my due date, I went into labour, so David took me to hospital and dropped me there, there being no question in those days of a man being present at the birth. We were confident that our baby would be born within a few hours, but how wrong we were! Our baby daughter, Angela Mara, arrived seventeen hours later, at 11 a.m. on 1 July – 'a funny little Pip-Squeak', said David, gazing into her somewhat wrinkled face. From that moment on, she became known as Pip, sometimes interspersed with Squeak. She was a great delight to Jill, since at eight years old she was happy to both help look after and play with her baby sister.

I remained with Betty for a few extra weeks, David returning to Tsavo by air, piloting the Park's new Supercub registration 5Y–KTP, known to all thereafter as Tango Papa, and it was in Tango Papa that David took Angela and me back home to Tsavo. In the interim, Peter had arrived back from his honeymoon and had 'dealt' with Huppety as threatened. He had taken her back to the Galana River, not far from a wild herd of zebra, who had taken a great interest as this pretty young filly emerged from the back of a truck. I hoped that in time

Huppety would become a mother herself and enjoy her life back in the wild. Although I was upset at first, I was relieved that I did not have to worry about Huppety and her impish ways. I was busy enough looking after my new baby.

Angela was just over five months old when Kenya became fully independent on 12 December 1963. We sat listening to the radio as the announcer described the lowering of the Union Jack and the hoisting of the new Kenyan flag – a shield and crossed spears against a black, red and green backdrop. The Duke of Edinburgh represented the Queen, handing over the instruments of government to Jomo Kenyatta, the new President of Kenya. There had been changes in the Royal National Parks also, which again became just the Kenya National Parks, dropping the 'Royal' prefix. The first 'expatriate' to be 'Africanized' was the founding director, Colonel Mervyn Cowie, but down in Tsavo we carried on pretty much as usual, answerable now to a new Kenyan director, Mr Perez Olindo, who was accommodating and amiable. Most of the white members of the Board of Trustees were replaced by indigenous black Kenyans, and many of our Game Department colleagues took their 'golden bowlers' and either retired into civilian life or left the country, also replaced by local Africans.

Since the arrival of our Supercub, safaris had become much less frequent as David could now cover the Park by air, communicating with the field patrols through the plane's radio network. So when he had to make a journey by car to the Athi, I decided to go along, taking Angela on her first ever safari. It was with some degree of nostalgia that we passed the baobab tree where Gregory had been born, the nests still clustered along its mighty boughs, and when, further along, we passed the high ground where our camp had stood during the floods, I thought with fondness of Old Spice. I have to admit that this safari was something of a challenge. Our six-month-old baby required a serious amount of paraphernalia, and the heat of Tsavo made her fractious, so there were frequent stops en route to fill up the little canvas basin, plonk Angela in it and sponge her down. Once settled at our old Kitani ya Ndundu campsite, I sat Angela in the portable seat that hooked on to the outside of the car door and then proceeded to spend most of each day trying to wash soiled nappies, which took on the colour of the brown river water, or sterilizing bottles and teats in cleaner river water collected in a hole dug in the sand. Our campsite was just a shadow of its former self, many of the huge shade trees and doum palms lost to the 1961 floods. However, it was encouraging to find that rhinos were still numerous along the river, and every drive from our camp was an adventure, with huffing and puffing rhinos charging as we passed by.

During one early morning drive we came upon six crocodiles feeding on a waterbuck in shallow waters, and we watched as the crocodiles spun over and over, twisting pieces of flesh from the carcass, throwing their heads back and gulping it down with snapping jaws. Several marabou storks stood around, bravely taking an interest in the scraps that drifted their way. As usual, my sympathies were with the victim, visualizing the desperate struggle that must have taken place before our arrival. David had once witnessed a crocodile seize a waterbuck doe in shallow water, and in response to her agonized bellows, her mate ferociously and repeatedly tried to horn the crocodile in an attempt to force it to relinquish its hold. The crocodile never even flinched, steadily dragging its terror-stricken victim to a deep channel where soon only a few bubbles were evidence of the doe's last struggle for life. The male watched the place where his mate had disappeared for several minutes, breathing heavily, before turning and slowly walking back to the bank. Of course dramas such as this were enacted several times a day, every day of every year, in the natural circle of life, but witnessing the suffering of any animal was very painful for me.

On arriving back home, we learned that our young orphaned rhino, Rufus, had been involved in a scuffle with a fully-grown wild rhino that had rushed out of a nearby thicket and with a tremendous snort tossed him high into the air, injuring him where it hurt most. His keeper had shinned up the nearest tree in fright, leaving Samson to come to Rufus's rescue, which he duly did, trumpeting and charging at the aggressor. Since the departure of Fatuma and Kanderi, Samson and Rufus had become comically inseparable. When they played, Samson would kneel or lie down, whereupon Rufus would lower his head, roll his eyes until the whites showed, snort defiantly and charge at Samson, butting him as hard as he could with his horn. This never made much impression on Samson, who managed to ward off the impact with his trunk, wrapping it around Rufus's neck in a vice-like grip that almost throttled him. Puffing with indignation, Rufus would then have to hastily reverse in order to disentangle himself but within a few seconds would mount a fresh onslaught, which ended up exactly as before, until eventually Rufus would accept defeat and begin to wander off. Angela adored all the orphans, clapping her chubby hands in delight every time she saw them. A great treat for her was a ride on Rufus, sitting on his broad back held in place by either David or myself. Rufus didn't mind a bit and even seemed to enjoy the extra attention, as well as the sensation of having Angela aboard.

Interestingly it was Rufus who donated the most intriguing sample to David's 'museum'. This was my husband's ongoing delight, a treasure trove of artefacts painstakingly collected over the years. He was always looking for intriguing items to add to his collection, though I did not think that a large beetle-like bot from Rufus's freshly passed dung would have been of so much interest. Carefully housed in a bottle with a layer of soil at the bottom and a closed lid in which small holes allowed the passage of air, the bot very soon disappeared into the soil and the jar was placed in a corner of the room where we promptly forgot all about it. All of us that is, except David, who a few weeks later noticed a large metallic blue insect inside the jar.

This creature turned out to be the gyrostigma fly – this one artificially hatched – a curious insect whose very existence depends upon being able to locate a living rhino within five days of being hatched, so that it can anchor its tiny white oblong eggs firmly in the soft indentations of the rhino's skin. After six days, tiny looped worm-like creatures the size of a comma emerge which, it had been assumed, gained access to the stomach through either the nose or the mouth of the rhino. However, we soon discovered that they simply bored straight through the hide to enter the bloodstream and from there somehow finally ended up as the large beetle-like bots present in the stomach of almost every living rhino. Even today very little is known about this fly other than that different established rhino populations have their slightly different versions of the fly that have evolved alongside them down the ages. Most of the fly's life cycle is thought to be in the bot stage, actually inside its host's stomach, feeding off the contents in a seemingly symbiotic relationship, though David felt sure that a high infestation might turn parasitic when the rhino became old or fell into poor condition during periods of drought. How long the bot stage lasts within the stomach of the rhino before being expelled remains a mystery, but one thing we did find out was that the bots had the ability to assess conditions in the outside world at the onset of the wet season by appearing briefly at the anal opening and, if the prospects were not to their liking, retreating back from whence they had come. If conditions were looking good, mature bots emerged with the dung, pupated in the ground and eventually emerged into the metallic blue, wasp-mimicking fly that David found fluttering in his bottle.

It was rare that David had much time for his 'museum'. By the mid-60s the Park was busier, with more visitors coming in each week. The new self-catering bungalows at Aruba Lodge, bordering David's man-made lake (this, his original Aruba Dam, was large enough to be termed a lake), were particularly popular, being booked up months in advance. A small shop had been established, selling tinned food and soft drinks, and petrol was available through hand-pumps. David had stocked the lake with tilapia, and by now a thriving fishery at the lake edge brought in a steady stream of income for the Park as well as providing a fresh source of protein for the rangers, keepers and other members of staff. Gill nets were set at night and the morning's catch was gutted and stored in large insulated tanks that were filled with the dry ice brought up twice a week by a supplier, who came to collect the tank's contents to sell them in Mombasa. Angela and I were often down by the dam as the nets were brought in to get some of the fish for our supper.

I was living a full and varied life, deeply in love with David, but happiest when Jill returned from school and my family was complete. David was a wonderful and loving father to Angela and a very attentive and caring stepfather to Jill, and he was careful never to usurp the role of her real father. With an aircraft now at his disposal, aerial surveillance sorties of the Park became a daily routine. David would take to the air after the 7 a.m. radio exchange between the Nairobi Headquarters and all field stations, fly for several hours and, on his return, buzz the house, throttling back the engines and shouting out of the window: 'Get the coffee ready.' We could hear his words clearly from the ground, and at the sound of 'coffee', the person nearest to the kitchen would switch on the kettle. I was also immensely busy during this period and the days would whiz by in a frenzy of activity. Evenings were special, especially when David and I could have some time for ourselves and discuss the day's events.

With the poaching threat of the 1950s having receded, the elephants now understood that Tsavo provided protection for them; their numbers multiplied and this had a massive impact on the Park's vegetation. David worried that browsing species such as gerenuk, kudu, dikdiks and rhinos might be affected adversely and continued to press for an in-depth scientific study to try to unravel the effects of such changes. He was resolute in his wish to avoid the artificial slaughter of elephants, South African style. There, elephant numbers were being strictly regulated by the annual cull, which, although surgical in proficiency, was particularly cruel and unpalatable to those who understood the very human emotional side of elephants. We knew only too well that there, family units were targeted from helicopters using the immobilizing drug scholine, in order to avoid contamination of the meat that would render it unfit for consumption. Scholine collapsed the muscles, leaving the elephants fully conscious yet unable to move even an eyelid while they waited for the gunmen to move in on the ground and systematically finish them off with a shot through the brain. Sickening scenes were recorded on film of men jumping on huge inert bodies to get a better vantage point from which to end the life of others, paralysed elephants knowing exactly what was going on and having to watch helpless as their family members were butchered one by one. We were stunned at the distressing images of panic-stricken calves crying for help from adults incapable of movement. Calves that might be able to survive without milk were then captured for subsequent sale to circuses or zoos. The fully milk-dependent tiny calves were usually the last to be slaughtered, but at least they were spared a lifetime of suffering and bondage in far-off lands where animal welfare was still apparently a very alien concept.

Once the entire elephant family was either dead or subjugated, the merciless butchers then moved in to cut up the carcasses and remove all the meat to huge abattoirs for processing, after which it was either dried and sold as biltong, or canned for pet food and even for human consumption. And having completed the grisly annual slaughter, grieving elephant survivors were allowed a brief reprieve of just one year to mourn their lost loved ones before the helicopters were mobilized and the carnage began all over again. We had been told that just the beat of a helicopter sent every elephant into panic-stricken flight, running for their very life, knowing that this time it could be their turn. In the elephant world, word silently spreads over distance like wildfire through their mysterious means of infrasound communication, so even those far removed were getting the message.

David had an intimate knowledge of elephant intelligence and sensitivity, of the strength of their family ties, and their very real sense of death. He knew how deeply they mourned their loved ones and that their powers of memory far exceeded our own. Few people understood what David had learned during the anti-poaching campaign and from the close observation of our orphans. We talked a lot about how best to handle Tsavo's so-called 'elephant problem', knowing that a cull had already been suggested by the powers-that-be. Before all else, an accurate count of Tsavo's elephant population was needed, for there was little idea of the true number. Fortunately, the British Army was willing to help in an intensive count as a training exercise. There was great excitement the day the Army Air Corps arrived, bringing with them three Beaver aircraft and two helicopters, maintenance and ground crew, petrol tanks, camouflage gear and all the usual equipment necessary for a training exercise. It so happened that on that day the orphans were feeding close to the Park's new state-of-the-art airstrip, so they came by and lent a hand, Samson rolling drums of fuel along the ground and inspecting the aircraft with his trunk and Rufus less eager to become involved, huff-ing and snorting suspiciously at the strange intruders into his territory.

Together with the commanding officer, David worked out details of how the count would be undertaken. The Park was divided into blocks, each of which could be covered in a day and, in order to avoid duplication, arranged so that adjoining blocks could be counted simultaneously by different aircraft. The aerial count went like clock-work; with military precision, each aircraft, with experienced observers on board, was assigned a specific block to count during the course of a day, at the end of which dots, each representing ten ele-phants, were marked on a map.

Final figures of the count showed that instead of the 5,000, as orig-inally estimated, there were in fact 9,000 counted elephants, with some 15,000 in the ecosystem overall encompassing an area of some 16,000 square miles, twice the size of the Park itself. 'Seeing is believ-ing,' observed David. He now had a minimum number, but suspected that there were probably more. Operation Count had been a huge success and it was with some sadness that we said goodbye to the sol-diers. They had been a lively presence in the Park and their assistance had been invaluable.

From regular aerial surveys over the Park, and now that the ele-phants were opening up the commiphora thickets, it was evident that the grazing species were proliferating and becoming much more vis-ible. Formerly small isolated groups of zebra, buffalo, oryx and other antelopes were joining up to form sizeable herds in what were now becoming open plains. However, the untidy debris of trees knocked over by the elephants, which littered the landscape, was the focus of public attention and pressure was mounting through the press for something to be done. Conditioned to the belief that only a reduc-tion in the number of elephants South African style would save the Park from degenerating into desert, armchair experts raised their voices in growing numbers. Every scarred baobab became a talking point, and every pile of bones was linked to starvation and the 'destruction' of the habitat caused by 'too many elephants'.

In order to gather evidence of the landscape in earlier times, David spent hours reading the diaries of the early explorers. He analysed the descriptions of Lord Lugard, the first white man to walk the length of the Galana River from the coast inland through what was now Tsavo; of Joseph Thomson, who walked through Masailand; of Krapf and Redman, the first to notice the snow-clad dome of Kilimanjaro as well as the snowy summits of Mount Kenya; of Meinertzhagen and Selous, who hunted in what was now the Park and wrote of enormous herds of ungulates which were extremely low in numbers when the Park was proclaimed in 1949. Through the analysis of such details, David believed that the demise of the commiphora-dominated thickets was perhaps being lamented out of all proportion, and that what we were witnessing was simply the reoccurrence of a perfectly natural vegetation cycle: woodland thicket to grassland and grassland back to woodland thicket, all triggered by the elephants having knocked out the trees to enable grasses to emerge for the grazing species, having planted another generation of trees in their dung, etc. He believed that the emerging grasslands would be beneficial, favouring an increase in biodiversity and generating a greater tourist appeal from easier viewing. It seemed ironic, in the aftermath of a successful anti-poaching campaign undertaken during times when we feared the annihilation of elephants, that we should now be accused of having too many.

Fortunately, we had an important ally visit us around this time. Dr Vesey Fitzgerald, an elderly naturalist, turned up unexpectedly and asked if he could spend a few days with us. He had recently cautioned the director of Tanganyika National Parks against a recommended buffalo cull that would have had far-reaching repercussions on many other species of the Lake Manyara National Park in Tanzania, bordering Lake Manyara, where David and I had spent our honeymoon. His belief that grassland in Tsavo would prove far more beneficial than dense commiphora thicket came as a welcome relief. Tourism would evolve into an important money-spinner for the country, and the new more open country provided easier tourist viewing. Like David, he thought the elephants should be left alone, that we should observe and learn from Nature's way of redressing any imbalance. This, he said, was the enlightened management of the future.

Shortly after this heartening visit, 'Chickweed' Parker came to see David to try and persuade him to support the tender of his firm Wildlife Services. He had just culled elephants in Uganda's Murchison Falls National Park, a grisly but lucrative task. Having abandoned the experiment of trying to create a viable occupation for the Waliangulu ex-poachers by way of the Galana Game Management Scheme, 'Chickweed' had established himself as a professional elephant cropper and in Uganda had worked closely with the scientist Dr Richard Laws. He hinted that the spin-off from any possible Tsavo culling contract could prove financially beneficial for all involved – including David. It was his view that some 10,000 elephants would probably have to be removed from the Tsavo population, three times more lucrative than the cull he had just undertaken. 'The elephants are going to go anyway,' he predicted pessimistically, 'and those of us who protected them all these years deserve some of the spoils.'

Parker was not alone in beginning to understand that corruption was creeping into the top echelons of independent Kenya. Prominent personalities and their relatives were beginning to dabble in ivory, rhino horn and charcoal as a means of enrichment. In fact it was this new development, coupled with the subtle innuendoes of Parker's conversation, that convinced David that if Tsavo's elephants ended up having to be culled, this would have to be done by officers of the National Parks Service rather than being handed out to private enterprise influenced by financial incentives. So David flew to Nairobi to try to pre-empt any decision that could have adverse long-term repercussions on elephants in Kenya overall.

He returned with the news that the grant-awarding American-based Ford Foundation had come up with money to finance an elephant research project in Tsavo, in which the dynamics of elephant population in relation to vegetation growth, climate and other related factors would be studied, and that Dr Laws, Ian Parker's colleague, would be heading Tsavo's research programme. In one way we were relieved that the burden was to be shared and that the matter was to be scientifically addressed. Our focus switched to building more staff houses, offices and laboratories to accommodate the new researchers. Under David's supervision, after much frenzied building, within a matter of weeks we were ready for the scientists.

With their arrival came controversy, not least startling assertions contradictory to our own views based on many years of experience. And so began a turbulent and difficult period of our lives.

10. Conflict

'It is not the critic who counts, not the man who points out how the strong man stumbled or where the doer of deeds could have done them better. The credit belongs to the man who is actually in the arena, whose face is marred by dust and sweat and blood, who strives valiantly, who errs and comes short again and again, who knows the great enthusiasm, the great devotions and spends himself in a worthy cause, who at the best knows in the end the triumph of high achievement and who at worst, if he fails, at least fails while daring greatly, so that his place shall never be with those cold and timid souls who know neither victory nor defeat.'

– Theodore Roosevelt

Dr Laws seemed pleasant enough – a large, soft-looking man with striking pale blue eyes, an English scientist known for his studies of whales. At first the work carried out by his team was not too invasive, but it wasn't long before he dropped a bombshell, announcing that he needed data from 300 dead elephants, a 'sample' cull.

We were baffled as to why Dr Laws would need uteruses, teeth and eye lenses for a scientific assessment of population dynamics in relation to vegetation, but he was so emphatic that the Trustees went along with it. He was equally insistent that Wildlife Services had to do the job, arguing that having been involved in the Murchison Falls cull, 'Chickweed' Parker and his colleagues were highly competent at taking and preserving body parts. Again, the Trustees agreed but decreed that the slaughter be done in a place determined by David, well away from the tourist circuit.

Dr Laws was in a hurry, and not surprisingly Wildlife Services were poised to start work. Both David and I burnt the midnight oil discussing this new development, both of us deeply saddened to have to be party to this great elephant betrayal. It had taken so much to gain their trust as to the sanctity of the Park, that this was a refuge where they could feel safe. There was pressure on David to select the killing field and it was with a heavy heart that he chose Kowito, on the north bank of the Galana River, off the tourist circuit and suitably remote. He imposed strict restrictions regarding access to the cull, mindful that elephants were a popular species and that images depicting the massacre of elephant families were bound to generate outrage among the animal-loving international public. Even though the 'cropping' was done by proficient marksmen on the ground, the Kowito cull was gruesomely efficient, and as I went about my daily routine on the appointed day, I couldn't help visualizing the chaos there, rivers of blood spilling out to blend with the red soil of Tsavo. The slaughter of an entire elephant family took only around three minutes. David returned from the massacre grim-faced, beset by contradictions that churned constantly in his mind. We would talk well into the night, unsettled by what was taking place. David was becoming convinced by the results of his own investigations that the natural role of elephants was one of recycling, rather than destruction, and that what was taking place was simply part of a natural cycle that had happened before.

Ever mindful of public criticism, the Trustees had considered it imperative that maximum use be made of the carcasses, a rather ironic twist of priorities in my view. In a procedure that reminded me of my father's biltong days, the meat was dried for sale; the feet sent to be converted into waste-paper containers or stools; the ears turned into handbags, briefcases or wallets; the hide cured to luxury leather; the bones crushed into bonemeal; and, of course, the ivory sold swiftly to dealers in Mombasa, with a share of the profits benefiting Wildlife Services. Pointing to his brand new plane some time later, 'Chickweed' Parker said, 'Your elephants.'

Dr Laws was soon immersed in a study of the collected body parts, during which he uncovered evidence of some remarkable facts. One old matriarch – now a statistic of his sample – had been totally blind from birth, eye lenses absent in both eyes. Yet for all those years she had led her family to water and to feeding grounds, negotiating difficult terrain. She had survived the poaching onslaught of the fifties and kept her family intact and safe. Now, just when the Protected Area was there to make her feel secure, she and her entire family had been gunned down. It did not bear thinking about, and when Dr Laws decided that he needed a further sample of the dead from a different elephant population for comparative purposes, David and I were overwhelmed by a feeling of helplessness. The Tanzanian authorities granted Dr Laws permission to supervise a cull in the Mkomazi National Reserve, which is part of the Tsavo ecosystem, and once again, Wildlife Services were ready with their heavy calibre rifles. This made no sense at all to David, who believed that the Mkomazi elephants did not in fact belong to a 'different' population but in his view merely formed part of the greater Tsavo population that moved within and without an ecosystem at least twice the size of the Park itself.

Nor did it end there. Having only been in Tsavo for three full months, Dr Laws boldly asserted that there were in fact ten discrete elephant populations in Tsavo, not just the one from which he had killed 300. He needed a similar sample of 300 elephants from each of the remaining nine; in other words a staggering 2,700 dead elephants, just for starters! David was incensed. From twenty years of practical observation of known elephants easily recognizable by their unusual tusk configuration, and as a result of our early marking experiments, we knew that an elephant could be in Voi one day or way north of the Galana River the next, sometimes in Tsavo East, sometimes in Tsavo West, or even sometimes in Mkomazi in Tanzania.

During a recent safari to the Serengeti in Tanzania, the Warden – our old friend Myles Turner – had warned David on the impending invasion of scientists in Tsavo. 'They're a bloody menace. Since they are about to invade your Park, make sure you lay down a stringent code of conduct about what they can and cannot do, before they spin out of control and have a field day, as they did here.' Something clearly was unfolding in Tsavo, not only due to the threat of a new onslaught on the elephants, but also because of the frequent clashes between David and the team of researchers living in the Park, whose behaviour had become somewhat problematic. Despite David's imposition of a strict code of conduct, they seemed to feel free to do whatever they liked – break the speed limit, enter the closed northern area without permission, fill their private vehicles from the Park's petrol pumps, order furniture to be made in the Park's workshop, etc. It was as if they were beyond the Warden's jurisdiction and that Park rules did not apply to them. Eventually, David decided that he had had enough. He publicly challenged Dr Laws's assertion that more elephants needed to be culled, and when the argument between the two men threatened to flare up in the public domain, the director of the National Parks Service summoned them both to Nairobi.

The Trustees listened to both sides, making allowances for the fact that twenty years of field experience was considered the equivalent of any doctorate. However, the argument became so heated that Dr Laws threw down the gauntlet, declaring that either David Sheldrick, who was the 'most un-cooperative Warden' he had ever come across, must leave or he and his team would have to do so. After a brief closed-door session, the Trustees delivered their verdict – while Dr Laws could be easily replaced, David Sheldrick, as Warden of Tsavo East, was irreplaceable. When David returned from Nairobi, I was on the verandah with Angela and he came towards us, smiling for the first time in ages. Looking out, he said: 'The elephants are safe, Daph, at least for the time being.'

Dr Laws and his team left without much ado, but their departure caused a regrettable family fall-out. Peter and Sarah had become friendly with a group of the researchers and took their side in the dispute. This angered David, who viewed it as a betrayal and breach of loyalty. He felt that Peter should be transferred, since tension in the ranks was not conducive to a good working relationship. As Peter was my brother, David put aside his anger and hurt, recommending that he be promoted to the position of Warden somewhere else.

This dissension in the family deeply upset my parents. By now Peter and Sarah had two young children and it was understandably a wrench for them to have to leave their much-loved home, especially under such a cloud. Peter was transferred to Meru National Park, about 300 miles north of Nairobi, a former National Reserve that had recently been upgraded to National Park status. In terms of infrastructure, he faced a challenge, since he would have to more or less begin from scratch, but in terms of habitat, Meru was a smaller, more picturesque version of Tsavo, with the advantage of being better watered. Many crystal-clear streams flowed through the Park from the high reaches of the Nyambeni Hills, where the climate was conducive to growing crops such as tea. The Park was home to a wealth of animals, and a healthy population of black rhino and some 3,000 elephants that moved in and out, their migrations dependent upon where rain had fallen. In time Peter and Sarah came to love Meru, transforming it into a miniature model of Tsavo, but resentment against David, and by extension myself, never really dissipated.

With the departure of the Laws team, David and a team of colleagues set up the Tsavo Research Committee, with a clear brief that any scientific study had to be relevant to the requirements of Park management, rather than simply as a means of satisfying scientific curiosity or acquiring a quick doctorate. Lessons had been learned from the previous contentious few months, and out of this came important new guidelines for future scientists working within Tsavo. In this new spirit of cooperation, the botanist Dr Glover was appointed to head the new Tsavo research team and he was joined by Dr Walter Leuthold, whose brief was to study elephant movements and settle the question of discrete elephant populations within the Tsavo ecosystem, as well as to monitor the smaller browsers most likely to be affected by the vegetation changes wrought by the elephants. Dr John Goddard was to monitor the rhinos, and scientists from Holland, Oxford University and other parts of Kenya were recruited to study the impact of elephants on soil surrounding permanent man-made water sources, to study the contribution to the environment made by the dead and to study dung beetles and other elephant-related insects. This new injection of researchers working within the agreed guidelines formed a cohesive team with whom we were on good terms. Moreover, Dr Laws's theory of ten discrete elephant populations in Tsavo was laid to rest when several elephants, both male and female, were radio-collared and their movements monitored over many months. It was established that they did, in fact, move vast distances, utilizing any area of the Park and beyond in response to rain, when the inland waterholes filled and green vegetation became available.

David had been correct on many fronts, although he was still being severely criticized for a laissez-faire style of management by those who remained convinced that the elephants would reduce Tsavo to a desert with the loss of many other species. But over time, as a result of the transformation of the commiphora thicket south of the Galana River into more open grassland, Tsavo in fact gained antelope species – the slender-legged, long-necked oribi and the dark-faced topi – neither having before been recorded there in living memory. Now that a large portion of the Park was more open country, the rangy Tsavo lions began to sprout sizeable manes and took to consorting in much larger prides. Buffalo emerged as the dominant grazer, forming herds that today can be numbered in the thousands. In the days of dense thickets it had been a talking point to see even a small group. Shy coastal topi made their debut and the fragile Hunter's hartebeest prospered. Acacia seedlings sprouted within the open plains, their seed pods, which fall during the dry seasons, a rich source of food for all. The elephants often shook the trees to make them fall, and I used to collect as many as I could and store them in a drum for my orphaned antelopes. To this day, Tsavo and its elephants owe a great deal to the courage of David's convictions and his steadfast stand against culling, which would have undoubtedly been abused in years to come when corruption became a way of life in Kenya. I was so proud of my husband, and while I could see that the fight had taken a toll of his health, we were always there for each other and our inner strength, love, core beliefs and resoluteness saw us through that exceedingly stressful period.

Meanwhile, our own elephant family had changed with the departure of Aruba, who had joined a wild herd, and just after she left, two young bull elephants arrived. We named them Raru (short for Ndara) and Bukanezi. The smaller of the two, Bukanezi, was so named after the Orma – one of the tribes living along the Tana River – word meaning 'the weak one' and he was, indeed, very feeble; in fact, at that time he was the youngest elephant we had so far managed to hand-rear. We dared not feed him milk, but got him through on hand-picked greens and sweet potato tops bought from the Voi market, along with pieces of apple and orange. These two new orphans soon became part of Samson's growing herd, settling into what was now a sizeable group, for in recent months three ostriches and half a dozen buffaloes had joined the ranks. The ostriches made us laugh. For some reason, they seemed to enjoy lining up with the Field Force rangers whenever they underwent drill inspections on the parade ground. As soon as the ostriches heard the sergeant-major bellowing, they would hurry along – ostrich style – to stand with the rangers, presenting a truly incongruous sight.

Each morning, we could hear the gate of the stockade being opened when Samson led his assorted herd down past the orchard – sometimes having to drag the ostriches by their necks – heading for the more lush vegetation of the Voi River valley. Although the river itself only flowed strongly during periods of heavy rain, rocky hollows in its bed formed stagnant pools in which to play and splash water over hot bodies, while brick-red mud wallows left by receding floodwaters or rain soon turned them all that distinctive shade of red that characterized Tsavo's elephants. It was just as well that the ostriches didn't fly, as their mud-caked feathers ended up plastered tightly to their bodies, giving them a decidedly bedraggled appearance.

Wallowing time was for playing, splashing, rolling and romping about. You had to be diligent to ensure that the ostriches were not handled too roughly or even ended up drowned, for sometimes Samson's idea of involving them in a game meant whirling them round and round by the neck. Many animals gathered at the pools during the heat of the day, so it was usually there that the orphaned elephants were able to mingle with their wild peers. Samson in particular found sparring with other young bulls of his age much more fun than taking on Rufus, who anyway was now more interested in challenging Reudi, a newly arrived young rhino, a casualty of a translocation exercise to remove rhinos from an area opened up for human settlement. Reudi was not as mild-natured as Rufus, and although the two became friends, they often had their differences, ending in tremendous battles. At such times Samson clearly felt obliged to intervene to restore order, and the combination of the rhino's huffing and puffing and Samson's trumpeting sent the ostriches and buffaloes in the opposite direction and the helpers up the nearest trees.

After the routine mud bath during the heat of the day, the orphans would gather around their helper as he sat down in the shade of a nearby tree to have his lunch. Afterwards he would stretch himself out in the grass, place his hat over his eyes and take a nap while the elephants stood guard nearby and the ostriches squatted, their necks protruding from the grass like three thin periscopes. The buffaloes lay in the shade, chewing the cud, a picture of bovine bliss, and Rufus and Reudi slept soundly nearby, breathing contented sighs through rubbery nostrils. The heat of noon, when the sun was at its peak, was a peaceful, sleepy time of the day, punctuated by the humming of insects, muted birdsong and the gentle slap of wet elephant ears as they fanned a cooling breeze across their red-mud-plastered bodies. We loved being a party to this scene and enjoyed a great view from the caravan of Philip and Mavis Hucks, who lived in the Park's public campsite during a five-year stint collecting and pressing for posterity specimens of Tsavo's plants and flowers, and had become close friends of ours.

It was about this time that Eleanor entered our lives. She had been discovered by Bill as a two-year-old orphan four years earlier in 1961, on the north bank of the Uaso Nyiro River in the Samburu National Reserve during a safari escorting the then Governor of Kenya, Sir Patrick Renison, and his wife Lady Eleanor. Eleanor was found standing alone on a sodden plain after a night of extensive rain, no other elephants in sight other than the carcass – minus the tusks – of what must have been her mother lying some distance away. Bill returned to a nearby lodge to recruit help in capturing the elephant and getting her to safety, which he managed to do with the help of some guests, the Governor and Lady Eleanor. Elephant 'Eleanor', who was named after Lady Renison, was housed for the night in an improvised stable on the verandah of one of the lodge chalets.

Fed patiently on hand-picked greens and treated gently and lovingly, Eleanor soon lost her initial terror of humans; once back at Bill and Ruth's Mweiga home, she got used to walking up a ramp on to a lorry every day, which transported her and her helpers into the lush Aberdare forest to feed. Her new home in the mountain National Parks was, of course, very different to the arid lowlands of her birth, so she suffered bouts of ill health until she became acclimatized. In the highlands the nights were damp and cold, and for much of the year mists masked the sun, the air damp with a frequent drizzle that laced the tips of the grass stems and leaves with an early morning frost. Eleanor soon became quite a legend among the local Africans, most of whom had never seen an elephant before, or even a picture of one, despite living so close to the Aberdare and Mount Kenya forests that were home to many wild animals, including elephants. Well-maintained deep ditches surrounding the Park boundaries confined the elephants to their forest strongholds, protecting them from the people and the people's crops from the elephants.

David and I had first seen Eleanor at the Nairobi Agricultural Show back in 1962, an annual event that drew large crowds from far and wide. There had been pressure on Bill to bring her to the show so that people could observe an elephant first hand, and from the moment we arrived, we could hear an excited buzz from the people pushing and jostling to get near to her. Whenever she reached her trunk through the bars of her stockade, they squealed and recoiled in terror. Even doing the most ordinary of elephant things, such as spraying water over herself with her trunk or scratching an ear, made the crowds roar with laughter and shout out in astonishment. Eleanor soon learned that noisy spectators could be easily dispersed by a shower of muddy water sucked up from her mud wallow and sprayed directly at them through her trunk. She was, though, rewarded for her tolerance when Lady Eleanor Renison heard that her namesake was at the showground and requested that the elephant be taken to Government House. Eleanor's journey from the showground caused quite a stir — heads swivelled and brakes screeched as motorists passed the unusual convoy. Upon arrival she was greeted by the Governor himself, and Lady Eleanor, and allowed to wander freely over their emerald lawns, helping herself to anything she fancied from the tempting array of exotic flowers.

Because she had been such a hit at the Nairobi Agricultural Show, the National Park authorities insisted that Eleanor should continue to be an ambassador for her kind by being on display at the Nairobi National Park Orphanage, just beyond the city limits. While this had been created with noble intentions to provide care and a home for orphaned animals until they could be returned to the wild, in reality it had proved so popular with local people that it had evolved into a zoo. It was hoped that Eleanor's presence would tempt more people through the doors and generate an increase in income, and indeed it did, as long queues of excited people waited to see her every day. But deprived of the exercise so vital to an animal that needs space and covers great distances, lacking the variety of food necessary for a balanced diet and the loving individual attention she so needed, the sparkle faded from her eyes and she became morose, obese and lethargic – just another one of many unfortunate innocents subjected to imprisonment through no fault of her own.

Eleanor would undoubtedly have died had it not been for Bill and David exerting unrelenting pressure on the National Parks authorities to allow her her freedom. In the end they managed to convince them that in order to save Eleanor's life she needed to make one last journey, this time to Tsavo, where she could join others like her. And so one bright afternoon on 19 March 1965, Eleanor arrived in Voi. To make her feel welcome, we had lined her stockade with an assortment of Tsavo's most tempting shrubbery. Upon arrival she walked slowly down the ramp and my heart lurched as I noticed that her stomach was severely distended from her sedentary life in Nairobi. Hesitantly, she extended her trunk in greeting to each of us in turn, rumbling pleasure deep in her throat, and then paused at the entrance to her stockade, startled by the strange sounds emanating from the two stout stables next door that housed the rhinos. Samson was already in his stockade and in his excitement at seeing another elephant was trying to scale the bars, and at the sight of Samson, who was larger than her, Eleanor needed a good deal of coaxing before she finally went in.

It took a little while for her to regain her physical health and psychological wellbeing and to adjust to her new surroundings. She was such a peace-loving and gentle individual that she strongly disapproved of the rhinos' rowdy squabbles, and was bent on separating them at the first hint of trouble by forcing her way between the two of them and flailing them both with her trunk before chasing them off in opposite directions. She adored Samson, who was thrilled to be the subject of such adulation and treated Eleanor with tolerance and genuine affection. With an older and wiser companion to lean on, she felt content, and she loved mothering the two smaller elephants, Raru and Bukanezi. At the daily mud bath she treated the ostriches more gently than Samson, taking hold of their bunchy tail feathers in her trunk and propelling them along by pushing from behind.

Samson was at the age when he began to feel, as young bulls should, that something was lacking in his life. Often he would scent a wild herd and become visibly restless, anxious to join them. At first it was not unusual for him to spend nights out, then weeks away and eventually months. Just as we were beginning to think that Samson had indeed made the transition back to being a wild elephant, he would reappear, usually accompanied by several wild friends who caused chaos and confusion around the Headquarters as soon as they found themselves among humans, scattering the workforce in all directions as they made a rapid getaway. It was touching to see Samson carrying on with whatever he was doing, puzzled as to why he couldn't keep his friends for very long. In the end David decided to resort to firmer measures in order to dissuade him from returning to base with wild friends, using thunderflashes as a deterrent. The time had now come when it was in Samson's best interests to sever his ties with humans completely and return to where he belonged. He came back unexpectedly one Sunday afternoon after a very long absence and my heart froze as he advanced towards Angela, who was toddling around, playing with her toys. I was terrified that having been made so unwelcome he might harm my daughter, but he stretched out his enormous trunk and tenderly touched the top of her head, rumbling a loving greeting at her delighted smile. As soon as he spotted me, he turned and hurried off, ears outstretched in anticipation of a reprimand, and that, sadly, was the last time I saw Samson, though David came across him occasionally during the course of his travels, sometimes on his own and at other times in among a wild herd. Samson adored David, and this made his transition from us to the wild much more emotionally difficult. With Samson gone, Eleanor slotted into her role as matriarch, accepting this responsibility with maturity, valiantly trying constantly to keep the peace between Rufus and Reudi.

Our orphans arrived unexpectedly, a variety of species, sizes and temperaments. We now had a dedicated, growing staff, trained to look after them. The smaller ones were cared for in small nursery stables and an enclosure adjoining the house, and once they could be trusted not to run away, they were allowed free run of the garden. These came to be known as the 'garden orphans' and included several antelopes, one of whom I fell in love with the moment she was presented to me, curled up in a shoebox, a perfect miniature Bambi. She made my heart melt with her big soulful black eyes and dainty features. I stroked her brown fur, tracing the reddish-brown crest on her forehead. And as she gazed into my eyes it was love at first sight.

We named this dikdik Wiffle because of her elongated nose, which was furred right to the tip of each nostril and 'whiffled' constantly this way and that, testing, examining, savouring and interpreting every faint scent that wafted in on the wind. She settled in happily and loved nothing more than a good bounce around the garden, turning with lightning agility, darting under foliage, leaping over walls, dodging Honk, our peacock, and ending up at my feet, panting with exertion. Her energy was infectious. She played endless games of hide-and-seek with Jill and Angela, sometimes waiting in ambush in a kneeling position, before bursting from cover to race off to another hiding place. When they tired of this, she moved swiftly on to a game of dodge, merely bouncing aside at an unexpected angle to avoid capture. Finally, when the children lay exhausted and laughing, she would tuck herself underneath a plant and keep a close watch on my movements.

Wiffle was a 'one-woman' animal and quite simply I was the most important thing in her life, the only person she allowed to pick her up and hold her; the only one from whom she accepted a bottle of milk; the only voice worthy of response and the only one on whom she lavished her affection. Her devotion to me was absolute, my reward for taking the place of her mother. She was like my shadow – whenever I was in the garden Wiffle would be just a few paces behind me. Since she experienced difficulty climbing the polished front steps of the verandah, I had to carry her on to the lounge carpet every evening, where she enjoyed her favourite food laid out as a banquet on a piece of newspaper – wild hand-picked delicacies with the odd rose or hibiscus flower. Gregory Peck seemed like an independent adolescent in comparison to Wiffle. Early one evening, as I was taking a bath, I momentarily disappeared from her view and within a second she had leapt over the side of the bath and landed right on top of me. The chaos that followed was spectacular, with Wiffle thrashing around wildly and me struggling to get hold of her before she succeeded in drowning herself. It was several seconds before I managed to lift her out, and a very bedraggled and subdued little dikdik lay shivering and sulking for hours after.

After her night-time milk feed – before which she rather puzzlingly had to nuzzle my watchstrap – we carried Wiffle to our bedroom, and for the first few weeks she was content to sleep on a blanket beside our bed. However, she decided very quickly that this was just not near enough to me, and that she should be entitled to a place on top of the bed, right next to me, just like David. For a few nights she hurled herself against the mosquito net until we capitulated and allowed her in. But then, restricted and frightened by the net, she thrashed about until we had to tuck the net halfway up my side of the bed and let her sleep outside it at the bottom by my feet. Just as soon as we got used to this arrangement, Wiffle began to cast a covetous eye on David and in a Goldilocks sort of way – the floor too hard, my bed too soft but David's just right – decided that she wanted his side of the bed all to herself. One night, following several trial runs, usually undertaken during the day when the bed was unoccupied, Wiffle made her stand, rolling on top of David in an attempt to dislodge him. But David was not going to give up his place in our bed to a dikdik, however sweet she was – 'It should be you that goes, Daph,' he laughed – and stood his ground, tossing and turning throughout the night. We were convinced that Wiffle would have difficulty remaining on board but she was grimly determined to stay put at all costs and stuck it out, even hopping back on when David kicked her off the end of the bed. This she didn't like one bit, the tuft between her ears erect to indicate her disapproval.

Actually we had recently discovered that Wiffle could scream, and while quite prepared to amuse herself in the garden during most of the day, after tea and until bed she expected to be entertained or at least kept company. Almost on the stroke of 4 p.m. she would appear at the front or back steps, calling with a soft, high 'Where are you?' twitter. If I didn't hear, which was usually the case, she would repeat it a lot louder and then, when I did not appear, she would emit a piercing scream that did not stop until I came to take her for an afternoon walk. Only demanding with me, Wiffle was otherwise a timid little thing and the larger orphans were a great source of concern to her. Lollipa, my favourite orphaned buffalo, was particularly partial to terrorizing her, even though Eleanor's gang only came into the garden to snatch a few forbidden titbits when in daredevil mode. One morning when they appeared unexpectedly around the hedge, Wiffle was engrossed in a game with Honk, the peacock, and was caught completely unaware. Stopping dead in her tracks, her doe eyes filled with alarm and she let out a terrified nose whistle, leaping off in a series of enormous bounds; when we located her, some hours later, under a thornbush right at the very back of the garden, she was still trembling. Nocturnal visitors around the house were another source of terror, for while we humans could sleep oblivious to any happenings outside, even when supposedly asleep Wiffle was always alert, for her eyes never closed completely, and she was conscious of movements and sounds outside some distance away. Every now and then she would stand up on the bed, eyes wide open, muscles tensed as she stared out of the window. For a good night's sleep, the best we could hope for was a visit to the garden pergola by an old giraffe who squeezed his large frame through, lifting it in the process. This scared Wiffle so much that she would retreat under the bed and remain there until sunrise.

When Wiffle was mature, in a motherly, controlling sort of way I took it upon myself to find a mate by visiting the Nairobi National

Park Orphanage to look over any likely suitors. But in the end I didn't have to do terribly much, as I soon noticed that our afternoon walks took on a greater significance. By now the two small glands situated below Wiffle's eyes were active, and she would rub the tar-like substance they produced on to the ends of any small twig protruding from a shrub or on to the tips of coarse grasses. Many such twigs and grasses selected for this purpose were already tipped with small balls of this glandular secretion, and each 'signpost' was eagerly scrutinized and carefully smelled before Wiffle added her own contribution. David noticed that when the glands were moist a certain small species of fly was attracted by the secretion, clustering around each gland and causing Wiffle a good deal of irritation. Need-less to say, it wasn't long before David had some labelled and stored in the shallow drawers of the insect cupboard in his museum.

I had been under the impression that Wiffle was far too attached to me to ever feel the desire to seek the company of other dikdiks, but it seemed that Nature's dictates proved compelling. When she was grown, she took to disappearing for the odd hour or two during the day, and one afternoon I was surprised and unsettled by the deafen-ing silence from the garden at four o'clock. This marked the beginning of Wiffle's separation from me, for she began to spend whole days away and then whole nights and days away. Like any anxious mother, I was keen to know where she was going, so one morning I followed her and was astonished to find her walking bold as brass into Dr Glover's garden, straight up to a male dikdik with whom she seemed remarkably well acquainted. It became clear that this was not as ideal as it at first looked, for this mate already had a wife, a somewhat dis-concerting discovery since dikdiks mate for life. Nevertheless Wiffle obviously presented the eternal triangle, for over the coming weeks she was repeatedly seen together with this mate and his wife and, what is more, provided tangible evidence of the male's infidelity, as she steadily grew more portly. Wiffle was expecting.

By now she was spending more time in Dr Glover's garden than our own, which was not popular with his wife, Barbara, who kept beautifully pristine flowerbeds and a lush lawn. I did my best by pro-viding biscuits and grain to try to take the edge off Wiffle's appetite, but even so, the ends of all of Barbara's most treasured plants were routinely nipped off. Towards the end of her pregnancy Wiffle was waddling about, lethargic and bloated, not the bouncy dikdik she had once been, and when we heard she had given birth, I hurried over to the Glovers' house. However, although the baby had obviously been born, it was clear as we searched the foliage surrounding the house, with Wiffle strolling nonchalantly behind us, that we were not going to be allowed the privilege of seeing it. Not until six weeks later did Wiffle bring her baby out, and thereafter the baby dikdik accompanied her mother everywhere. Wiffle made herself even more unpopular with Barbara Glover, for she took to nipping her with the incisors on her lower jaw every time she was discouraged from a flowerbed. In the end Barbara had to resort to donning gumboots whenever in the garden, and complained bitterly to me about being 'bitten' by my dikdik, something which, at first, I could scarcely believe, until I witnessed it for myself.

Some months after the arrival of her first baby, Wiffle stepped into the role of principal wife to the male, whose other wife had mysteri- ously vanished, probably having fallen prey to some predator. She also acted as guardian to the first wife's youngster, which was roughly the same age as her own, and all three of them could be regularly seen together pruning the shrubs around Barbara's garden. Soon Wiffle was again taking on a matronly look, and seven months after the arrival of her first fawn, her second baby was born. This time we were fortunate in being able to have a peep before she sequestered it properly. Wiffle went on to have seven offspring before she vanished entirely and I sadly lost contact with her for ever. Over the years I would become preoccupied with a host of other orphaned antelopes, but Wiffle was a particular favourite of mine. She taught me so much about her species and I have loved all members of the antelope family ever since.

In a life such as ours there was always loss to contend with, and while each loss left me extremely heart-sore, it was, of course, far worse when people we loved died. At the age of eighty-seven, Granny Chart succumbed to stomach cancer and was laid to rest in the

Nakuru cemetery alongside our beloved Granny Webb. Granny Chart had been the eldest of Great-Grandpa Aggett's eight pioneering offspring and a formidable icon of courage, resilience and strength. We mourned her passing deeply. We had also recently lost our good friend Philip Hucks, who one night woke up in his caravan, asked his wife, Mavis, if she had fed the regular night-time wild genet that came for its bowl of food, and then fell back, dead. The Hucks' legacy lives on to this day, for they had pressed, photographed and documented every known plant in Tsavo; these today lie preserved for posterity at Kew Gardens, the National Museum in Nairobi and sadly, in a state of disintegration at the current Tsavo Research Centre's Herbarium.

There was a severe drought in 1970 that brought loss on an unimaginable scale. Day after day, the sun beat down from a brassy sky with a fierce, desiccating intensity, and it became increasingly pitiful to watch the weary resignation of the elephants as many became emaciated. Although dying from malnutrition was not starvation, and was the natural end for an elephant at the end of its long life once the last set of molars was too worn to be able to ingest a sufficient quantity of food to maintain strength, the immense emotional suffering among them was so intense that it left us dejected and depressed. It was ironic that while people seemed able to detach themselves from the emotional impact of the organized slaughter of large numbers of elephants, easily satisfied by that magic word 'cropping', there was no such emotional reserve when Nature stepped in to do the job for them, quietly, peacefully and in a way that could never be achieved by artificial means. David and the Trustees were left reeling from the public outcry accusing them of allowing the Tsavo elephants to starve to death because they had opposed them being artificially culled. It was stressful to find ourselves embroiled in rampant press intrusion, with journalists turning up unannounced and unexpectedly from all corners of the world, bent on sensationalizing what was essentially a much needed die-off of mainly females and young, which would impact on recruitment and bring the Tsavo elephant population in balance with the modified habitat.

Of course, it wasn't only in Tsavo that elephants were dying from malnutrition. The drought turned out to be the severest on record, affecting a wide swathe of the country as far north as the border with Somalia, where thousands of cattle and even camels perished. Elephants also died on the neighbouring Galana Ranch and in Tsavo itself, the worst affected area being Kowito, where Dr Laws's sample of 300 had been taken. It was extremely doubtful therefore whether the large-scale die-off in Tsavo and beyond – 10,000 elephants in all – could have been averted, even if the elephants had been artificially culled. And where were the scientists when this natural event of such importance was taking place – the first time a natural mass die-off of elephants could be monitored and documented? It fell to David and my cousin Tim Corfield to number and chart the sex of every elephant that died, to record the location, to remove the lower jaw, label it with a correlating number to the body and dry and store it in the purpose-built shed at the research centre. They found that female herds were hit most, for they were anchored by weakening offspring and spent a great deal of time sleeping near permanent water, lacking the strength to venture out to browse. What we were witnessing was the enactment of Nature's most powerful tool – natural selection, where only those units led by an energetic and strong leader survived, and the sick and weak were removed en masse from the population, leaving the gene pool pure and strong.

Eleanor received each of the drought orphans with compassion, but usually by the time they reached us they were too far gone to be saved, the shock of capture proving the final straw. Those that were still milk-dependent had no chance, for we had yet to unravel a suitable formula that could keep an infant elephant alive. Eleanor began to associate lying down with death, refusing to allow her charges to sleep. As soon as they wanted to lie down, she would lift them to their feet to satisfy herself that they were still living. At this time we never quite knew how many elephants we would have each day, for Eleanor would collect odd waifs and strays down by the Voi River and bring them back home with her. Such additions did not always end up as permanent residents, particularly if they were independent little bulls that wanted to break free from the orphans' unusual routine and human companions.

We had recently been forced to try to release Rufus back to the wild after he had inadvertently wounded a stand-in member of the caring team — as it turned out, fatally, although the man's death was actually due to negligence, the local hospital's failure to investigate the extent of his arterial bleeding. He had apparently tossed stones at Rufus to dissuade him going where he wished, and as a result Rufus turned aggressive to all Africans. We were astounded that he had developed this dual personality, for he was still perfectly well behaved with David and me; we could scarcely believe that this was the same docile rhino we had allowed Angela to ride.

We settled him at Aruba, where a deep elephant and rhino ditch surrounding the compound prevented him from gaining access to the lodge. There he would be situated near permanent water and within hearing range of human presence, and we could monitor him. It broke my heart to see Rufus go, though quite obviously we had no choice but to remove him. David reminded me that black rhinos were a solitary species, and since Rufus was now almost fully grown, being alone was no hardship for him. It was, David said, far preferable to being expelled to a foreign zoo or spending life incarcerated in the Nairobi National Park Orphanage where Eleanor had been so unhappy.

Some time later, while driving home over the Ndara plains, rangers travelling with David spotted vultures hovering over a dead rhino, its horns intact but its body lacerated by deep gashes and bites. He saw immediately that it was Rufus, killed by the onslaught of a pride of lions. The wounds were septic, evidence that the lions had failed to kill him outright but had left him so severely injured that he had succumbed to a slow and painful end. I was haunted by the image of the vultures pecking out his eyes. Rufus had been such a gentle, sloppy favourite of our orphan group. I realized that we had been able to gift him a longer and happier life than had he not been rescued, but I couldn't help feeling terribly sad about his brutal end.

For David, even sadder news was to come. While flying near the Galana River on his way home, David spotted a young lone bull that was obviously wounded. As he circled to get a better look, he could see that the elephant could barely put one foot in front of the other, his eyes sunken and great bones protruding at angles from beneath loose skin hanging in dry, flaking folds. After each agonizing step, the elephant stood for a long time, feeling his front leg carefully with his trunk, and even from the air David could see that the leg was three times its normal size. There was, he thought, something achingly familiar about this elephant, so he landed on a nearby sandbank in order to investigate further. As he walked to the wounded bull David knew in his heart that this was Samson, in the last stages of the effects of the deadly acokanthera arrow poison, and he knew too that there was nothing he could do now to help him other than end his suffering with a merciful bullet from his trusty .416 rifle.

David held a very special place in his heart for Samson, for he had known him for over twenty years. He had rescued him when a helpless calf, saving him from certain death; nurtured him through his formative years and learned so much from observing him, gaining a valuable insight into the elephant psyche, a complex range of emotions and compassion. Memories and thoughts flooded through his mind in the brief moment before David raised his rifle to end his beloved Samson's life with a shot to the brain. And in that brief moment Samson looked up and there was a flicker of recognition in his eyes before he fell. Hurrying to his side, David caressed his face as he lay in the throes of death, David's own eyes moist with tears. Samson's eyes seemed to be looking straight back at him until David drew the lids gently down and closed them. He spent a long time sitting silently beside Samson's inert body, his gun at his side, enveloped by the sounds of the bush and by an overwhelming sadness tempered by a deep underlying anger. Eventually, taking his knife from his belt, he cut into the swollen and rotting foot and removed the arrowhead. He was disappointed that it was unmarked, which would have enabled him to hunt down Samson's killer.

When David came home I knew that something had happened, as he was visibly troubled. Being a man of few words, taught from a young age to keep his emotions in check, I could also sense that he did not want to talk. It was much later that I learned of Samson's tragic end – 'Having to shoot a trusted friend is the hardest thing I have ever had to do,' said David, and he never spoke of it again. He asked the Field Force rangers to remove Samson's ivory and he placed the tusks in a corner of the ivory store. There they remained for many years, David unable to add them to the annual pile that went for auction in Mombasa.

After the quiet decade of the 60s and the elephant die-off of the early 70s, once again the price of ivory began to rise on the world market and yet again Tsavo's elephants found themselves under pressure, not only from the effects of the drought but also from opportunists in search of ivory. Very early on David recognized the escalating threat and tried to impress the seriousness of the situation on Kenya's newly independent government, but invariably political considerations intervened and his warnings fell on deaf ears. Where there was life, there was death, and we certainly had to contend with a lot of death in those drought-ridden days. But David's dictum, 'Turn a new page and put it behind you,' proved useful, for just as soon as we lost one orphan, another arrived and it was all hands on deck nurturing it back to life. These little lives depended on us, on our skilled workers and above all, on the tenderness of Eleanor and the other, more robust and settled orphans.

Our orphan group was about to expand to its biggest yet.

11. Discovery

'I've watched the zebra herd in panic fly before the menace
of the stalking pride. The dusty, sun-soaked thorn bush at midday; the
solitude, star filled at latest night. The hour when hills are dark, and far
away, with rose-blush peaks, in false dawn's lovely light.'

– Larry Wateridge

The composition of Eleanor's herd was constantly changing and her
assorted orphans had to adapt to new animals with differing temperaments, some more compatible to communal living than others.
One orphaned rhino arrived in a pitiful state of advanced malnutrition, her mother having been shot on the neighbouring sisal crop
estate. She was extremely aggressive, expending her last ounce of
strength pounding the door of her stable – and anything else that
caught her eye – and her behaviour prompted us to name her Stroppie. We weren't actually able to handle her until she collapsed into a
coma, and for the next ten days we were involved in a desperate
struggle to save her life. The soft skin behind her ears became a pin-
cushion from the endless injections needed to cure the ailments that
assailed her – pneumonia, tick fever, even trypanosomiasis – all having taken hold due to stress and malnutrition that had compromised
her immune system. She was old enough not to be milk-dependent,
but every morsel of food needed to be hand-fed, so I spent hours
feeding her one leaf at a time, willing her to make the effort to live.
It was a real struggle and we would have lost the battle had it not been
for the timely arrival of another feisty newborn zebra that we named
Punda – a name we had used before on the biltong safari and for
Huppety, but one we wanted to use again.

This latest addition had trailed a zebra-striped minibus for several miles until the passengers insisted on picking him up and depositing him on our doorstep. After the experience of Huppety, I was not over-keen to take on another zebra, but I was incapable of rejecting a needy animal. Through trial and error, we had learned by now that both rhinos and zebras thrived on the full-cream Lactogen baby formula that Jill and Angela had been raised on, so having given the new arrival a feed, we steered him to the nursery, where poor Stroppie was hovering between this world and the next.

From the moment he arrived, it was clear that Punda was a busybody, keen to know what was going on even if it had nothing to do with him. As soon as he entered the enclosure and became aware of Stroppie, he immediately made her his business, gripping her button-like horn between his teeth and tugging at it. The indignity of this was too much for Stroppie, even in her fragile state, prompting her to open one rheumy eye and attempt a bubbly, sickly sort of snort that sent Punda bucking and kicking around the enclosure. At this, Stroppie's eyes opened a fraction wider, and as they began to focus a little better, a look of outrage crept into them as Punda was advancing for another onslaught on the horn. And so it went on – the more determined Stroppie was that she would not have her horn chewed, the more determined Punda was that it would be chewed – and in those moments Stroppie realized that it was necessary for her to live. As she began to recover the two became inseparable. In fact, over time it became apparent to us that Punda saw himself as a rhino.

When the rains eventually ended the great drought of 1970, Eleanor became happier and more settled, less worried about the fate of her charges. She and the other elephant orphans often left Punda, Stroppie and the buffaloes with Ali, their keeper, while they wandered off to investigate the scent of other elephants along the banks of the Voi River. Raru loved these excursions. He was not at all daunted by larger elephants and took all sorts of liberties not usually permissible to bulls of his age. While Eleanor and Bukanezi would hang back hesitantly, Raru would daringly jump the queue at waterholes or force his way among strange cows in search of a playmate. I was surprised that he did not take these opportunities to attach himself to a more mature elephant matriarch, but his devotion to

Eleanor never wavered and he was always in the column that filed back to the stockades each evening.

During these outings, it wasn't long before Raru and Punda recognized a devilish mischievousness in each other – two kindred spirits who may never have otherwise been united, but a special relationship blossomed between the two of them. They played for hours, tussling together in what to me seemed overly rough on Punda, who soon began to resemble a battle-scarred old warhorse, tusk marks and weals marring the beauty of his striped coat. But with incredible tenacity he would come back for more and more – and more. There were occasions when Punda would find himself caught with his neck wedged between Raru's tusks like a yoke, or his head in a vice-like grip beneath Raru's chin, but the two continually energized each other. It was amusing to see such an unusual friendship.

One day, down near the Voi River, as Raru and Punda were busy playing, Eleanor halted abruptly in her tracks, spreading out her ears and testing the wind for scent. Ali stopped too, intrigued as to what Eleanor was sensing. Vultures were clustered in tall riverine trees beyond a bend in the riverbed, from where came a faint chopping sound. Clearly agitated, Eleanor stood for a few minutes swaying and listening before deciding to venture forth. Silently, she and Ali rounded the bend to find two men busy hacking the tusks from the skull of a recently deceased elephant, while at the same time keeping a wary eye on a group of wild elephants led by a seasoned old matriarch, who was advancing slowly towards them. Engrossed in hacking and watching, the men were totally unaware of Eleanor's approach until she was almost within trunk range. Ali shouted '*Simama!* – Stand still!' The two poachers almost leapt out of their skins, aghast at being caught red-handed, and also scared witless by the proximity of an elephant with outstretched ears and a raised trunk. Then, as the rhinos, Punda and Raru rounded the bend, followed by an assortment of buffaloes and ostriches, the poachers became incoherent, fearing witchcraft and pleading on their knees for mercy. Ali, who was not normally the bravest of the brave, suddenly found he had all the courage in the world, backed up as he was by the assorted orphans. The wild herd retreated, leaving Ali and the orphans in charge.

Meanwhile Eleanor was carefully investigating the carcass of the dead elephant, running her trunk up and down the gleaming surface of the tusks. With one foot on the skull, she gripped them firmly in her trunk and with a sickening crunch tore each one from its socket. Holding each tusk aloft, she waved them about for a few moments before flinging them deep into the bush. It was as if, despite leading a sheltered life, she realized that herein lay the cause of the persecution of her kind in their wilderness home. In so far as we knew, this was the first elephant carcass she had ever seen, other than that of her mother, which she was probably too young to remember clearly. I wondered how she knew that a tusk could be pulled from the socket and what she was thinking, but to us it seemed abundantly clear that her complex and convoluted elephant brain was endowed with inherent knowledge already programmed at birth with the power of reasoning – an instinctive aid to survival in an animal that lives three score years and ten.

Ali declared that he would consider sparing his captives' lives, as he trussed them up using his belt. By now the poachers, convinced that the forces of evil were afoot, marched swiftly, terrified of the elephants, two rhinos, about six young buffaloes, a zebra and three ostriches walking behind. Somewhere along the way, Punda managed to get his hoof wedged into a discarded milk-can that no amount of bucking and kicking could dislodge, making a metallic clank as he walked. From somewhere the Field Force sergeant appeared, wanting to take over the captives. However, Ali was determined to hand them to David personally, and this resulted in a loud shouting match between the two men as the column made its way up the hill towards our house. The sight of the sergeant in uniform triggered great excitement in the ostriches, who danced about with outspread wings, anxious to halt the column and line up on parade.

It so happened that David and I were enjoying a rare moment of relaxation by the lily pond at the time the convoy came into view. Once Ali had recounted, in glorious detail, what had taken place, David thanked him profusely, handed over the prisoners to the sergeant and enlisted the help of the rangers to remove the milk-can from Punda's hoof, which ironically proved the most problematic manoeuvre of the afternoon.

As time went on, we despaired of Punda, for his obsession with rhinos extended beyond Stroppie to the wild rhinos. At least once a week, Ali would relate how Punda had pursued a wild rhino, nipping at its heels and even grabbing it by the tail. Inevitably, disaster struck, though it came not from a wild rhino, but instead from one of our own buffalo orphans, who, tired of Punda's incessant teasing, swung his horn sideways and opened up his stomach. In great pain, Punda managed to stagger home, Ali, Raru and Stroppie by his side. David did what he could to clean and stitch the wound, but tragically Punda died during the night. Sadly, we laid him to rest in a deep grave just behind the stockades so that he would always be close to Stroppie and Raru. He had become a loved member of our orphaned family, living out his life in a kamikaze sort of way. Raru mourned his passing deeply and Stroppie certainly noticed his absence, but Eleanor seemed unashamedly relieved, since together, Punda and Raru had never missed an opportunity to have a dig at Bukanezi when Eleanor wasn't looking. They would bait him with unbridled enthusiasm, causing disquiet in Eleanor's normally peaceful unit.

As David advised, we turned the page, and it wasn't long before a new orphan replaced Punda, this time a little female elephant calf that we named Sobo, after the huge lone rocky outcrop that rose from the flat landscape bordering the south bank of the Galana River. David spotted her from the air, standing forlornly beside her dead mother, drawing water from her stomach to spray over her body. It took some time for the rangers to reach Sobo Rock by road, capture the orphan and get her to Voi. Eleanor immediately took charge, experienced now in coping with Bukanezi's jealousy every time a newcomer threatened to divert her attention and affection from him. Sobo was a little older than Bukanezi, a forlorn and lonely little elephant, suffering the anguish of losing all her loved ones in her short life. But she startled us by stuffing lucerne into her mouth as though determined never to be hungry again, and before long her gaunt appearance softened into a healthier, more rounded shape and her skin took on the supple texture of wellbeing.

This was an intensely busy period for me. Not long after the arrival of Sobo, another orphan came in, this time a tiny infant – one of those I dreaded, being a milk-only candidate. He shuffled around fearlessly on unsteady legs, having been unloaded from the rescue lorry, ravenously hungry. This time, rather than cope on my own, I decided to enlist the help of Eleanor, who could furnish the love and attention this baby needed in addition to the milk which I would provide. Ignoring Bukanezi's frustrated bellows at the sight of the new calf being placed by her side, Eleanor gathered the tiny, hairy newborn to her, embracing him with her trunk and rumbling reassuring endearments. Then, she coaxed him beneath her to suckle her breast, the moment I had been hoping for. Armed with a bottle of diluted milk, I scrambled beneath Eleanor's huge forelegs from the opposite side and substituted the bottle of milk for Eleanor's teat every time the calf attempted to suckle.

Being underneath an elephant is an awesome experience – dwarfed by an enormous body overhead, crouching between giant legs, I was very aware of tusks each as thick and as long as an arm, and the cool tip of an investigative trunk monitoring what was going on. From this position I was conscious of the elephant's latent power, knowing that the trunk alone was capable of crushing the life from my body. However, I trusted Eleanor implicitly and never felt threatened in any way. Deep rumbles from her throat, close to my ears, vibrated through my body and I knew that she understood and that I could count on her total cooperation. Ours was a deep and abiding mutual trust cemented by a shared love. Ironically, much more cause for misgiving came from the infant for whose benefit this was being done. Instead of showing appreciation, he meted out hefty shoves, sending me hurtling backwards to land in disarray among the pile of vegetation in the far corner of the stockade. I let out a yelp and Eleanor came over to feel me tenderly and establish that I was all right; even Raru put his trunk through the crossbars, anxious to ascertain that I was in one piece. Rubbing a sore bottom, I reflected on the strength of even a tiny elephant and the need to cultivate its friendship, rather than risk its ire.

Broadly, though, the first day's attempt at feeding the new calf beneath Eleanor had gone well, so I decided that he should be fed on demand, as would be the case were he with his mother. To accomplish this, I had to enlist the help of Ali and his assistant, whom Eleanor trusted, so after they had done the next couple of feeds under supervision, we operated by shifts. Every time the calf disappeared under Eleanor in search of milk, one of us had to be there to substitute the bottle, which meant that all the paraphernalia necessary to mix and reheat the milk had to come along as well. We managed this pretty well between us – despite regular thwacks and shoves from the calf – but trouble came from the other members of Eleanor's herd, who remembered being bottle-fed and wanted to be in on the act again. Bukanezi began to throw monumental tantrums, his frustrated bellows echoing for miles around, and after a few weeks of this, Ali, his assistant and I were all exhausted. Returning home, battered and weary, I offloaded my woes on my sympathetic husband, who suggested that I was taking on too much.

We named that little calf Gulliver because he had the hairy, wizened look of a little old gnome, shuffling about on legs that lacked coordination. Eleanor adored him, as did Sobo, who took on the duties of a nanny, stepping in to care for Gulliver whenever Eleanor needed a break. I was happy that Sobo enjoyed this role, for it gave her something to focus on outside her grief, although there lurked the distinct possibility that the new arrival might not make it. I dreaded Sobo having to endure another loss all over again. As days turned into weeks, Eleanor began to rely more and more on Sobo, content to entrust Gulliver to her care whenever she felt like a wallow or went to investigate something unusual in the bush. The rapport between Eleanor and Sobo was enlightening, and it enabled me to understand the depth of bonds that bind family members together, that these gentle giants were not so different from us. Gulliver was never left unattended for a moment and I became convinced that Eleanor and Sobo communicated telepathically, for each knew instinctively what the other intended to do. Whenever Eleanor decided to move off, Sobo was there to take over, and when Sobo wanted a drink or needed a wallow, Eleanor would be there for Gulliver.

Sadly, however, the weak cow's milk mixture that we were feeding Gulliver did not suit him and I could see that he wasn't thriving, but instead becoming progressively weaker and sick. Changing his feed to 'Trilk' milk substitute made no difference, and I was distraught that all my attempts at finding a suitable diet for a milk-dependent newborn elephant had failed yet again. After struggling for three weeks, Gulliver died. He was by Eleanor's side. We buried him in the tiny graveyard that nestled beneath the dappled shade of the large melia tree David had planted as a tiny seed thirty years earlier. Now it stood in its beauty, a living testimony to the passing of the years, along with the passing of all the newborn elephants we had tried to save. Gulliver was laid to rest just as the first raindrops began to fall to relieve the drought and mingle with tears of sadness and frustration that I would never manage to unravel the secret of how to save a newborn infant elephant.

It was Sobo who felt the loss of Gulliver most keenly. She remained morose, her grief exacerbated by the recent loss of her mother and elephant family. During the funeral, she stood listlessly beside his lifeless form and came forward to touch him lovingly with her trunk as he was lowered into the grave. Even after the grave had been filled with the dampened red earth of Tsavo and decorated with pure white ipomoea blossoms, Sobo stood beside it for a long while before walking away, and each evening thereafter, as the orphans filed back up the hill, she left the column to pay her respects at Gulliver's grave. As days passed into weeks we were saddened to witness her detached solitude as she lagged behind the herd and stood apart when the other orphans were playful during rainstorms.

Sometimes after rain, as a family, we enjoyed a visit to what we called the red waterhole below the Headquarters, savouring the fresh vegetation and the heady scent of warm wet earth and new growth. A stroll with David was always a natural history lesson, filled with interest as he interpreted for us the signs and signals around us. Near the red waterhole, we would select a tree beneath which to wait and see what the day would unfold. It amused me that Angela always mapped out an escape route well in advance, for she loved nothing more than shinning up trees, particularly as she was better at it than anyone else, except perhaps her father. Jill, being a good deal older, was more sedate, while my ineptitude in this respect was well known and a source of great mirth to my family. My attempts at climbing

trees were legendary, for inevitably I ended stuck halfway up, unable
to go either up or down, much to the amusement of my family, who
stood underneath offering ridiculous suggestions until David had to
come to the rescue.

A few weeks after Gulliver died, David and I took a walk to the
waterhole where we were delighted to encounter our orphans enjoying the green feast spread before them. We watched Eleanor and the
others until an excited trumpet made us look up. To our amazement,
Sobo was rushing towards a wild herd as fast as her legs could carry
her, emitting happy trumpets and rumbles as she went. Without hesitation she raced in among them as they reached the waterhole and
was greeted with unrestrained joy. We knew at once that this particular group was part of her past, for she was obviously well known to
them. At four years old, Sobo had found the remnants of her lost
elephant family; those fortunate few who had managed to survive
the drought. Trunks intertwined with hers, fondling, feeling and
smelling her tenderly as the entire herd milled around, urinating
with excitement and rumbling lovingly, sounds that echoed against
nearby Mazinga Hill. The reunion had been spontaneous and ecstatic,
and we knew that the pain in her heart would now heal. Among that
family were probably her aunts, possibly even a grandmother, little
cousins and even older brothers and sisters. And as the wild herd
began to move off, without a moment's hesitation Sobo went with
them, passing in a heartbeat from our world back into hers. It was a
joyous and very satisfying moment that brought tears to my eyes.

Not all our time was spent at home with the animals, for we enjoyed
an excellent rapport with our neighbours on the Galana Ranch. We
enjoyed get-togethers with them reminiscent of the old Voi Hotel
days. Following the collapse of the Galana Game Management
Scheme run by 'Chickweed' Parker, a consortium of wealthy white
ranchers from Laikipia, with financial backing from an American,
had purchased almost a million acres of marginal land neighbouring
Tsavo's eastern boundary, where they combined eco-tourism with
cattle ranching. Scrub cattle purchased from the northern pastoral
tribes were fattened on the ranch before being walked the 100 miles

to Mombasa for slaughter or export. This had fast become a highly successful enterprise, the blueprint of how to manage such marginal land. They established an attractive rustic lodge overlooking the lower reaches of the Galana River beyond the Park boundary, erected game viewing platforms over waterholes and ran mobile tented camps which, like the elephants, followed the rains and the resultant flush of green where animals concentrated, and provided photographic opportunities. Strictly controlled sport hunting by licensed professionals was also permitted on the ranch, and many of these employed Waliangulu ex-poachers as trackers – men who could follow an animal footprint rapidly and enable a paying client hunter to get within range for an accurate shot.

The Galana Ranch was an ideal rehabilitation retreat for many of our orphaned buffaloes and inevitably the day came when it was the turn of my favourite, Lollipa, to leave the fold. From a very young age Lollipa had been one of our garden orphans and I was very attached to her, but she had recently taken to chasing the children and had to go. Whenever I was with her, she would lay her head lovingly against my shoulder in a touching show of affection unusual from an animal with such a fearsome reputation. On the ranch and in among the cattle, Lollipa formed a very strong attachment to one particular castrated male steer and this anchored her within the cow herds, although she would periodically leave to seek out a wild buffalo mate, returning to the cow herd pregnant. During her lifetime, she gave birth to five buffalo calves, all born among the domesticated cattle herd.

One day we received news that she had given birth to a stillborn baby, the same day on which another buffalo orphan arrived. David decided that Lollipa's loss provided us with the opportunity to offload the new orphan as a replacement for her stillborn calf. Over the radio network he suggested that her dead baby be skinned, so that when we arrived with the orphan, the skin of the dead baby could be wrapped around it in the hopes that Lollipa would accept and nurture it as her own, thereby saving us a great deal of trouble, not to mention the expense, of having to purchase tinned milk.

We made haste to the Galana Ranch with the new orphan held by a ranger in the back of the pickup. By the time we arrived, the cattle herd that contained Lollipa had been brought close by, and although I had not seen her for several years, as I called her, after hesitating for a few moments, she walked straight up to me and laid her head against my shoulder just like old times. The Galana herdsmen were flabbergasted at seeing me cuddling a buffalo, for they were extremely wary of buffaloes generally, and were careful always to keep at a safe distance from Lollipa. At the ranch this incident earned me the reputation of being a magician. Sadly, however, our plan to offload our latest buffalo orphan on Lollipa failed. While she smelled it with some interest, she concluded that it was not her own and tossed it away, the end result being that we had to take our baby back and rear him as another buffalo addition to our growing orphaned herd.

Lollipa's attachment to her steer friend eventually proved her undoing. She remained loyal to him throughout her life, even after each of her calves had grown up and left to join the wild buffalo herds. On three occasions she walked the 100 miles with him and others to the slaughterhouse in Mombasa, and when they tried to separate her friend from her she created such mayhem that they had to spare him and walk them both back again to the ranch. However, in the end, both ended up shot within the slaughterhouse compound, supposedly for endangering human lives. It was some months before the ranch owners came clean about Lollipa's tragic end. I had difficulty in understanding why our Galana neighbours could not spare this one steer, since he was, after all, just one out of many hundreds of others and surely would not have been missed. Furthermore, David and I would happily have paid the butcher's price for Lollipa's sake, but it was not to be. During my time in Tsavo, I would rear twenty-three Cape buffalo calves, sixteen of which were transferred to Nairobi National Park, forming the foundation of the Park's current buffalo population, now numbering over 100. However, for me Lollipa stood out from all the others, a buffalo calf I shall never forget.

I was coming to understand the contrasting characteristics of rhinos, having now hand-reared four orphans. Like the elephants, they were capable of extreme gentleness and affection in captivity and loved nothing more than a tummy rub, which invariably induced a state of collapse, falling over with their legs outstretched in a condition of comatose bliss. Yet, unlike the elephants, when confronted by strangers of their species unknown by scent, or whenever they felt threatened, they would instantly go into 'auto-mode', their subsequent reactions dictated not by thought processes but by instincts beyond their control. At such times they were definitely unpredictable and dangerous, earning them their fearsome reputation. Our orphan Reudi was now almost fully grown and not far off two tons in weight, sporting a sizeable horn that he had sharpened like a dagger. He was beginning to display warning signs that made us afraid he might skewer the two younger rhino orphans, Stroppie and Pushmi, or even put another orphan attendant at risk. David decided that the time had come to try and rehabilitate Reudi and return him back where he belonged, among his own wild kind.

Since the rhino population had been seriously thinned out on the north bank of the Athi River during the 1960 drought, we decided this would be a good place for him, so a stout stockade was built near to the Tsavo Safari Camp in which to confine him for a week or two in order to become accustomed to his new home. Although Reudi seemed to settle well, his presence attracted an old cow rhino and her half-grown calf, who broke into the stockade one night and set about attacking him. The commotion was indescribable. Deafening rhino roars woke up all the tourists in the camp and brought the manager, who bravely managed to fling open the stockade gates, enabling poor Reudi to escape into the night, hotly pursued by the cow and her calf. He had been outmatched, and few expected to ever see him again. Fearing that he would die of injury out in the bush, David instructed a Field Force patrol based in the area to try to track him down, but the spoor became obliterated by rain. Astonishingly, two days later we heard via the radio network that Reudi had hobbled back into the lodge grounds, bruised and battered, with a deep wound in his side. He had apparently taken to lying in the soothing waters of the river to escape his attackers, a very sorry-looking rhino, obviously not finding independent living to his liking at all.

Reudi's convalescence was long and painful, during which time his wounds were treated on a daily basis. Rubbing his tummy meant he would lie down, so this was easily accomplished, after which he would take to the river again. Nothing anyone did could induce him to return to his stockade, as it clearly held sinister connotations. Instead he preferred to put water between himself and his opponents at night, wading in either to sleep in the river, or to lie right beside it on the opposite bank. Unfortunately, but probably unavoidably, visitors to the lodge lavished attention on him, the one thing we were hoping to avoid since he was supposed to be in training for a natural life, which meant severing his links with humans altogether. Instead, he was encouraged to come into the large bar tent, where he would rest his massive head on the counter, open his mouth to receive any contributions, then shuffle away to sleep off the effects in the grass outside.

When his wounds had healed, Reudi plucked up the courage to venture further afield in order to browse, his enemies still very much in evidence but more accommodating to his presence, having initially forced him to retreat back to the lodge compound. It was Reudi who taught us most about how sensitive the reintegration of rhinos into an established rhino community was, and that the key to success lay in the communal dung piles and urinals and a lengthy introduction through chemistry and scent, something that even David had not fully appreciated.

While at first the presence of a fully grown rhino at the camp, eating from the visitors' hands, was an added attraction, invariably the tour operators became nervous, fearing litigation should a client be injured. Demands began to be made for Reudi's removal. He had become so accustomed to the bar handouts that when they failed to materialize he would display irritation, snorting and tossing his head. Had he not been corrupted by the visitors, he might well have been able to live out his days in Tsavo, establishing a truce with the old cow and her calf as well as other rhinos resident in the area. We gave the matter of Reudi's removal a great deal of thought, reluctant to have to put him through the same painful process again, so we approached the wealthy American owner of Solio Ranch, near Nanyuki, who was establishing a fenced wildlife sanctuary as a birthday present for his wife. A twenty-five-square-mile area within the ranch was being stocked with wild game animals. Reudi would be the first of some twelve other rhinos due to be brought in from elsewhere, and since none would be established territorially, he would be spared the inevitable battle for the right to belong. Instead he would be free to establish the boundaries of his own territory unhindered, secure from poachers, as well as from the privation of Tsavo's droughts and floods. And so once again he was enticed into the travelling crate to face another long journey, this time to Solio Ranch, and as he passed through the Voi Park Headquarters I clambered aboard to wish him well in his new life. Gently, he accepted the Lucerne handout I had brought him and allowed me to rub the side of his face. By now he was a magnificent specimen in his prime, with a long sweeping horn. He did in fact settle down well at Solio, and in the fullness of time became the dominant breeding bull of the sanctuary and a prime player in the salvation of the species. In the years ahead, due to rampant poaching, rhinos in the wild came close to becoming entirely annihilated, but thanks to Solio Ranch, which ended up holding a population of ninety black rhinos – mostly sired by Reudi – the black rhino as a species was saved from extinction in Kenya.

Meanwhile, back in Tsavo, my parents were anxious that David and I should bury the hatchet with Peter and Sarah and join them on a visit to Meru National Park. They were very proud of Peter's achievements as Warden of Meru, and Peter was anxious that David, as his mentor, should also see what he had been able to accomplish. David decided to combine this family visit with a recruiting exercise in order to bring the Field Force back up to strength, particularly as Parliament was about to debate a Bill that proposed merging the National Parks Service with the Government Game Department under the Ministry of Tourism and Wildlife. Despite the fact that this would compromise the National Parks by removing them from the jurisdiction of an independent Board of Trustees, and instead subject them to the whims of politicians, the passage into law of the new Bill seemed a foregone conclusion. David saw the urgency of recruiting the right sort of raw material for an effective Field Force that would be capable of dealing with a new threat of poaching, this time by armed Somali rebels who were just beginning to make an appearance around the boundaries of Tsavo. Through past experience David knew where to look for the people he needed for the Field Force – they would be recruited not from the classrooms but from the wild nomadic tribes of the Northern Frontier, who had the necessary stamina and skills to operate under challenging hot and arid conditions, totally at ease walking on foot in harsh terrain among wild animals.

Jill had by now completed her secondary schooling at the Loreto Convent in Nairobi, and in order to equip her to earn a good living, my parents urged Bill and me that she be sent to South Africa for a secretarial grounding, which after all had served me and both my sisters in such good stead later on in life. They felt also that she needed exposure to the urban sophistication of Cape Town, at that time a city much more akin to the capitals of Europe than Nairobi. And so David and I took Jill to South Africa and established her in a comfortable hostel in Cape Town, within easy walking through the gardens to her secretarial college in the city centre. Betty had some close friends who lived nearby who were happy to keep a close eye on my daughter and expose her to the attractions of South Africa in between her studies. David had inherited his mother's love of clothes and astute sense of fashion, so he took great delight in taking Jill shopping in order to equip her for an urban life as opposed to one in the bush. Jill settled down well into city life, but when she got wind of the recruiting safari she flew back home and surprised me by strolling in through the front door. At first I was convinced that I was dreaming and that she must be an illusion – it was soon to be her twenty-first birthday and I thought we would be apart for that – but I soon realized it was really her, that she would be coming along with us to Meru and beyond.

It was the first time I had been to Meru National Park, which was a well-watered mini-replica of Tsavo, with streams fringed by rust-coloured raffia palms, plains of corn-coloured grass, giant baobabs, and, near the Tana River, the same old commiphora scrubland thicket, reminiscent of the southern section of Tsavo before the elephants undertook their handiwork. The Park roads were ship-shape, the junctions marked by immaculate cedar signs similar to those that first graced Tsavo, while shallow concrete drifts spanned the many streams flowing through the Park from the Nyambeni Hills. Crossing one, we enjoyed the thrill of being roundly charged by a rhino that missed our truck by a whisker. We passed large groups of beautiful reticulated giraffe, beisa oryx and Grévy's zebra as well as peaceful elephant herds, indicating that Peter had also managed to get control of poaching.

Peter and Sarah's home was a colonial-style bungalow with an open verandah and living area, fronted by a verdant grass lawn and a rustic birdbath well attended at all times by a vast assortment of feathered friends. Below, a tiny stream fed by a spring flowed through a wire enclosure protecting a flourishing vegetable garden and the beginnings of an orchard, planted with seedlings of mango, avocado and citrus germinated by my mother in Malindi. My parents were already there, and were, of course, delighted by the unexpected appearance of their granddaughter, so our welcome could not have been warmer. It felt like home from home, with waterbuck and impala grazing the open area below the house and an old giraffe casually strolling past. A special bond existed between Jill and my parents, going way back to the time they had spent together when I was a young and inexperienced mother of twenty-one, about the same age, in fact, that Jill was now. Sadly, Angela, who was twelve now, couldn't be with us, for it was still term-time at her boarding school in Turi, situated about 150 miles west of Nairobi. My parents wanted to catch up on all her news too, and I was proud to tell them of her sporting achievements, riding skills and academic excellence – she really was a chip off her father's block.

Prior to our arrival, David had asked Peter to liaise with the local chief to arrange a gathering of nomadic Boran pastoral tribesmen for recruitment. David was keen to take on only the really raw warriors among them, and from these eight with the best physique were selected and asked to run two miles in a test of endurance, something they undertook with tremendous enthusiasm and laughter. The first five were then sent for a medical, and, having successfully passed this,

the Field Force had five new Boran recruits who accompanied us during the rest of the recruiting exercise. This entailed a 2,000-mile
adventure in which we journeyed through the colourful frontier
town of Isiolo; endured the stifling heat and powdery dust of the
Kaisut and Chalbi deserts; camped in the crater of the volcanic
mountain of Marsabit at Lake Paradise; survived a stay in North
Horr a few hours after a violent raid on the local people and livestock
by the gun-toting Amakoki horsemen; got blown out of our tents
during a night-time gale at Lake Turkana; and celebrated Jill's twenty-
first birthday at the relatively luxurious Loyangalani Lodge. On the
way David was able to recruit men from the Rendille, Gabbra and
Shangilla tribes, men who soon became part of our lives back at Voi.
On the way home, the astonishment of the recruits was plain; they
gazed with as much disbelief at the forested slopes and towering
peaks of Mount Kenya as at the traffic and buses on the road.

After four full days of travelling, it was good to be back in familiar
surroundings and to catch up with all that had taken place in our
absence. It was wonderful to be reunited with Eleanor, who welcomed us by lifting a huge foreleg for us to encircle with our arms. I
was looking forward to having Angela back home from school again
before Jill had to return to South Africa, so that our family could be
intact.

Now, intensive, relentless training of the recruits began in earnest
under the eagle eye of Sergeant Kimwele, who had served with David
in the 5th King's African Rifles during the war years. For the next
few weeks the recruits were drilled endlessly on the parade ground
– the ostriches often in attendance. The new recruits became radio-
proficient, were taught how to shoot and underwent target practice
at the Lugard's Falls firing range. They were also put through a tough
battle course designed on military lines, and after three full months
Tsavo East had a Field Force unit of disciplined and efficient men, of
whom David was extremely proud.

That was the last recruiting exercise undertaken in this way, and I
remain honoured to have been able to be a part of it, to have seen at
first hand how these proud tribesmen could be transformed into an
extremely effective paramilitary force, enduring conditions that

would undoubtedly have crushed the spirit of men softened by easy living. They had instinctive skills that could never be learned in a classroom, skills that were honed by hardship – the type of men that served Britain with such distinction in two World Wars. Deprived of rangers of this calibre in the future, Tsavo would never be the same again.

12. Expansion

'The world breaks everyone, and afterwards many
are strong in the broken places.'

– Ernest Hemingway, *A Farewell to Arms*

Whenever I had to be elsewhere, I missed the orphans, but at that time none more so than Bunty, a beautiful impala to whom I had grown deeply attached. She had arrived as a tiny fawn from a neighbouring ranch, where her mother had been killed by a lion. Initially she had been difficult to feed, rejecting every teat that we tried, until Jill sat up through the night in her bedroom, stroking Bunty's soft shiny russet fur, coaxing her to take milk from a bottle. She spent her initial nights in a cupboard in Jill's room, and then more comfortably in a night stable at the side of the house until she resolutely refused to sleep inside. The girls and I were worried that a lion would devour her, but David reassured us that the art of basic survival was the most important lesson in life and that there was no other way to hone instinct other than exposure to a wild situation, especially in an animal that had known no natural mother. For the first few nights I was alert to the slightest of sounds, peering from the window on to a world lit by a pale moon, where every shadow took on the slinky shape of a predator. Sometimes Bunty's alarm snort would sound in the stillness of the night and instantly I would be awake, knowing that she had been exposed to danger. David insisted that to have just been aware of the danger was half the battle and that our presence would simply put her further at risk by distracting her attention. So I had to wait impatiently for the morning to see if she was still alive, my imagination running riot in the meantime.

Despite my fears, Bunty did survive and shared her life with ours for the time she was in Tsavo. Very early on she instinctively knew that by night the garden was not the safe place it was by day, so as soon as the sun sank below the horizon, as the Honk peacock family began to settle in the branches of the car park tree and the curtains were drawn for the night in the house, Bunty left the garden and set off for the open space beyond the offices. There, she was a changed animal, no longer calm and confident of safety. Instead, every muscle was tensed, poised for instant flight, while her ears moved restlessly, straining to catch the slightest sound that might warn of impending danger. Her large deep-black eyes scanned the darkness constantly, searching, seeking and analysing every movement to determine whether it was friend or foe. All those latent instincts with which she had been born now came to the fore. During the night she was no longer the impala we had raised from a newborn fawn but simply another wild creature preoccupied with the important business of survival in a world where the odds were evenly cast.

I was so well attuned to Bunty's alarm snorts that one evening, while David and I were walking back from the office to our house – a distance of some 200 yards – I heard her alarm signal from far off, an urgent insistence in her warnings. I knew she was trying to alert us to the presence of danger, and sure enough, in the beam of our torch, we picked up four glowing red eyes and could make out the ominous shape of two crouching lions by the side of the path. Since lions rely on the element of surprise, it is not inconceivable that Bunty saved our lives, for the Tsavo lions were well known for their fondness of human flesh and were especially bold at night. In reality, lions are actually rather cowardly creatures, brave only when they are aggressors, so the best way to turn the tables on them is to rush towards them in a demonstration of aggression. Picking up some stones, David did just that, hastening their retreat with a hail of rocks. We were grateful for Bunty's presence that night and I silently thanked her as I reached the steps of the verandah with a rapidly beating heart.

Generally Bunty kept herself slightly aloof from the other garden orphans, particularly those that were a bit boisterous, but there was one she loved dearly and that was Jimmy, the kudu, who had come to the orphanage as a baby fawn. Since a kudu grows up more slowly than an impala, being a longer-lived species, he was small for a long time, and unusually, he would allow me to pick him up and carry him with his front legs dangling over my shoulder, right up until the time he became too heavy for me to lift and his long ivory-tipped horns were an obstacle to cuddles. He and Baby, a feisty eland – much larger than Bunty – were inseparable, but both accepted Bunty as their leader and deferred to all her wishes. It was at night that Bunty first met her own kind and came up against a male leader of over a dozen beautiful young impala ewes and their young. He was a magnificent specimen with sweeping lyre-shaped horns, and his nocturnal retreat happened to be the open area below the office. Each evening at dusk he ushered his wives out of the thickets to the safety of open ground, herding them along with a series a low grunting barks. To us, he became known as 'Father Ram' and he ruled his wives firmly – any that dared look to be straying from the fold were instantly rounded up and herded back in. However, he met his match in Bunty, whom he must have regarded as a particularly troublesome addition to his harem, for as soon as dawn broke and the sun painted the sky crimson and pink, she had only one thought in mind and that was to escape in order to return home and spend her days on the lawn near us. While Father Ram and his wives were excellent company at night, providing additional eyes and ears to detect danger, she looked upon us as her diurnal herd and her affection for us never wavered.

Escape from Father Ram was not easy, for he was constantly on guard against wayward wives, particularly since a group of handsome young bachelors, aspiring to the dominant position that entitled him to a harem, were always lurking around the periphery of his territory, waiting for a chance to oust him and take over. Some days you could see it had been a struggle for Bunty to get away, as she would appear on the lawn with puncture wounds in her rump, evidence of Father Ram's retribution. But Bunty was clever and she soon perfected a special technique to outwit him. She would wait until the workmen began filtering to work in the morning and seize the opportunity to escape, running as fast as her legs would carry her back towards the house with Father Ram in hot pursuit. Whenever he looked as if he was catching her up, she would jink sideways and head for the nearest person, and since he was fearful of any humans, Father Ram had to accept defeat and allow Bunty to amble away. He couldn't anyway afford to spend too much time away from his other wives in case they got ideas and allowed access to one of the bachelors.

And so, every morning, so long as we were home, Bunty would be there to greet us and we would hear Father Ram making what Angela called his 'showing-off noise' as he rounded up his other wives and warned the bachelors-in-waiting that he was still in charge, despite the loss of one member of his harem. If we happened to be elsewhere, Bunty wouldn't attempt to escape, yet as soon as we returned, she would arrive the instant we started to unpack our cases. At first it was a mystery how Bunty could gauge our return so accurately, but there was no doubt that she could because it happened with convincing regularity, leaving us in no doubt that Nature had endowed her with powers of telepathy. The bond between Bunty and me was that of mother and child – we were incredibly close – and on any return journey I would think of her and the other garden orphans as we neared home, hoping they were safe and sound. Later, I would come to see the same pattern of behaviour repeated between Bunty and her offspring, and this proved to me that the antelopes – and indeed many animals – are able to pick up thought processes and that telepathy is a real means of communication, especially among family members with strong emotional bonds. I had no difficulties reaching this conclusion; for me, the natural world was – and still is – so full of mysterious wonders that we humans have yet fully to understand.

Bunty was very much a one-woman buck. She was fond of David but in a second-best sort of way, and loved Jill and Angela when they were around, but I basked in a love that was given without reservation, my role as her mother rewarded by a devotion and loyalty so complete that it spanned the years and eclipsed even the call of her own kind. She also came to understand that whenever David appeared in casual trousers and the suitcases came out, we were about to leave home, so she would butt him repeatedly, angered that he would be taking me away. As our car pulled out of the yard, she would make her way back to Father Ram, no different for a time than any of the other wives, and over the years she came to produce seven children with him. It was an unwritten understanding in the family that all Bunty's children had to have names beginning with the letter B, so over the years there was Bouncer, Bonnie (the only daughter), Bullitt, Bravo, Biscuit, Bimbo and Bandit, each born after a gestation period of six months, all born just below the garden and just before midday, the heat of the day, when predators were most lethargic and inactive. Vulnerable during labour, Bunty was always careful to select a spot where her russet colouring blended with the red Tsavo soil, so as to be camouflaged and not conspicuous against the green grass of the lawn. I would know when her time had come because she made it quite plain that she and I needed to be elsewhere. So, taking a camp chair to sit on and a book to read, I would accompany her to the place of her choice and sit quietly beside her during the birthing process. As long as I was there, she was relaxed, for she knew that both she and her baby would come to no harm.

It was both an amazing learning curve and a real privilege to be a part of the birth of her wild babies. During labour Bunty would alternate between lying down, standing up and walking around a little and even feeding, until two tiny black hooves appeared, then another contraction produced the front legs, another the head and shoulders and the final one expelled a very wet baby that plopped out in the lying position. Even before the umbilical cord was severed, Bunty licked her fawn clean, and before half an hour had lapsed, the newborn was up on unsteady legs searching for her udder. With every passing moment the fawn became stronger, and in no time at all found what it wanted and began suckling strongly. After an hour or so Bunty expelled the afterbirth, which she devoured immediately, and she made such heavy weather of it that I couldn't believe it was such a delicacy. However, always the farmer's daughter, I knew this was an essential task, vital in disposing of evidence that would jeopardize the survival of her newborn in addition to being a rich source of nutrients for the mother. Natural instinct dictated that no trace of an afterbirth be left to attract a host of terrestrial and airborne predators.

Bouncer weighed in at twelve and a half pounds. I had taken the kitchen scales to record his weight but after that I never touched Bouncer again – nor any of Bunty's other children subsequently – for fear of contaminating them with human scent. By late afternoon Bouncer was sufficiently strong for Bunty to usher him to a patch of long grass below the big orphans' stockades, where he quietly sank down; whereupon Bunty turned and walked away without so much as a backward glance. I ran to tell David, worried that she was abandoning him, but he warned me not to retrieve Bouncer: 'Don't interfere, Daph. She knows what she's doing, so just observe and learn from her. Bouncer won't be strong enough for at least ten days to run with the herd and for now, being devoid of scent, his best chance of survival throughout the night is without her. Remember, too, that his survival is dependent upon hers, so she is far better protected with the many eyes and ears of Father Ram's nocturnal herd.'

Nevertheless, I spent a fraught night worrying, hardly able to sleep, and at the first sign of light I was up and out, just in time to see Bunty returning, slowly, pausing every few yards to scan her surroundings, her instincts fully alert. As she approached the spot where she had left her baby the day before, she stopped, and with a very soft sound barely audible to human ears, called him several times. To my immense relief, he popped up and ran to her for his first meal of the day and then accompanied her to the lawn, where he was greeted with great curiosity by Baby, the eland, and Jimmy, the kudu. Bunty wouldn't let Baby go too near, head-butting her away, but was quite happy for Jimmy to investigate her baby, which he did very gently. This nocturnal hiding period lasted ten days, after which Bouncer began licking the earth, triggering his natural scent, and from then on – his 'passport' to his species secured – he accompanied his mother constantly.

It surprised both David and me that each one of Bunty's six sons kept in touch with their mother throughout her lifetime, returning periodically to the garden. We came to know when one of her children was on its way, as Bunty would stand at the edge of the garden, concentrating deeply, sometimes for many hours, and later one of her sons would appear. Of course, this merely reinforced our belief that telepathy was at play. On the day that Bunty's fifth son was born,

Bimbo, son number three, just happened to turn up afterwards. Having greeted his mother fondly and shown interest in his newborn brother, he walked away, and half an hour later returned accompanied by Bouncer, whom we had not seen for six months. I had been surprised when Bimbo had gone off so quickly, but when he returned with his brother it just reinforced my firm belief that just like us and the elephants, antelopes have enduring family ties and the ability to communicate meaningful messages to one another.

At night the young bachelor males, including Bunty's offspring, were permitted to mingle with Father Ram and his harem in the interest of security. When dawn broke, however, they became competitors to Father Ram and were rowdily expelled to the bachelor-herd-in-waiting. Only Bonnie, Bunty's daughter, became a permanent member of Father Ram's harem of wives and, unlike her mother, never risked his displeasure by escaping back to the lawn. Jimmy the kudu was fond of all Bunty's sons, although Bimbo became his firm favourite. Sometimes the sons brought back with them wild bachelor friends, most of whom never repeated the experience, fleeing back to the herd once they caught sight of us humans.

Jimmy was a gentle kudu who lovingly embraced all the garden orphans, irrespective of species. However, as Bouncer grew up and his horns developed, he took to threatening Jimmy by prodding him whenever he was in range and this was an injustice that Jimmy never forgot nor forgave. Jimmy's horns grew more slowly, but once he was suitably equipped and felt sufficiently confident, he was bent on settling the score and one day challenged Bouncer to a full-blown duel in the garden. I was beside myself with worry, since both were going hammer and tongs at each other and it looked as though it could only end in serious danger for one or the other. David told me not to interfere, saying that it was far too dangerous to do so, hence I could only hold my breath until, to my immense relief, Bouncer broke free and found himself chased out of the garden by the victorious Jimmy. Nor was he ever allowed back again, relegated to being a permanent outcast, although all five other sons were welcomed whenever they chose to return, and treated with affection by Jimmy. Like elephants – and some of us humans – antelopes have long memories.

Baby, the eland, was Angela's firm favourite and the two of them were often seen playing a game of 'dinks' with her Matchbox toy cars or racing each other around the Headquarters, Angela on her bike and Baby leaping over any obstacle by the wayside. Elands, the largest members of the antelope family, grow to the size of a cow and are incredible jumpers, effortlessly clearing obstacles six to eight feet high. On our regular afternoon walks, the entire garden entourage would accompany us, Angela on her bike, racing in among the exuberant members of the herd, with Bunty and any visiting sons following at a leisurely pace alongside David and me. These walks were the day's treat for us all. At the appointed hour we would all stop what we were doing as the animals either lined up at the front steps of the house, or came with the children to join us at the office. It was a very special feeling to be accepted and loved by so many different members of the animal kingdom and for our children it was a most magical experience.

By the early seventies, the Park had come a long way. In 1949, with just one lorry and six labourers, David had been given the task of developing 5,000 square miles of the pristine wilderness that comprised Tsavo East into a tourist attraction that could accommodate overseas visitors and bring revenue to the country. Now, there was a beautiful 200-bed lodge situated on the slopes of Worsessa Hill, just behind the Headquarters. This site commanded stunning views over Tsavo's expansive wilderness, a vast uninterrupted vista of the plains, with the deep blue massifs of Ndara and Sagalla to the right and the thin ridge of the long Yatta Plateau on the northern horizon. From your window in the lodge you might see tall delonix or acacia trees fringing distant waterholes; the stark contorted beauty of the twisted commiphora; terracotta anthills; herds of wild elephants, zebra or buffalo, small groups of antelopes, and smoky blues and mauves where the sky merged with distant horizons. Sometimes dark clouds drifting over the saffron yellow plains held the promise of rain, and the drama of lions targeting solitary animals at the lodge waterhole was an exciting and ever present possibility for tourists staying at the Voi Safari Lodge.

Within the Park, there were now almost 200 miles of all-weather roads, twelve airstrips, additional research and staff housing, five entrance gates serving Tsavo's distant boundaries, new staff quarters; camping grounds with washing facilities; rustic rock elephant-proof road signs at all intersections; boreholes, dams, bridges, and of course the causeway to the north, built by hand with much sweat and toil. We had a sophisticated radio network embracing all entrance gates and outposts, able to keep in touch with all the mobile anti-poaching patrols, each section of which was fully equipped with a workshop trailer, a mechanic to undertake field repairs and a water bowser to enable the patrols to cover waterless country and remain in the field for weeks at a time. The Park's transport fleet included more than twelve heavy earth-moving machines, twenty-two trucks and Land Rovers, twenty-five stationary engines, generators, pumps, trailers and all sorts of implements, including a lathe and the huge hydraulic press which, in addition to its usual tasks, was useful for squeezing the juice from the fiery red chillies that David so enjoyed at meal-times.

Now there was an urgent need to modernize the entire Headquarters complex and particularly to improve the workshop facilities to cater for the increased workload. We needed a new office block, since the original offices and stores were now bulging at the seams. The ivory store was filled to capacity with tusks and rhino horns, since a recent presidential decree precluded ivory being sent for auction in Mombasa as it had been before. This had come as a bombshell, since it impacted heavily on the working budget, reducing it considerably. David pleaded for the funds he needed, but all the accounts department at Headquarters in Nairobi could release was the paltry sum of £700, insufficient for one modest office, let alone what David had in mind.

There had been a tendency for some of the established Parks to expand in disjointed ways as additional units were added piecemeal, mushrooming into untidy villages in the heart of pristine wilderness. David was determined that this would not happen in Tsavo East and despite the absence of funding resolutely refused to compromise his vision. Unexpectedly, fortune favoured him from a surprising quarter – the railway – which up to this time had been something of a thorn in our flesh, responsible more often than not for the destructive fires that plagued the new grasslands created by the elephants. Every dry season, sparks from the boilers of the steam engines ignited wild fires, fanned by the prevailing strong south-easterly winds, destroying huge swathes of the Park. Perhaps it was to make amends for this that the railway offered David the old dak bungalow, on condition he undertook to demolish the entire building and remove it completely from the station yard.

The dak bungalow was the rest-house at the station, dating back to the turn of the century and the early days of the railway when no dining cars were attached to the passenger trains. Many such bungalows existed along the line but once the daily passenger train had a dining car attached, they had become obsolete. David was jubilant, for the dak bungalow was a substantial building with about ten good-sized rooms and massive steel girders supporting an iron roof. The doors were made of rosewood and teak, imported from India, though sadly since plastered in glossy white paint. The dak bungalows had always been important meeting places for the early settlers, my old pioneering relatives included – and I had heard many a tale about the excellent bacon and eggs and a variety of alcoholic drinks, served by Goan waiters clad in starched white uniforms.

Rubble from the demolished walls of the dak bungalow became concrete blocks for the walls of the new Headquarters complex, faced with Tsavo's beautiful flat quartz stones; those same steel girders supported the roof, and the painted rosewood and teak doors separated the various rooms. David was able to incorporate spacious offices for himself and his assistant; a large conference cum operations room; and offices for the accountant and the radio operator as well as a secure armoury, flush toilets and a guardroom with a built-in siren. David planted a baobab sapling nearby to mark this important milestone in the Park's development, and when all the building had been completed, he hoisted the green National Parks flag with its rhino logo alongside the flag of Independent Kenya. It seemed fitting to me that the dak bungalow, so steeped in history, including that of my own family, should become the working Headquarters of Tsavo East.

And so the dak bungalow was not lost but simply recycled. In designing his own office, David had pandered to a particular whim of mine and built an aquarium into the wall behind his desk. Its tranquil presence had a soothing influence, since we were all anxious about the impending amalgamation of the National Parks with the Game Department into the Wildlife Conservation and Management Department, which was to be responsible for all wildlife throughout the country, both within and beyond the established Park boundaries. We all feared for the future of wildlife, as there were such fundamental differences in the way the two organizations operated. The National Parks had evolved in a way that allowed its wardens the autonomy needed to deal with contingencies rapidly and efficiently and provide services to the public quite outside the scope of government, where the procurement of much-needed goods was subjected to a rigid and cumbersome tendering procedure bedevilled by corruption. It was no secret that many contracts were allocated to unscrupulous businessmen in exchange for what was becoming known as 'kickbacks'.

We were fearful, too, of a return to poaching within the Park by the Wakamba and opportunists from the coastal tribes. A sudden rise in the price of ivory on the world market meant that a poacher could now expect to receive 140 Kenyan shillings per kilo for a tusk as opposed to the four Kenyan shillings of previous years. It wasn't long before just about every able-bodied Mkamba tribesman re-armed himself with a bow, arrow and their lethal acokanthera-poisoned arrows and set out in pursuit of any elephant they could find. Since a presidential decree had banned legal hunting in the country, the remote hunting blocks were now wide open to nefarious activities, some of the worst offenders now being corrupt game scouts and highly placed officials within the Government who were heavily embroiled in the lucrative ivory racket. As elephant numbers rapidly dwindled beyond the Park boundaries and survivors fled for their lives to the safety of the Park itself, so the bows, arrows and poison followed them.

We also had environmental concerns, one being the silt-load coming down the floodwaters of the Voi River, which was affecting

Kanderi, one of the Park's loveliest natural waterholes. Since independence, laws prohibiting cultivation along riverbanks had fallen into abeyance, and this combined with poor farming practices in the high forested Taita Hills meant topsoil was being washed down in huge quantities every time the heavy rains caused the seasonal Voi River to flood. Previously the waterhole had been a permanent scenic paradise for water birds, with rich vegetation behind and the twin massifs of Ndara and Sagalla mirrored in its glassy surface. Snow-white egrets and sacred ibis were always perched on skeletal inundated trees in the centre of the pool, while wild ducks, Egyptian geese, storks, darters and cranes gathered in the shallows to feed on the abundance of frogs and fish. Recently, however, silting had caused the river to keep altering its course and the Kanderi waterhole had turned into a treacherous swamp. A sun-baked crust on the surface lent the illusion of stability, but beneath lay a soft quick-mud bog that was proving a death trap for elephants and other large herbivores.

Although elephants were usually careful to avoid walking anywhere that might prove problematic, the Kanderi waterhole was so deceptive that it fooled them; having broken through the crust, they sank down in the mud until they almost disappeared completely, with just a portion of their body and head visible above the surface. Several elephants perished in this way before we realized what was happening, as they were not easily detectable from the road. Thereafter, we kept a close watch on the swamp and managed to extract at least twelve, towed out of the mud by the Park's Michigan bulldozer.

It was clear to me that these animals understood perfectly that they were being assisted, lying still so that David could position the steel cable from the tractor beneath their heads and around their bodies before towing them to firmer ground. Several of them, having struggled for many hours to the point of complete exhaustion, were too weak to get up unaided once out. It requires a lot of effort for an elephant to stand up from a recumbent position, first throwing back its head in order to rise front legs first, but many of the victims could not even summon the strength for this initial effort. By digging the bulldozer blade beneath them to include a protective cushion of earth, it was possible to lift them on to their feet, and, once up, not one of them made any attempt to attack either the tractor or the people standing about but instead ambled off, understanding that they owed their lives to the humans around them whom they would normally have viewed as their enemy.

There was one small elephant that didn't appreciate our efforts to extricate his bogged mother and older brother, and on this occasion rescue efforts were severely hampered as he bravely chased everyone around in an attempt to protect his family. It fell to me to try to keep him at bay, using the Landcruiser to drive him off, but it was heartwarming to witness the joyful reunion with his mother and brother, after which he showed no signs of further aggression.

During one short safari to the Tiva River in the northern area of the Park in 1973, David had to shoot two elephants, both victims dying from the effects of arrow poison: one a beautiful young bull with two hits in his hindquarters, and the other a marvellous old matriarch with three youngsters who had one arrow projecting from her hind hip and another from the top of her trunk. She was clearly in great distress, moving painfully and laboriously, constantly brushing her hip wound with her tail. David ended her agony with a shot to the brain, and it was heartbreaking to see the emotional suffering of her offspring, who crowded round their fallen mother, desperately trying to lift her and coax her back to life. As we drove away I couldn't hold back my tears, knowing that they would be keeping a lonely vigil by the side of their mother for some days until the oldest calf assumed the responsibility thrust upon her and led her siblings away in search of food and water. On the way back we spotted another female elephant in among a herd of others, her intestines hanging out of a burst arrow abscess on her stomach, and this time we could do nothing to help because she was in the midst of wild elephants hell-bent on protecting her.

It was patently obvious that poachers had again invaded the Park in great numbers and the elephant herds were now visibly fearful, consorting again in large numbers. The Field Force patrols in the northern area of the Park reported seeing poachers' tracks everywhere, and they intercepted gangs carrying ivory. Scuffles between rangers and poachers were taking place on an almost daily basis, and we also had to deal with a distressing in-house poaching incident incriminating David's long-serving and trusted sergeant along with members of the old Field Force. Sentences imposed by the local magistrates were ludicrously lenient; one poacher who had been arrested six times was charged only 100 Kenyan shillings – the equivalent of about £3. In despair, David flew to Nairobi to appeal to the Attorney-General, the result of which was the transfer of our poaching cases to a First Class Magistrate Court in Mombasa, where stiffer penalties were likely to be given. The downside was that this involved a great deal more inconvenience, since Mombasa was 100 miles from Voi.

By September 1973 the price of ivory on the world market had risen again. Official figures published by the Customs Department in the first three months of 1973 were revealing, putting Kenya's ivory exports at $2.2 million compared with only $285,000 during the same period the year before. By May, just two months later, this figure had risen to $5 million. And whereas in 1972 Kenya's elephant population was around 500,000, by 1973 it was estimated to have fallen to 300,000. In March 1974 the ivory rooms in Mombasa were closed and the sale of all ivory and rhino horn banned, but it was reported that the day after this declaration, a staggering nine tons left the country for China followed by even larger consignments, the volume of which far exceeded the stockpile that had been legally registered for auction, proving yet again that the black market trade in ivory and rhino horns was flourishing.

David was undeterred by this deceitful corruption and set up Operation Mshale – *mshale* being the Swahili term for arrow. Our recruits were based on top of the Yatta escarpment, directed by radio from a base at Lugard's Falls. The Attorney-General agreed to make a magistrate available so that cases could be dealt with on the spot. The new rangers were smart, well-equipped and fully briefed. Poachers attempted to conceal their tracks by walking along rock seams or doubling back to confuse and hold up the rangers – even sometimes walking on their toes or heels, hoping that the prints might be mistaken for those of a hoofed animal, or wearing their tyre sandals back to front so as to appear to be going in the opposite direction. How-ever, none of these tricks could fool the skilled Shangilla trackers, who could follow spoor at a run, keeping in touch with one another through their special 'yipping' signals.

David was constantly in touch with the patrols from Tango Papa, and as soon as he had word that the rangers were closing in, he circled low overhead, forcing the poachers to take cover. In this way the rangers were able to catch up, close in and capture the offenders. Within just two weeks some 125 offenders had been caught, charged and sentenced by the magistrate, who, on the instructions of the Attorney-General, handed out more effective sentences than his urban counterpart. David estimated that for every animal positively identified as having fallen victim to poachers, another five had almost certainly been killed. This alarming assumption meant that the Park had probably lost at least 1,040 elephants during the first six months of 1973 alone.

Our ivory stores were soon bulging at the seams, packed with tusks, rhino horns, leopard-skins, bows and arrows. Ominously, the local Game Department representative in Voi began taking an inter-est in our stockpile, wanting to know how much we had accumulated. David informed him that we couldn't divulge any information with-out the authority of the Trustees, who seemed to be in a confused sense of limbo as they awaited the passage of the new Merger Bill. Then, out of the blue, came an instruction from the Game Depart-ment to send all the ivory to Mombasa, despite the closure of the ivory room. We spent two full days and nights extracting all the ivory and rhino from our stores, to correlate each tusk and horn with the number and weight in our trophy register and eventually to load it on to the waiting trucks. We sent 3,710 tusks weighing 31,203 kilos and 950 rhino horns weighing 1,564 kilos to Mombasa in a convoy of eight trucks.

David led that ivory convoy, keeping in radio contact with the eight trucks, each one with two armed guards aboard and with a Field Force sergeant, also armed, in a separate vehicle at the rear of the col-umn. It was, in essence, an immeasurably sad elephant and rhino funeral procession, for the contents in those trucks represented the remains of over 1,000 elephants and 400 rhinos. In Mombasa the attendant was visibly shocked, having never seen such a massive haul, and had to find extra storage space. When David returned, he was morose, declaring as he kissed me that we needed a break to escape from 'all this madness' and restore our sanity.

It was not like David to express his emotions forcefully but I knew that he meant what he had said, so I packed up just what we would need for a few days away and soon we were heading to our special retreat – the Ntharakana blind on the slopes of the Yatta, overlooking the Tiva Valley and 3,000 square miles of wilderness. This was a place to soothe troubled souls, a place that imparted a mysteriously healing and uplifting magic, touching the human soul and reminding the subconscious of its primeval home. The natural waterfall tumbling down from the rock-face made a welcome splashing sound in this hot, dry land, and the pink, red and crimson blooms of the desert roses that sprouted from the surrounding rocks lent a surreal beauty to an otherwise arid setting. Wild creatures, of all shapes and sizes, came in a steady stream to drink from the pool below, hesitant during daylight but confident under the cover of darkness. Lost in quiet contemplation of the animals and our surroundings, it was easy to appreciate the intrinsic beauty of wilderness and the need to preserve it in its wild and natural state.

Inevitably, it was just a matter of time before our reverie was shattered. A magnificent bull elephant with long sweeping tusks approached the waterhole, clearly in excruciating pain, pausing at almost every step to touch the horrendous wounds on his body. We could almost feel his pain, the agony of the poison seeping through his blood, and we could see there was no hope for him. After he had quenched his thirst, David followed at a safe distance to avoid distressing him further – and quietly ended the elephant's suffering beneath the shade of a giant baobab tree. As he fell, the earth seemed to tremble under his great weight. His mournful soft brown eyes gazed one last time through the great boughs of the tree before David closed them.

The death of this great elephant evoked in us a lament for all the wild creatures of Africa and the vanishing wilderness that had protected and sheltered them for so long. It was symbolic of the ten-uous future all wildlife faced in a continent where poverty bred corruption and greedy people in faraway lands created the demand that fuelled the killing. The bull's very size and magnificence height-ened the sense of tragedy, for there is nothing so profoundly dead as a five-ton elephant with the allotted lifespan of a human, who has died before his time simply to supply some unthinking Westerner with a trinket. Those beautiful tusks were worth a small fortune to any trophy hunter, but for the elephant they were the very mark of his majesty and rank, a symbol that elevated him among the elite within his community – the identity that generated respect and awe from his peers and made him a dominant breeding bull. We knew that the beneficiaries of these splendid tusks would be the unscrupu-lous and corrupt 'big names' who by their avarice had violated this precious wilderness and inflicted so much chaos.

It was with sadness that we drove back home, diverted only from despair by stopping to watch the subterranean naked mole rats who were busy clearing out debris from one of their tunnels, sending puffs of earth flying. I had never seen these creatures up close before, so David picked one up to show me. He was not a thing of great beauty – his skin was soft, pink and naked, but for a few sparse hairs, and his eyes were somehow undeveloped, probably only equipped to determine shades of darkness in order to gauge the depths of the tun-nels that linked his underground country. Two ferocious-looking incisors protruded from his tiny whiskered face and his feet were equipped with the tough claws needed for tunnelling in hard earth. We didn't keep him long, aware that the sun would be damaging to his tender skin, and he was soon gone, disappearing at the speed of light down the tunnel he had just cleared.

Naked mole rats are the subterranean animal equivalent of ter-mites, bees and wasps, living in colonies and travelling through a network of tunnels in order to mine roots and tubers for a livelihood. We stood for a while looking at the soft earth mounds as I asked David about these odd little rats, and it never ceased to delight me how he could enlighten me on just about any animal in Tsavo. He explained that their society was rigidly segregated into categories of workers and soldiers, the females infertile and the males subservient, all under the matriarchal dictatorship of a dominant queen rat who employed a hands-on system of 'shoving management' to keep everyone in line and ensure that the colony functioned as it should. She shoved the workers from behind to keep them tunnelling, bullied the females to keep them infertile and gave the largest males a hard time to make sure they didn't rise above their station. She made a point of 'shoving' each and every one of her subjects constantly, in between giving birth to another generation, for she was the sole breeding female of the colony, suckling the babies in the same way as other mammals. Her mate enjoyed the privilege of having to endure less shoving than the others, whose Sisyphean task it was to clear the subterranean tunnels of their homeland and excavate fresh ones to access new feeding grounds, passing each other in little lay-bys and shoving loose earth from the tunnels to puff out at the surface, using their hindlegs. Inhabiting the arid regions of Kenya, Somalia and Ethiopia, they have long remained an enigma to all except the most discerning of naturalists, and watching them that day, after the tragedy of our fallen elephant, I marvelled again at how the wilderness is filled with wonders, that there is always something to observe and be amazed at, that Nature is awash with living miracles.

That year another very large elephant died – the legendary Ahamed – king of the northern Marsabit Mountain. Unlike the Ntharakana bull, Ahamed had died of malnutrition, his sixth and last set of massive teeth worn too low in old age to enable him to ingest the quantity and variety of vegetation needed to sustain his huge frame. Because of his magnificent ivory tusks, which reached in perfect symmetry to the ground, Ahamed had become world-famous and a target of international trophy hunters. Two American hunters had let it be known that they were out to 'bag' him, but because of the subsequent press outcry and the iconic status Ahamed enjoyed, with people journeying from all corners of the world, President Kenyatta had afforded him special protection. Five ranger bodyguards were assigned the special task of guarding him, and when he died near Lake Paradise, the President declared that his body must be preserved for posterity. Ahamed's tusks weighed 140lb each – heavy enough – but it was their length of 9 foot 6 inches and 9 foot 10 inches that was most impressive. On his death they were insured for 20,000 Kenyan pounds and supposedly secured in the vaults of a local bank. To this day a replica of Ahamed stands in the courtyard of the Nairobi National Museum, a lasting monument to the memory of this great elephant.

Marsabit was a long way off from our orphanage in Voi, but it was one of Ahamed's descendants that enabled me to unlock the mystery that had eluded me for so long.

13. Turmoil

'The greatness of a Nation and its moral progress can be judged by the
way its animals are treated . . . I hold that the more helpless a creature, the
more entitled it is to protection by man from the cruelty of man.'

– Mahatma Gandhi

She was the smallest elephant I had ever seen – still covered in the soft
fuzz of elephant infancy, her tiny trunk tinged with pink, toenails of
pale yellow – soft and brand new. My heart sank. She had come from
far-off Marsabit, having fallen down a disused well, and was sent to
us because apparently we would know what to do and would be sure
to keep her alive. I remember thinking: but we don't, not one this
young. We looked at the hind side of her ear, which I could see was
as soft and pink as the petal of a flower, and I knew that this baby was
younger than three weeks old. She was far too young to be handed
over to Eleanor, for she needed milk and only milk. I stroked her
head – we had never managed to rear an elephant as young as this and
with the death of each one, the sense of failure deepened. David
often said that it might be kinder not to even try, to simply accept
that the hand-rearing of infant milk-dependent African elephants
was impossible. But my conscience could not agree with this, for it
would be even more distressing to hand out a death sentence without
even trying. Nature intends elephants to live three score years and
ten, the same as ourselves, and we would never turn a baby away for
fear of failure. I knew I had to persevere.

The garden orphans had all gathered around, for the arrival of any
newcomer caused interest in varying degrees: Bunty and her visiting
sons decidedly disapproving; Baby and Jimmy curious; our peacocks
and guinea fowl chattering excitedly, stretching out their necks to

stare. I took a deep breath. I was under no illusion as to how much work this tiny newcomer would entail – three-hourly feeds day and night, constant companionship, relentless clearing up. But this was nothing compared with the desperation of, in all likelihood, having to watch her decline daily, with the prospect of burying her in our graveyard beyond the lily pond. But, I reminded myself, only by trial and error would a suitable formula emerge, and as the newcomer was steered towards the orphan stables, trailed by a retinue of furred and feathered onlookers, I steeled myself for a tricky few weeks.

Feeding an elephant is not easy at the best of times. You have to mix gallons, not pints, and the bottle and teat have to be elephantine. David and I consulted the thick 'orphans' file that contained an assortment of ideas on how to simulate elephant's milk. To our knowledge there had not been a single success story involving a newly born, milk-dependent elephant baby, due to their intolerance to the fat in cow's milk. That night we fed the little elephant only water and glucose and went to bed with the problem still unsolved.

Throughout the night, shrill bellows from the nursery stables forced me to succumb and I fed her a very weak mixture of cow's milk, dreading the fallout the next day. And the next few weeks were indeed the nightmare I had predicted, as I battled with different milk concoctions, mixing, measuring, sterilizing, cleaning and changing the formula time and time again. Meanwhile, the little elephant declined rapidly, developing the dreaded skeletal look of starvation: the sunken eye sockets, pronounced cheekbones and feebleness that heralded the end. I desperately wanted this little elephant to live, for she was putting up such a brave struggle and I had come to love her dearly. Gentle and obedient sometimes, depending on the mood of the moment, just like a human child, a baby elephant captures your heart entirely – so utterly dependent and incredibly intelligent. Although a baby elephant duplicates humans in terms of age, they are certainly much more advanced than the human equivalent in early infancy and much more responsible and wiser in childhood and adolescence.

We had deliberately avoided naming any very tiny elephant orphan that came to us, simply because we suspected that they would not be with us for long, but because I had a hunch that this baby was a direct descendant of Ahamed, possibly even a daughter, we gave her the Arabic name of Aisha. A few weeks later, on one of our afternoon strolls with the garden orphans, Angela and I encountered a group of German tourists. Aisha was on the alert – her soft pink ears stood out like round dinner plates from her tiny face as she gave a mock-charge that ended with a squeak, an early attempt at a trumpet. This unexpected sound startled her and she backed away with her head up, looking down her trunk. 'Schmetterling, schmetterling,' laughed the tourists. 'What does that mean?' asked Angela. 'I suspect it means elephant,' I suggested, but I was corrected. 'No, no, Fräulein. It means ze botterfly.' And they were right: standing there with her tiny ears outspread, the baby elephant did look rather like a butterfly. From that moment on, Aisha was known affectionately as 'Shmetty'.

The day came when Shmetty was too weak even to get to her feet. Sitting with her head in my lap, the tears rolled down my cheeks as I wondered just how I was going to keep her alive. I walked back into my store and stared at the rows of different formulas that I had been trying one by one. Only one, which had been given to me by Ruth Eden, a sympathetic English visitor, remained to be tested, and as I read through the ingredients I saw that it contained coconut oil. I remembered once being told that coconut oil was the nearest substitute for the fat of elephant's milk, so my spirits lifted – all was not quite lost yet. I mixed it as directed on the tin and went to relieve Shmetty of her hunger.

It worked! I was overjoyed. I hardly dared believe that I might have unlocked the mystery of how to rear an infant elephant. As the days passed, Shmetty began to lose her gaunt appearance, her skin became more supple and soft, and then one day she began to play, charging Bunty and Baby, scattering the Honk family and grabbing Jimmy by the back leg. As if in joyful recognition that this moment marked the beginning of Shmetty's recovery, everyone was soon involved, Baby in the thick of things, bucking and kicking and leaping over the terraces with such ease. In her exuberance Baby speared the flower basket left lying on the lawn with one horn and charged with it attached to her head, resulting in total disarray. Honk, his wives and the guinea fowl set up their loud alarm squawking, Bunty made her snorting noise and her sons beat a hasty retreat to the relative calm of the bachelor herd. Even our newly acquired warthogs were drawn in, shooting out of the garden with their tails in the air, nearly colliding with David who was on his way up from the workshop.

The four baby warthogs – Balthazar, Oliver, Cleo and Justine – had been found as tiny trembling piglets cowering by the side of the road near the Aruba Safari Lodge. Bloodstains on the road and the signs of a scuffle were evidence that their mother had been eaten by a lion. The wife of one of the scientists had brought them to me, but when she saw my face drop at the prospect of more babies to rear she gallantly took charge of the initial bottle-feeding stage. So it was not until the piglets were three months old and on solids that they joined the fold as part of the Garden Gang. David made them a long, low trough from which they took their daily rations of gruel and grain, and they were soon at home, wandering around all over the place, eager to get into the house. They were a disruptive influence in the garden, chasing the peacocks and guinea fowl, nudging the antelope orphans whenever they took a rest, forcing them to get up and move, or nipping at their legs forcing them to run. They were exceedingly mischievous, and Jimmy and Baby, who by now sported sizeable horns, began to lose patience with them. We reckoned it was just a matter of time before one of the warthogs got badly hurt, so we tempted the piglets away from the garden by excavating a burrow for them. This was a great diversion, each of them spending hours rootling away with their snouts like miniature bulldozers chucking puffs of earth in the air around them. As they became more adventurous they spent their days around the main entrance gate to the Park. Returning home, a squeaking, grunting discussion took place about the evening's plans. If the decision was to stay around, they would lie down at the front steps of the house in a line and wait to be carried to their stable for the night. But if the consensus was to go out, all four tails would shoot up erect and off they would trot in single file, heading for a culvert down by the main entrance. In time they became independent, sometimes returning individually to see what was going on or catching up with Eleanor's herd down by the Voi River. It was when Cleo returned with four tiny piglets in tow that we knew our orphaned warthogs had successfully made the transition back where they rightly belonged.

Meanwhile, Shmetty was thriving. I hardly dared believe I had found at least a part of the mystery of the milk formula that had been eluding me. Shmetty was living proof that I was doing something right, happily playing for hours in the little mud wallow that David had made for her. At first she wanted me to come in with her, but she soon hooked up with three little ostrich chicks recently brought in by a tourist bus, ruthlessly hauling them in when they came within trunk range. The chicks provided the companionship so vital for a baby elephant, attaching themselves to her as a mother figure even if she was a rather rough one, dragging them around the orchard by their necks. But wherever Shmetty was so were they, squatting patiently by her as she slept or when she played, racing around, pirouetting in circles with their ridiculously tiny wings outspread. They were the barometers that reflected Shmetty's changing moods, and Angela, having read a romantic fairytale, rather poetically named them 'Shmetty's handmaidens'.

Shmetty was very demanding, and as it was impossible for me to be with her at all times, David asked one of the rangers to 'elephant sit'. Attaching Shmetty to her sitter entailed careful planning, since she was fully aware that he was not me. Only by throwing my apron over her head to cover her eyes could I make a dash for the gate, so that by the time she had managed to disentangle herself, I was nowhere to be seen. Bizarrely, as long as the ranger put on my apron, she would remain with him without too much fuss, but it was never really enough, for two round ears were constantly slightly raised, denoting unease, listening intently for the creak of the gate. When she spotted me, she rushed over bellowing loudly, almost bowling me over. Her loving rumbles usually ended in a loud roar that had to be muffled whenever Eleanor was in earshot. We had to keep these two apart while Shmetty was milk-dependent, otherwise Eleanor would assume the role of mothering without having the vital means to sustain her.

There were days when Shmetty was not herself, her stool showing signs of becoming too loose. Diarrhoea in elephants leads to life-threatening dehydration, and it took the combined efforts of David, the sitter and me to restrain Shmetty while we inserted a sulphadimidine pill down her throat during the five-day course. Often, the tablet would be ejected as she shook her head from side to side in irritation and distaste. There was no chance of getting it down disguised in her bottle of milk either, for she would immediately detect its presence and refuse the entire feed. After being dosed, she would head off to the kitchen and stand dejectedly with her head in the box that housed the gas cylinder, seeking comfort from the feeling of being underneath something large. She missed being tucked beneath her mother, and only the gas box seemed to give her this particular comfort and feeling of security whenever she was upset. It always tugged at my heartstrings to see her head in the box – there were some things I just couldn't provide.

Teatime was a fixed routine in our home, much loved by all the orphans because not only did the rattle of teacups indicate that the afternoon walk was imminent but it also meant the appearance of the teatime biscuits I baked, made from a recipe handed down from generation to generation in my family. Most of the orphans viewed these as a treat, particularly Jimmy and Baby. Gazing over the verandah ledge with drooling mouths and looks of such longing in their large liquid eyes, they pleaded with every fibre of their being and were impossible to resist, even though feeding them the biscuits was rather like posting letters, so rapidly were they downed. After observing this handout for some time, Shmetty decided she should have one as well. It was hilarious to watch, as she clearly had absolutely no idea what to do with a biscuit, waving it around in her trunk, popping it in and out of her mouth and her ear and finally sucking it up in her trunk until it got blown out in an elephant sneeze, making us all jump. However, the biscuits weren't popular with everyone, and as soon as Bunty and her sons heard the teacups, they would walk over to the car park and wait patiently for us to assemble for our afternoon stroll.

The sandpit by the office was almost as special as the little waterhole and so the walk had to be routed this way. There, Shmetty would play in the sand just like a child, climbing to the top and sliding down on her bottom until her ears and trunk were full of sand and it was time to press on. We had to arrange our return for just before six, because we couldn't risk any noisy protests as Eleanor and the other orphans were coming up the hill back to their night stockades, and Shmetty had a terrific sense of time, objecting loudly if her feed was just a few minutes late. Nevertheless, despite such precautions, Eleanor was definitely suspicious that I was hiding something from her, for she would pause by the side of the house to listen for a long time, then shake her head in irritation before moving on. I have no doubt that she could detect Shmetty's presence just by the amazing elephant intuition and was probably extremely puzzled as to why this particular calf had not been handed over to her as usual.

The days turned into six months and our little elephant was still alive. Every month I would get out my tape measure and every month when she was half an inch taller, I felt on top of the world. I dreaded the day when I would have to part with her by handing her over to Eleanor. It would be Eleanor and not I who would introduce her to the wild world and tutor her in the way of her species. Of course I could not do that, and so I lived each day with her for as long as I could. A very special feeling flooded through me when I thought about my orphans – the sort of feeling I knew David must have experienced over and over and over again as he created the Park. It was a feeling of achievement and identity, a warm glow, a deep satisfaction that I was contributing something to the wilderness I loved so much. It was rewarding to be able to offer a second chance of life to any animal. When I recalled the dark days of working in an office in Nairobi, yearning to be in Tsavo with David by my side, I was struck by how lucky I had been and how I would not have chosen any other life on earth for myself other than this one I was now living. But failing Shmetty – as I inevitably did – left me so desolate and distraught, and to this day I can hardly bring myself to think about her death.

When Jill announced her intention to marry Alan, her South African boyfriend, I instinctively felt that like my own first marriage this union might not stand the test of time. However, I couldn't voice such doom-laden predictions: Jill appeared happy and in love. Bill and I greeted the news with cautious enthusiasm. Two weeks before the wedding I went to join my mother at Betty's home in Muthaiga, to prepare for the reception in her beautiful garden. Although I settled Shmetty with an experienced sitter who had overseen the orphans, she missed me so much that her condition deteriorated rapidly. No amount of comfort or medication for her diarrhoea helped. With the wedding day imminent, it was impossible for me to leave, so all I could do was pray that my return would not be too late.

My daughter looked radiant in her silver-threaded bridal gown as she entered the church on Bill's arm. Three hundred guests, many from our extended family, had travelled from far and wide to share in the celebrations, as Jill was the first of her generation to get married. By doing all the catering ourselves, we kept the costs at an affordable level, as both Bill and David earned a pittance. The cake, decorated skilfully, mirrored the three peaks of Mount Kenya, which was fitting for Jill, who still held the record for being the youngest girl to have scaled Lenana, the third highest peak, under Bill's supervision when she was just ten.

Like my mother, both Jill and I always had difficulty holding back tears when parting and it was no different as she left for her honeymoon. Back at home I burst into Shmetty's stable and as she struggled to get up to greet me, she collapsed in my arms. Cuddling her close, I wept tears of grief, for I knew her life was ebbing away. With her head cradled in my lap, she managed one last loud cry that ended in a sigh and then her body went limp. I had not noticed David's approach until his arms encircled me and held me close. He was also overcome; this little elephant had so captured our hearts and her death left us bereft. I remained with Shmetty's body cuddled close until it turned cold. Only then did I disentangle her and let her go. She was laid to rest in the little graveyard – a new fresh mound of red Tsavo soil to add to the long line of other newborn casualties. Of them all, however, this particular baby elephant would always be the most special for me and live in my heart and my memory for ever.

In the months that followed, I struggled to turn the page, finding solace with my garden orphans, who lent such magic to the garden.

Inevitably the time came when Jimmy and Baby answered the call of the wild and one morning disappeared together, causing me the usual anxiety. That afternoon we decided to take a game drive along the Voi River circuit, hoping that we might see them, and sure enough, to my relief, by the airfield stood a herd of eland that would not have looked unusual but for a striped kudu in among them. A few days later Jimmy returned alone. Obviously Baby's eland peers did not relish having a kudu in their midst, so he had decided to come back home to Bunty and the garden.

It was many moons before we saw any further signs of Baby, until one afternoon while having tea on the verandah we spotted a lone eland. Baby didn't stay for long, as her best friend, Jimmy, was by now also elsewhere. He had acquired three beautiful females, whom we spotted with him during one of the afternoon strolls, and while the females bounded off with alarm barks, Jimmy, now a fully grown stately bull with ivory tips to his spiral horns, simply walked up to us, as friendly and as tame as ever. His coat had turned from the original baby brown to a kudu bull's adult gunmetal grey, with white lateral stripes for perfect camouflage within the light and shade of the thickets. From then on we used often to see him and his entourage, and while he always said hello, he never stayed long, conscious of keeping his wives under close surveillance. Being bush dwellers, he and his wives preferred denser cover, and contact with them became more infrequent. However, both Jimmy and Baby were unmitigated orphan success stories, and during the time they shared their lives with us, like Bunty, they contributed greatly to our understanding of their particular species.

And then one day my parents arrived, unexpectedly, the bearers of devastating news. There being no telephone connection between the outside world and us, they had come in person, and it took my father some time to find the words to break such sad tidings to us. While on holiday in South Africa following Jill's wedding, Betty and Graham had found a mysterious lump on their eleven-year-old daughter's right thigh and within just a matter of days, Sally's whole leg had been amputated from the hip. She now had to embark on a long and gruelling course of chemotherapy in an attempt to stop the spread of this particularly virulent form of bone cancer. This meant that her family had to move to South Africa as soon as possible. Fortunately Graham's firm were willing to transfer him to the South African branch, so at least his continued employment was assured. My parents decided to move with them to South Africa to offer emotional and practical support to Sally.

It seemed that everyone near and dear to me was converging on South Africa. After their honeymoon, Jill and Alan left for Cape Town, where he worked as a rigger. I was already missing Jill, my close confidante and proficient helpmate with the orphans. She was so passionate about animals that I felt sure she was going to find it difficult to adjust to urban living in a far-off land. Now that my parents, sister and her family were off there too it unsettled me greatly, and a few months later, for our annual leave, David and I went to South Africa to see how they were all getting on. I had other plans while we were there too. David had recently been complaining of a 'cramp' between his shoulder blades, and knowing that his father died at fifty-six, having suffered a heart attack during a polo match in Nyeri, I was worried. At that point in time, apart from the normal electrocardiograms, there was little else that could be done to diagnose and, moreover, correct heart conditions. However, some of the best heart specialists of the day were in South Africa and I planned to book David in for a thorough check-up. David had dismissed these cramps as inconsequential, and indeed nothing untoward had been found at the annual check-up for the renewal of his pilot's licence. The doctor even said that the cramping was due to sitting for long periods in the cockpit of Tango Papa.

At the doctor's in Cape Town, David was insistent that he be alone during the examination, sending me off to buy presents for our family. Before I could protest, he was ushered into the surgery and the door was closed, but I was waiting when he emerged and was relieved to hear the doctor say: 'I'll see you in two years' time for another check-up.' David looked relaxed and told me there was nothing to worry about; he had been diagnosed with 'just a touch of angina' and this could be corrected through medication and diet. I was happy to believe this and vowed to myself to keep an eye on his diet.

*

55. Playing with Aisha on a sand pile.

56. With Aisha.

57. Aisha having her mud bath.

58. With Eleanor in the 1980s.

59. Myself with Boobalub, one of our orphaned eland.

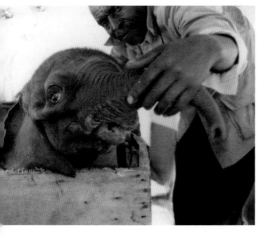

60. Olmeg was rescued from Maralal on 4 March 1987, estimated one month old, sunburnt and emaciated.

61. Olmeg, two years later.

62. With the orphan elephants, Voi, 1990s.

63. Eleanor with the Tsavo orphans.

64. Ithumba orphans in the mud.

65. Myself and David Read.

66. Angela's wedding, 1996.

67. The Nairobi nursery, 2007.

68. Communities visit the orphan project.

69. Nursery, 2009.

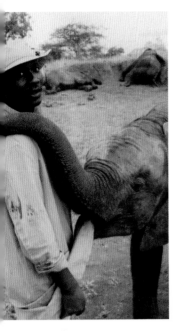

70. Mishak, 2005.

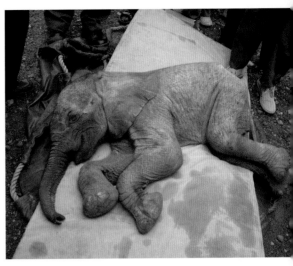

71. Baby Mara just after being rescued.

72. Suguta with keeper Benson.

73. Myself and Wendi, 2011.

74. With my grandchildren. *Back*, Emily, me and Zoe; *front*, Roan and Taru.

75. I am made a Dame Commander of the Most Excellent Order of the British Empire.

76. Jill, 2009.

77. Angela with Makena as a nursery baby.

On our return, the dreaded amalgamation of the National Parks with the Government Game Department was officially enacted by Parliament on 13 February 1976, bringing the National Parks under direct government control. A new organization, known as the Wildlife Conservation and Management Department, immediately took control of all wildlife throughout the country, under the direct jurisdiction of the Ministry of Tourism and Wildlife. Amalgamation will always remain a sinister word for those of us that remember the events of that time. It was the beginning of what turned out to be a tragic, shockingly dark period in the proud history of Kenya's National Parks. For their wild inhabitants, especially rhinos and elephants, who became instant targets, it was the death knell. The ink had hardly dried on the new legislation before National Park funds were frozen, with cheques, outstanding invoices and purchase orders declared invalid. Within a few days the five entrance gates to Tsavo East had run out of tickets and the Park's petrol pumps had run dry. Fortunately David had some fuel stored in metal drums out in the bush, so the Field Force rangers could still remain operational. I sought solace with my orphans, glad to be able to satisfy their needs and enjoy their company.

An inventory officer paid us a visit that would have been amusing had it not been so indicative of the new regime. He floundered around looking confused at the workshop lathe, power drill and other sophisticated equipment that he was unable to even name. When David told him that in order to catalogue the Park's equipment he would have to make a 3,000-mile round trip, expressing the hope that he had brought his own petrol with him, the official took off, never to be seen again. He obviously had not missed the giant trophy tusks still held in the ivory store – especially one pair far larger than those of the legendary Ahamed at Marsabit. A signal arrived from Nairobi the following day with instructions that any big tusks still held in the Tsavo East stores be delivered immediately to a specific government office in Nairobi.

With these changes came a new position for David, a supervisory role over all the National Parks and Reserves as Head of the Planning Unit, focusing on the country's numerous undeveloped National

Reserves. He was allowed to take Tango Papa, the Supercub aircraft and our Toyota pickup, known as the 'Poon wagon' after the lady who had gifted it to us. He was allocated an office within the Ministry at Jogoo House in Nairobi and benefited from a substantial pay rise, the promise of a house within the Nairobi National Park, and he was able to take several rangers to work with him.

When he told me this news David held me tight and I could feel the strength of his arms around me, as if he recognized the need to keep me upright. All I could hear was 'leaving Tsavo, leaving Tsavo, leaving Tsavo' and I felt a part of me die. I cried for days, but as usual David was prepared to turn the page and kept a stiff upper lip, although I knew that the proposed move pained him as much as it did me. For him it meant abandoning thirty years of painstaking work and leaving the elephant and rhino population at the mercy of poachers and their corrupt masters. It also meant leaving our vibrant house and garden that we had nurtured so lovingly, and – most upsetting of all – abandoning our precious orphans to an uncertain future. Our world was collapsing around us, and I did not have David's unflinching courage and strength. I marvelled at his ability to always move forward and focus on what needed to be done next rather than commiserate about the past.

I was deeply afraid for the safety of our precious orphans, knowing that one of the Game Department officers would be taking our place, most of whom were inveterate hunters. I feared for Bunty and her children, living wild just below the offices; for Jimmy and his wives, who were, thankfully, much more independent, and for dear Eleanor, Raru and Bukanezi; for our treasured, almost fully grown rhinos, Pushmi and Stroppie; for our buffalo orphans; for the Honk peacock family and the 100 or so vulturine guinea fowl that paraded around the garden on a daily basis. It would be easy to arrange a good home for the twenty or so peacocks, but not so the resident guinea fowl, which would most likely be seen as 'perks for the pot'. We weren't too worried about the buffalo orphans, as they were pretty much attached to a resident herd that watered at the Voi Safari Lodge and we were confident they would eventually be absorbed there with relative ease.

Our immediate concern focused on Pushmi and Stroppie, who although still young and dependent carried a small fortune on their noses. By now rhinos everywhere were in mortal danger, due to the demand and the market price their horns were fetching in the Far East, for their supposed mythical medicinal properties, and from the oil-rich elite emerging in the Middle East, who valued them as invincible dagger handles. Recognizing that the rhinos would be in dire jeopardy, David arranged to relocate Pushmi and Stroppie to the Solio Ranch, where Reudi was happily settled. It was another sad day when Stroppie and Pushmi boarded their travelling crates, enticed by sugarcane handouts. David and I accompanied them on the long journey to Solio, stopping twice en route to cool their bodies down with water and feed them freshly cut vegetation.

We returned home to the unenviable task of packing up our home and sorting out belongings accumulated over the past thirty years. I was recovering from a gynaecological operation, so I directed proceedings from the sidelines. Eventually it was time to say goodbye – the day I had been dreading with all my heart. To this day I am not sure how I managed to get through those goodbyes – hugging Bunty in the garden for the last time, wrapping my arms around Eleanor, Raru and Bukanezi as they browsed down by the Voi River, and surveying the garden, which I knew would now fall into neglect. The animals could sense my distress; as the cool tips of trunks caressed and investigated my tear-stained face and as I turned to look at them for the last time before leaving, I prayed fervently that they would remain both safe and free.

We hit the road, heading a convoy of five trucks carrying our worldly possessions to our new home. As we entered the Nairobi National Park our spirits lifted, for we passed zebra, wildebeest and other plains animals on the way to the house David had selected for us. It was a relatively new house, previously occupied by the last Warden, but upon arrival it was locked up and the keys were nowhere to be found, nor was anyone who seemed able to help us. Wearily, we set up our tent on the lawn, dined on a tin of sardines and fell asleep to the roaring of not-too-distant lions. It had crossed our minds that the absence of the keys was perhaps intentional, territorial tactics to remind us, as new arrivals, of our place within the pecking order.

The next day, as David went to Ministry Headquarters to tell them we were going to have to break into our house, the keys miraculously turned up after a phone call from the Permanent Secretary. Meanwhile I explored the premises of our new home and much to my disappointment discovered that apart from a glorious pale lilac bougainvillea below the house, the garden was non-existent. I nearly jumped out of my skin when I came across a cage behind the house in which sat a half-grown and very unfriendly leopard, crouching low and snarling at me ferociously, hatred in her startling green eyes. Later, we learned that Lulu had been a particular favourite of the Warden, providing an ongoing attraction for his guests and other curious passers-by, most of whom had never seen a big cat that close. It disturbed me to see her so confined, and when David returned, I implored him to do what he could to improve her situation. The first priority, he said, was to get her more used to our presence by feeding her, so when the Warden called, I offered to relieve him of that responsibility. Over the next weeks, while David got to grips with his office in Jogoo House, I spent a lot of time with Lulu, talking to her gently whenever it was time for a meal. I settled into our new home and started work on the creation of a garden. Here, things grew easily and I found myself enjoying this task, planting some old favourites I had brought from our Voi garden as a nostalgic reminder of our Tsavo home.

David's new job was challenging. He was in charge of twenty National Reserves, covering a staggering 5,237 square miles. Whereas National Parks were areas set aside exclusively for wildlife where humans, other than those working there, had no right to live, National Reserves were areas in which wildlife was protected but resident humans took priority. He set up files on each one, detailing the date of gazettement, Land Registration number, acreage, expected rainfall, topography and roughly the number of people who called it home, plus what he called 'shoats', i.e. cattle, sheep and goats counted during his aerial surveys. Since the office he had been allocated in Jogoo House was unsatisfactory, we converted one of our bedrooms so that he could work at home and I could be on hand to help out. From a series of meetings with the local chiefs during his air recces, he had a good idea of what needed to be done, and he seemed energized by his new role despite the ongoing cramping between his shoulder blades. Nevertheless, he was in good spirits. We both knew he had a Herculean task ahead in designing the infrastructure needed to make each Reserve viable for tourism, but David was never daunted by a challenge and embraced his new role with commitment and dedication.

After a few desk-bound weeks, David was ready for our first field assignment – the Lake Bogoria National Reserve – an area of 26,441 acres. Lake Bogoria itself was one of several soda lakes cradled within the Great Rift Valley, surrounded by high escarpments and hills. The geysers along its shoreline, which blew pungent steam and boiling water high into the air, were reputed to be rich in minerals and detoxifiers. Hot springs bubbled along the lake edges as well as in the middle of the lake itself, which was home to a multitude of greater and lesser flamingoes, turning it bright pink and contributing a graceful beauty to its stunning setting. To the local people, the lake was an eerie place where, by night, they believed the murmuring of the flamingoes was the ghostly voices of ancestral spirits. President Kenyatta was a regular visitor who came to the lake to benefit from the medicinal properties of its natural saunas.

We set off for Lake Bogoria in the Poon wagon, now equipped with long-range petrol tanks. I had suggested that we flew, but David quietly vetoed this. I was beginning to notice that he was reluctant to allow me to fly with him of late, finding any excuse as to why it was not possible. During his first months in Nairobi he had flown on many reconnaissance sorties and I had asked to come with him, but he had told me each time that he would probably be accompanied by an official. On his return, I would learn that in fact he had flown alone. I was disturbed by this and wondered about the possibility that perhaps he knew more about his cramping than he had confided in me, but there was no point in trying to argue with David once his mind was made up. Besides, I would enjoy the additional time we would be spending when travelling by road.

On the way to the lake we somehow found ourselves caught up in the presidential motorcade, escorted by police and motorcycle outriders. We sped along in the midst of the convoy, all other traffic halted by the roadside and people standing beside their parked vehicles as a mark of respect. I began to panic. 'Enjoy the moment,' laughed David. 'It's not often we can enjoy being VIPs, so just wave and watch the amazement on the faces of those we happen to know.' Sure enough, as we neared Naivasha town there were many people we knew standing by their cars, and as we swept by with a royal wave, the puzzled looks of sheer disbelief made us both laugh. Nevertheless I was uneasy, fearing the possible repercussions should we be found out, but it was a glorious day, with herds of zebra grazing along the highway and David was in a jovial mood. As we approached Nakuru town I saw my old primary school up on a hill, with its imposing clock tower and red tiled roof, and when we reached the tree-lined promenade leading to the State House, the President and his escorts turned right, while we merely drove straight on without anyone even noticing.

We arrived at the shores of Lake Bogoria in the late afternoon. The atmosphere of the brooding lake, combined with the whoosh and hiss of the steam jets, and the toss of the boiling water, made us feel like spectators at the creation of the world. Strolling along the lake edge we discussed names for the steam jets, standing in the spray of the largest geyser to inhale the supposedly medicinal vapour. The geyser gurgled and growled as it hurled boiling water aloft, and we examined the curious red-coloured algae clustered around its edge until the first stars began to appear in the dome of the sky and it was time to return to camp for an evening meal under the stars. Retiring for the night, David pulled my camp bed close to his, saying, 'Since we are obviously going to spend so much of our time like this, I am going to have to design a double camp bed!'

Breakfast the next day was a culinary first – an egg boiled in the boiling waters of one of the smaller geysers, after which David embarked on a foot recce of the area he envisaged for the proposed new Headquarters. Then we went to meet the local councillors, who welcomed us warmly, treating us to a convivial lunch of *nyama choma*, charcoaled roasted meat, after which David showed them the site he had selected. They confirmed their willingness to relinquish the land and were so enthusiastic about the entire project that David was somewhat taken aback. Meanwhile, I busied myself gathering fallen flamingo feathers for Angela, as she loved piecing them together on plywood, creating colourful feather-flower pictures that she offered for sale to family and friends to earn herself some pocket money. Like my mother, she had been endowed with natural artistic talent and was also resourceful, just like her father.

David was extremely upbeat about the way things were going. We spent the next day exploring the lake, enjoying a leisurely picnic beneath a huge fig tree, where I shed my shoes to paddle in a stream but had to jump out swiftly as a hungry leech attached itself to my leg. David had to persuade it to release its grip by lighting a match and warming its rear end. Later, while lying together in the shade of the fig tree, David talked fondly of Tsavo and said that when we got back to Nairobi, he would take the plane down to have a look at how the Park was faring. 'Can I come?' I asked, almost knowing what the answer would be before it was even spoken. 'No,' came the now usual reply, 'since I will be circling low over the Park in the heat of the day and it will be hot and bumpy.' I didn't press the point, at one level relieved not to have to confront our former home and its many treasured memories only to find it was no longer the same.

On the way back we called on Jonathan Leakey and his wife. Jonathan was the eldest son of the famous palaeontologist Louis B. Leakey, who had been a Trustee of the National Parks. Jonathan was an expert on snakes, milking them for their venom, from which was made the serum that saved victims of snakebite. He and his wife showed us their venomous cobras, mambas and vipers, but just before he fed a living mouse to a huge hairy baboon spider, I found an excuse to leave the room, although I could hear the little mouse shriek with pain as the spider pierced it with poisonous fangs before feasting on its body juices. Later that evening, after an enjoyable supper with our hosts, David experienced the cramp he had been having of late, but apart from a brief interruption to down some aspirin, he slept well and woke rested the next morning.

During the next phase of our journey we began dreaming of what we would do during our eventual retirement, when, David said, we would be able to make many such excursions and spend as long as we liked in wild places. 'We'll just bring our double camp bed and our tent,' he said, 'and we'll become true nomads, foot-loose and fancy-free, with no responsibilities other than our immediate family. It will be wonderful to spend such carefree days together.' We stopped for lunch on the top of the escarpment, a breathtaking panoramic view below us, and while I prepared the food, David pottered about, returning with a posy of sweet-smelling white and red *Carissa edulis* blossoms – the so-called 'Daphne flower' of my childhood days. He presented the bouquet to me with a deep bow, popping it into the buttonhole of my sweater. I thanked him with a long kiss, more deeply in love with this amazing man than ever before.

At Maralal, we stopped to examine plants and flowers before visiting the local game warden, and as we drove through the game scouts' lines we were greeted with waves and the words 'Saa Nane', which could be heard spreading like wildfire as more and more heads appeared. I was surprised that David was known here, but he clearly was. Later, we set up camp in the forest high above the town, David building a crackling log fire to keep us from the bitter cold at this elevation. It began to rain, so we took ourselves to bed, David insisting that I share his camp bed with him. We fell asleep in a tight squeeze to the music of nocturnal forest animals, wrapped in each other's arms. In the dead of night, David was seized by excruciating chest pains, writhing in agony, drained and pale. I knew at once, as I had secretly suspected all along, that the cramps were symptoms of something much more sinister than I had dared believe. Fumbling in the dim light of the torch, panicked and unsteady, I searched for the pills David had been given. He remained calm, instructing me to look in the medical box for a specially prescribed pill that was to be put beneath his tongue in the event of a severe cramp. Once this was done, the pain subsided and we held each other through the rest of that terrible night, a night that haunts me to this day. When I suggested that he could be suffering a heart attack, he turned away. 'God knows, but whatever it was, it was very unpleasant.' In the morning

I suggested we return to Maralal town and contact the Flying Doctor service, Peter or Bill through the Game Department radio network, but David would have none of it, asserting that he felt better. He did tell me that the pills he had taken, the ones that I thought had been prescribed for cramps, had in fact been given to him in case of 'mild angina'. I tried to argue, but I could see by the set of his jaw that it was useless to press him further. He turned to me and said quietly, 'If I'm not going to be able to live the sort of life I want and do the things I like, then I would rather just meet my Maker and go.' I knew that he meant it, but I still could not bring myself to even contemplate that what he said might be true.

So we set off to the final meeting with the Maralal councillors, as though nothing was amiss. During the meeting only I knew that David was in pain, due to the flexing of his jaw muscles and his greyish pallor. When we returned to the car he asked for another pill, and as the pain gradually fell away, he told me how much he had enjoyed our time together and how the meetings and plans for the Reserves could not have gone better. The road from Maralal to Rumuriti was, to put it mildly, diabolical. We bounced, bumped and banged our way from one pothole to the next, so much so that all the crockery in the lunch box was smashed, as were the binoculars and David's prized large camera lens. I was relieved when we arrived at Thomson's Falls, for the road from that point on was tarred. While at Thomson's Falls, David insisted on negotiating the steep slope to get a better view of the 300-foot cascading waterfall, named in honour of the early explorer Joseph Thomson, and I reprimanded him for doing this, noticing that he stumbled on the way back, ashen and drawn. He asked for another tablet and I remonstrated with him as we set off once more, but he was silent.

Finally we hit the outskirts of Nairobi, and I suggested that we should drive straight to Nairobi Hospital, but he adamantly ruled this out, saying that all he needed was a warm bath and his own bed, promising however to ring the doctor as soon as we got in. Once at home, uncharacteristically, he allowed me to do the unpacking and went straight in for a bath, during which an old friend from our Tsavo days popped by. David emerged in his dressing-gown to greet him and in the comfort of our living room, over whisky and soda, they discussed the Rhodesian Unilateral Declaration of Independence. Leaving them to it, I rang John McCaldin, our doctor, who asked to speak to David directly. Dr McCaldin said he would come to the house if David was worried, but David assured him that this was not necessary and that he would come to his rooms first thing in the morning. Dr McCaldin thought that the symptoms suggested a gall-bladder problem.

Once our guest had left, I suggested David go to bed, and although it was early, I turned in myself, feeling utterly exhausted from the night before. Sick with anxiety and worry, I just wanted to get through the night so that we could get to the doctor. David was composed and relaxed, insisting that I lie with him while he read. I was overwhelmed with relief that we had made it back in one piece, and that help was not far off. I fell into an exhausted, jittery sleep.

14. Grief

'He lieth under the shady trees in the covert of the reed, and fens.
The shady trees cover him with their shadow; the willows
of the brook compass him about.'

– Job 40: 21, 22

During the night David asked for another pill, and as he placed it under his tongue, he asked the time. It was 11.30 p.m. Before I could answer, he fell back gasping, his eyes rolling back in his head. I knew at once that he was dying.

My hands shaking uncontrollably, I fumbled for the phone and called the doctor at his home number, but there was no reply. I dialled Sheila instead and stammered out a cry for help. Lifting David's head, I tried slapping his cheeks but he didn't respond, so I put my mouth to his and desperately attempted to breathe life back into him. His eyes were open and unseeing. I dashed to the back door, calling out in my distress until Mwangangi, our loyal member of staff who had come with us from Voi, emerged, bleary-eyed. As soon as he saw David, he jumped into action; together we hauled the mattress off the bed with David on it and carried him to our station wagon, hurriedly putting down the back passenger seat so that he could lie in the back with his legs sticking through the boot door. Mwangangi sat holding David's lifeless body to stop him falling out of the car. Barefoot and in my dressing-gown, I drove to the Nairobi National Park Service entrance, yelling for someone to come and open the gate, and it seemed an eternity before anyone did. At breakneck speed I made straight for the hospital, screeching to a halt just outside the casualty section. I ran in, shouting for help, and though it was only a few moments later, it seemed like an eternity before a stretcher, an oxygen cylinder, a doctor and nurses were mobilized and hurrying past me to the car to collect David.

For the next twenty minutes everyone battled to try and restore him, and as they did so, I went out into the dark car park and prayed to God to please spare him and not let him die. When the doctor came and stood beside me, I did not need any words because his silence and his arm round my shoulders said it all. The world seemed to stop turning. I was in such deep shock that I felt as though I would faint. The doctor was talking, but I had no idea what he was saying. I wanted to die as well.

They took me to him. He was lying on a concrete slab clad only in his kikoy. He looked his handsome self, peaceful as though just sleeping. But when I bent to kiss him for the last time, I was shocked to feel that his body had already turned clammy and cold, and as reality began to dawn, so came the tears. The nurses covered his face with a blanket and I began to cry, silently and slowly, overcome with grief as I turned to leave the room. Upon hearing the doctor mutter 'post mortem' I spun round, for I could not bear the thought of David being hacked around. I pleaded through my tears to spare us this indignity. The cause of death was surely obvious – massive cardiac arrest. The doctor promised to prevent any interference. It was distressing enough that David was going to be taken to the mortuary. I wanted to take him home with me.

By now the sun was beginning to rise above a distant horizon, the world around me stirring to greet a new morning. I was outraged that life could go on as normal. Startled, my thoughts turned to Angela, away at boarding school in South Africa, not knowing that her beloved father had died. It was impossible to think that David would never see his Pip again, not live to see her grow up and become a woman. I needed to speak to Betty and my parents and ask them to go to the school to break the news to Angela and bring her back to me. A feeling of immense hopelessness seized me – how could I face the future alone, without my soulmate by my side? This wasn't supposed to happen now – David was only fifty-seven, I was only forty-three, and we had just spent many happy hours talking about our retirement plans. All our dreams for the future were now as nothing.

Sheila and Jim came to the hospital and took me back to their home. A deep weariness seized me, and as I sank into an exhausted sleep, a strange calmness overcame me as I realized that nothing worse could ever befall me in my lifetime. For too long I had suppressed what I suspected – that David's cramps were a manifestation of something grave – and now at least that nagging worry was ended. I knew that he would want me to have courage, to face the coming days with his spirit of moving forward, and in a dazed semi-consciousness, I vowed to do my best for his sake.

The following days were a blur of messages, flowers, tears, people and more people, letters, telegrams and a great void in my heart. Betty arrived with a grief-stricken Angela, who had mysteriously sensed that her father had died even before being told. When she, Jill and I were reunited, at least we had each other, and I felt less alone. My father's health had deteriorated and my parents were unable to travel to the funeral, but Betty and her family came to be with me. Actually, everyone rallied round, not least the officials of the Wildlife Conservation and Management Department, who could not have been kinder, as stunned as anyone by David's sudden death. The director assured me that I could occupy the National Park's house for as long as I needed, a compassionate gesture that I appreciated enormously.

The Karen church was filled with so many people that they spilled out into the courtyard and beyond, from all walks of life, and from all races. It seemed as if time were suspended, all these people brought together to share in my grief – it was incredibly touching. As my daughters, sisters and I walked past the sea of eyes to the front row, Jim filled the church with soothing organ music and the scent of the many wreaths and bouquets permeated the air. David would have liked this combination of pathos and beauty. His coffin was brought to the church in the back of our treasured Poon wagon, draped in the National Parks flag that had once proudly fluttered above the dak bungalow offices in Tsavo. It seemed right that it should be buried with him to mark the end of an era – the end of an era in more ways than one.

My husband's coffin was carried in to the tune of 'Amazing Grace', borne by his closest family, friends and colleagues. The padre – an old school friend of Peter and Bill's from their Patch days – gave a moving sermon drawing on the books of Isaiah and Job, highlighting how God cared about the natural world and his creation that inhabited such places as Tsavo. He reassured us that David would find favour with the Creator for devoting his life so selflessly to Nature's protection. 'Thou shall not hurt nor destroy in all my holy mountain' were the words from Isaiah that I chose to be engraved on the huge Tsavo rock that would later be brought to the cemetery in Nairobi to provide the headstone for David's grave. The address was followed by 'Abide with Me', most of us now in tears, and David was carried out to the signature tune of the old King's African Rifles, 'Funga Safari' ('Pack for Safari'), a tune he often used to hum as we set off to do what he loved most – being out in the bush.

David was laid to rest in the Langata Cemetery. When the coffin was lowered into the ground, I broke down – my daughters the only comfort to me at this, the bleakest of my life's moments – as I tossed the soil into the ground. We gathered for a wake at Sheila's house, and I thought if only David could have seen all this admiration, respect, fondness and love for him, as well as the disbelief and grief, he would have been so touched. I returned to his graveside the next day and had a quiet, private talk with him as I planted a seedling of the yellow-barked fever tree that his friend Leslie Brown had germinated for me. This type of acacia epitomized the places David loved most, a vibrant tree that Rudyard Kipling had immortalized in one of his Just So stories, 'The Elephant's Child'.

Angela, Jill and I went to my parents, who had returned to be in Grandpa Webb's little bungalow in Malindi. It was a huge comfort to be with them at this hour of need, and I unburdened my heart to them. When it was time for them to return to South Africa with the girls, I headed to Nairobi with Sheila to begin the painful process of picking up the pieces of my shattered life. I was worried about earning a living – having no wage or pension to speak of – and about where I would set up another home for Angela and me. Before too long another official would take over the Nairobi Park house that David and I had shared. I even thought about asking the Director if I could erect a tent in the Park until I sorted out my life, but miraculously, Granny Webb's dictum – 'when one door closes another opens' – came true and within a few months I was offered both work and a place to live permanently.

Bob Poole, Director of the Nairobi Office of the African Wildlife Foundation, commissioned me to write wildlife articles for the magazine of the country's Wildlife Clubs. These had been established in many of Kenya's schools to generate awareness among local children of the value of their wildlife heritage, wildlife having hitherto been viewed in negative terms, simply as a nuisance, out to destroy crops and kill the odd pedestrian on the footpaths of the forest. Peter, Bill, John Sutton and other close friends managed to obtain permission from the Government for me to erect a small dwelling in the Nairobi National Park so that I could continue working with the wildlife. Mrs Poon, the kind Samaritan who had gifted the Poon wagon to David, generously stepped in to provide the wherewithal to erect a small Timsales prefabricated wooden bungalow for me. All the while I was convinced that David was still nearby, and this was reinforced when I found myself in the house of a spiritualist. I had never met her before and she had no idea who I was, but she described David accurately, assuring me that he was with me.

Peter and I chose a spot for my new house. The one stipulation made by the Wildlife authorities was that my new home had to be constructed within range of the existing Nairobi National Park power and water points, so we chose a place on some rocky terrain overlooking a small seasonal watercourse about 200 yards from the home I now occupied. I liked the idea of being near a little stream, even if it only carried floodwaters at certain times of the year, for having lived so long in arid country, the possibility of the soothing sound of running water was very appealing. The actual site for my new home was bleak, devoid of shade trees and surrounded by low croton bushes and rock. But the Park forest was not far off, and my brother pointed out the advantage of having a ready-made rock seam as a firm foundation for the building. At that point in time I would have been content to be anywhere, or in anything, as long as the natural world was within reach, for all likes and dislikes were nothing more than trivia. I was profoundly grateful to the Kenyan Government for granting me the unique privilege of residing in the Nairobi National Park, my chance at least for stability.

People were immeasurably kind to me during this period and I was profoundly moved by their solicitous empathy. Bob Poole, Peter, Bill and John Sutton were there to support me every inch of the way. Unbeknownst to me they were hatching another plan that would end up shaping the rest of my life. Through Bob Poole and the African Wildlife Foundation, they initiated the David Sheldrick Memorial Appeal, aimed at disbursing the stream of donations in David's memory and to solicit additional funds in support of conservation projects. The response was amazing, and Bob suggested that I head a small committee to identify projects that would have had David's blessing. I was delighted to oblige – proud and deeply touched by the legacy David had left. His accomplishments remained very much alive in the mindset of people all around the world. Tragically, just a few months after David's death, Bob Poole was himself killed in a car crash on the Mombasa road – another good man snatched from the conservation world who, like David, was far too young to die. His death came as another great blow to me, especially as he had been with me just the day before, and had told me that his parents were long-lived, so he would be at the helm of the African Wildlife Foundation to oversee the David Sheldrick Memorial Appeal for many years to come.

It took a year before my Timsales house was ready to occupy. I watched it being erected, as it was so close to where I was living. During the construction the foreman, Mr Muturi, and I became good friends, discussing a great many things, from the Mau Mau emergency to the recent accession of Daniel Arap Moi, the new President of Kenya, appointed after the death of Jomo Kenyatta in 1978. Mr Muturi very kindly ensured that I had bookcases to house David's collection, shelves on which to place my ornaments, and a large fireplace in the lounge to add warmth on cold bleak nights. He was kindness itself to me.

On moving day, Mwangangi, Mr Muturi and I laboriously manhandled all my belongings through the barbed wire fence that segregated the Park Staff compound from the Park proper. My first night alone in the new house was particularly lonely. Jill was in Namibia, and Angela had recently returned to school. I longed to have a piece of Tsavo with me, so the next day I asked the Director of Wildlife, Daniel Sindiyo, whether when next a lorry was coming from Tsavo it could possibly bring some flat Galana rocks. He agreed, and when the rocks arrived, Mr Muturi organized for them to be laid on the verandah. Much later on, when I needed an office attached to the house, he very kindly built it for me, lining it with cedar panels so that it reminded me of Cedar Park.

I sourced mineralized sediment from the shores of Lake Magadi, another of the Rift Valley's extremely saline lakes, and spread it on the rocks near the Park forest for the animals to enjoy, since Nairobi Park was deficient in certain minerals craved by larger species such as rhino, buffalo and giraffe. I noticed that the rocky terrain between my house and the Park forest served as the path for many wild creatures en route from the forest to the plains below, so giraffe, buffalo and rhino appreciated the salt lick, as did elands, bushbuck and a small impala herd that I watched with a deep and aching nostalgia. The wild animals were my solace, my companions and my sanity, and because of them I was never entirely alone, at least during the hours of daylight. However, the nights were long, empty and very lonely without David. At such times I thought about the elephants and felt humbled, knowing how stoically they dealt with the loss of loved ones on an almost daily basis, how deeply they grieved but how they did so with courage, never forgetting the needs of the living. Their example gave me the strength I needed to 'turn the page'.

I kept myself busy during the day, writing the wildlife articles, passing on all that David had taught me about animals and opening my eyes to the wildlife that lived around me. I fed the birds, enjoying them as they became tamer, lining up each afternoon for their daily handout of mealworms and crumbs. Some that I named the 'Chippy Chips' included the robin chats, tropical boubous, yellow-vented bulbuls and an olive thrush that knocked at my window each morning. I was amused by the warthog family living in a burrow nearby who were quick to take advantage of my presence as protection from predators. When the mother pig appeared with her one remaining tiny piglet hobbling along holding a broken leg off the ground, I was in a quandary as to what to do, hesitant to alert the Wildlife authorities for fear that the piglet would be taken from its mother and would end up as an exhibit in the rather dubious zoo, or whether I should look after the mother and piglet myself. In the end I fell back on David's philosophy of 'when in doubt, don't', feeling it was better for both mother and baby to remain together.

The piglet's leg healed and, apart from a slight limp, Grunter – as I subsequently named her – grew up to lead a normal wild life and, in fact, became one of the main players in the ongoing warthog drama which taught me a great deal, revealing many things about warthog life unknown then to the scientific world. The drama involved the 'Ever Hopefuls', another family comprising a mother pig, her four piglets and a daughter from the previous litter chosen to be the nanny. Warthogs give birth to only four piglets at a time, and for the first three weeks of life they hide their babies away, their presence given away only by the mother's elongated nipples. What I didn't know was that as soon as babies are brought out of hiding, they immediately become the target of infanticide by all other warthogs in the area. Despite her slight handicap, Grunter displayed a sinister cunning in attempting to exterminate every new generation of the Ever Hopefuls, hiding in ambush and bursting out to seize, slaughter and eat one of the newborn piglets. Such cannibalistic tendencies came as a somewhat distressing surprise. I knew that as omnivores, pigs like meat as a small supplementary part of their mainly vegetarian diet, but I really didn't know that it included eating babies of their own species!

I came to understand that an inexperienced first-time mother is at risk of losing most, if not all, of her litter. However, like domestic pigs, warthogs are extremely clever, and more experienced mothers only expose their babies at a time when there are not many other pigs around. The tiny piglets soon learn that in order to survive they must run in tight circles, which the adult pigs find difficult to negotiate. Assuming they can avoid being murdered during the first few weeks of exposure, things soon settle down and the new piglets become accepted as part of the resident warthog community. Second time around, the wiser mother will select one of her litter, normally a female, to act as nanny to the next litter, to help protect and rear her mother's new babies. How the nanny is chosen and her subsequent devotion to the task she has been allotted remains one of nature's most intriguing mysteries. The nanny will even sacrifice her own life protecting her mother's piglets from others, yet her immediate siblings will be among those bent on infanticide. Once the nanny is mature and ready to breed herself, she will synchronize her heat with that of the mother so that they both give birth to four piglets around the same time. They then share all the offspring, cross-suckling them and caring for them as if their own. Should one of them fall victim to a predator, the other adult will take over all the piglets.

I named the Ever Hopefuls' nanny 'Little Ever Hopeful', and the mother 'Fat Ever Hopeful', and I watched as they successfully reared several litters of piglets and, with my assistance, managed to avoid Grunter. But then disaster struck. One day Little Ever Hopeful appeared in a pitiful state with a wire snare tight around her snout. With the help of Mwangangi we managed to throw a blanket over her head so that the snare could be removed, but in the meantime Fat Ever Hopeful had taken seven of the eight piglets out of their burrow and run into a pride of lions not far from my house. Later bloodstains on the ground remained the only evidence of the tragedy, since the lions had either devoured or carried off the entire family. Meanwhile, Little Ever Hopeful, relieved of the snare around her snout, returned to the resident burrow where the runt of the litter, Tom Thumb, was still in hiding. In due course she appeared with him, whereupon Grunter did her utmost to do him in, but with some help from us he managed to survive and grew up to be both a fine boar and the constant companion of Little Ever Hopeful, his mother.

When she gave birth again there was no female nanny to call on, so Tom Thumb stood in – albeit reluctantly – something I found extraordinary, since normally males were extremely aggressive towards any newborn piglets. There were many amusing occasions when we could see that he did not exactly relish this new role; days when he quite obviously had second thoughts and would leave the piglets to try to follow his peers, but he would hesitate, turn back and resume his nanny duties, tolerating an exuberant welcome back from his adoring litter – with high-pitched squealing and grunting as they clustered around nuzzling him.

During my writing assignment for the Wildlife Clubs I had to read many scientific papers, and due to my first-hand field experience I discovered that some of the content was definitely flawed. I attributed this to the fact that science precluded researchers from interpreting animal behaviour in an 'anthropomorphic' way, and as such they came up with complicated explanations as to why an animal was behaving in a certain way, when, in fact, the answer was pretty simple. One simply had to compare it to the likely response of the human animal if subjected to the same set of circumstances.

Just before he died, David had cooperated with Simon Trevor in making a documentary to highlight the extent of the poaching menace in Tsavo. Simon had been one of our assistant wardens but had since become a documentary maker. Now Somali 'Shifta' gangs armed with AK 47s were gunning down entire elephant herds within Tsavo, one of the victims our precious orphan Bukanezi, who died alongside sixty other wild elephants slaughtered en masse in the Voi River Valley, not far from the Voi Park Headquarters. I was even more upset to learn that Eleanor was being driven to the roadside and made to stand beside the busy tourist routes so that her corrupt keepers could extract rewards from passing tourists. Tsavo, like all National Parks, was fast becoming a 'no-go zone'. Tourism had all but evaporated as the situation became more desperate.

To Simon, and to those of us who cared about Tsavo, there seemed just one course of action left and that was to sensitize the new President, Daniel Arap Moi, to the catastrophe that was unfolding on a daily basis. We knew, of course, that Simon's film, *Bloody Ivory*, would be controversial, since it highlighted the failings of the new Government department in charge of wildlife, but we also knew it was our duty to reveal what was taking place and that David would expect no less of us. With help from Richard Leakey, who was then in charge of the National Museums and knew President Moi personally, an interview was arranged at State House.

Simon had kindly agreed that his film be the fledgling David Shel-drick Memorial Appeal's first fund-raiser, dedicated to saving Kenya's black rhinos from extinction. As David had predicted, the thirty rhi-nos we had left in Tsavo, who used to drink regularly at the Voi Safari Lodge, were now no more, their horns in far-off lands. There had been around 8,000 rhinos in Tsavo out of 20,000 countrywide but by now they were mostly all gone, with just a few outliers holed up in thickets widely separated from one another, effectively a dying breed. Being fiercely territorial, the few remaining isolated survivors would never meet up to be able to perpetuate the species, so something needed to be done rapidly.

Peter sought overseas funding to establish Kenya's first ring-fenced official rhino sanctuary, electrically fencing Lake Nakuru National Park, which had recently attained National Park status as a flamingo and water bird spectacle. Made secure, it could duplicate as a rhino breeding sanctuary to accommodate the few black rhino survivors – those that could be captured and relocated so that they could come together and breed successfully. On the appointed day we gathered at what was now State House, where Eleanor had walked when it was the official residence of Kenya's colonial gover-nors. Richard introduced us and the President welcomed us warmly. He was a tall man with striking amber eyes. The film cer-tainly made an impact on him, for he hailed from a small tribe around the shores of Lake Baringo, where rhinos and elephants had long been extinct, so it was apparent that he knew very little about either species. However, he listened attentively and we left feeling that our mission had been accomplished, because not only did he agree to attend the première of *Bloody Ivory* as our guest of honour but he also provided a fitting statement for inclusion in the pro-gramme.

I dreaded the première. Not only did I fear public speaking, but I just did not know how I could cope when faced again with moving images of David, how I would be able to hold back the tears seeing my Tsavo home and garden, with scenes of Shmetty, Bunty, and the other garden orphans, as well as Eleanor and the elephant and rhino orphans. The ordeal took on even more momentous proportions when our guest of honour failed to turn up and the audience became restless. At first we were told that the President had been delayed, but eventually it became obvious that he would not be able to get there in time.

Somehow I managed to stumble through my speech and endure the film, closing my eyes to maintain my composure when David or the garden orphans appeared on the screen. Afterwards, in the foyer, people crowded around me, many in tears. I responded to their kind words as though from the depths of a dream. It was only when David Read, David's best friend from his Second World War years in Abyssinia and Burma, came and hugged me that I felt stronger. Now that he was Nairobi-based, he had decided to make it his mission to cheer me up. David Read had been a frequent visitor to Voi, and I never tired of hearing him talk about his incredible childhood, running wild with his Masai peers while his mother struggled in a small shop at Narok in Masailand. His first language had been Masai, and his best friend a Masai boy who was now a tribal elder. He had a twinkle in his eye and a ready smile, providing a precious link with my David.

Some months later, there came another surprising development. A cardinal from the Vatican approached the Kenyan Government proposing a visit from the Pope, adding that the Holy Father would like to bless an elephant while in Kenya. With the Tsavo orphans in mind, the Director of Wildlife asked for my help. As no young elephant was available at the time – Eleanor was now grown up – I saw this as a golden opportunity to highlight the rhino's predicament instead. Furthermore, I knew of the perfect recipient of such a blessing – a newborn orphan rhino at Lewa Downs, near Isiola in the north of the country. My advice had been sought when she looked as if she might die, having been wrongly fed on cow's milk rather than the tried and tested formula that I had in fact already passed on to the management at Lewa. It surprised me that they had chosen to take the advice of their local vet rather than mine, since I had already successfully reared four orphaned rhinos on Lactogen without any difficulty.

The Director approved of my suggestion and told the visiting cardinal, who promised to get back to us. However, five months passed

before he did so, by which time the Lewa rhino had trebled its size –
rhinos develop twice as fast as an elephant and live half as long.
Nevertheless, on the assumption that she would be as docile as our
Tsavo orphans and that the Pope would simply fly to Lewa and per-
form the blessing there, I figured it would be fine. Not so: I was told
in no uncertain terms that the Pope would bless the rhino not at
Lewa, but rather in the Masai Mara, Kenya's showcase tourist attraction. My heart sank, for this would entail moving the young rhino
under sedation, always a risky business, and although I protested, the
Director was adamant that this had been determined at a high level
and he was banking on Peter and me to make it happen.

Peter was by now in charge of the Wildlife Department's rhino
programme, so together we drove to the sanctuary at Lewa, where
we were introduced to Samia, the soon-to-be-blessed orphan, and
the lady who had raised her, Anna Merz, to whom the rhino was
firmly attached. We knew from our own experience that unaccom-
panied baby rhinos feel severely threatened without the protection of
a 'mother', as they risk being killed by the wild rhino residents until
known by scent, and that rhino orphans tend to bond with the person that feeds them – in this case, Anna Merz. I had learned the hard
way that it was prudent to get an orphaned rhino attached to several
people, and I could see that Samia was extremely jumpy when Anna
was not actually physically with her.

Just two weeks remained until the papal visit, during which time
Samia would have to become a great deal calmer if she were to be
trusted in the presence of the Holy Father. As she was, she was far too
feisty to risk close contact with the Pope and his entourage. After a
great deal of discussion, Peter and I decided that there was just one
course of action – to separate Anna from her rhino immediately, fly
the calf to the Mara and install a surrogate Pope, clad in white robes,
to set about getting her used to that sort of presence for the big day.
Understandably, this suggestion was greeted with outrage, so it was
under a dark cloud that we nevertheless left by air, along with the
sedated Samia and a vet in attendance.

As soon as we arrived in the Mara, an officer from the Wildlife
Department, dressed in a white sheet, began the process of training

and taming. I trebled Samia's milk ration and gave the papal substitute ample stock of rhino treats to reward for good behaviour. It was with mounting anxiety that we went back home, anxious for daily feedback as to how things were going. At first the trainer had to be pretty agile to avoid being flattened, but after a few days the increased milk rations made Samia more replete and she became a lot calmer. Within a week she was much less jumpy around strangers and, most importantly, calm around the white-clad figure whenever he approached, anticipating both her milk and a reward.

On the big day, as the Pope and all the attendant dignitaries flew to the Mara to enact the blessing, Peter and I were nervous wrecks, glued to the radio, hoping against hope that nothing would go amiss. Mercifully, the blessing was an enormous success, although the Pope was advised to stand behind, rather than in front of Samia. The ceremony was televised worldwide, so the plight of the rhinos received the intended publicity, though the downside of the operation was that Anna Merz never spoke to me again, even though her rhino arrived back a lot plumper and calmer.

Meanwhile, as I had feared, Jill's marriage to Alan Craven had not worked out and they had separated. She returned to Kenya to be with me, and with the help of friends we erected a small rustic hut for her near my Timsales home. It meant a great deal to me to have Jill back, not only for the congenial company she provided, but also because she was equally dedicated and committed to the wildlife cause, happy to lead a simple eco-friendly existence surrounded by nature. She got a part-time job with a friend who operated a safari business, devoting the rest of her time to the many orphans I now seemed to be acquiring – in particular two baby duikers, retrieved from wheatfields up-country during the harvest period. Elspeth's Huxley's novel *The Flame Trees of Thika* was about to be made into a television series, and the cast for the film included wild orphans as well as a host of domestic animals. We were asked to loan our little duikers for the duration of the film, and we agreed on condition that Jill could be on hand to look after them. This resulted in her being offered the job of general animal supervisor, and so our duikers were set to make their on-screen debut.

The filming was a transformative experience for Jill, for not only did she have to look after chameleons, chickens, a rooster, dogs, cats, oxen, mules, horses, a goat and wild birds in cages, but she also became extremely attached to the Frenchman who was in charge of the props. Communicating by means of a dictionary and a lot of improvised sign language, she realized they had a lot in common. When the filming was over he invited her to France, and because Jill had never left Africa, this seemed like a wonderful opportunity to see some of Europe. Having returned the duikers, along with a bare-necked rooster known as the Baron that she didn't want ending up in the pot, she left for an extended overseas holiday.

In the meantime Angela had completed her secondary education and was now studying graphic art at Cape Town University. She had blossomed into a stunning beauty, taking great delight in fashion and enjoying urban living. Angela easily excelled at all she undertook, from sport to anything artistic. I often wondered how David and I had managed to produce such a sophisticated daughter who coped so easily in a city situation.

No sooner had Jill left for France than I received a call from the Director of Wildlife asking me to help with two orphaned baby elephants that had just come into the orphanage at the Park Headquarters, both victims of the rampant poaching that now gripped the country. I was flattered to have even been asked, and after the experience of Shmetty I felt more confident of success, so I promised to do my best. Armed with the formula that had succeeded previously, I drove to the orphanage taking with me a large wine bottle, an egg whisk, scales and a spoon, vital components for preparing feeds for any baby elephant.

The two little elephants had already been named: the baby bull was Juma and the little female, Bibi. Both were no more than a couple of weeks old, their little bodies covered with baby fuzz. The rangers at the orphanage were not terribly enthusiastic about the three-hourly milk feeds throughout the day and night that would be necessary, nor about cleaning the babies' bottoms after runny stools that had to be immediately covered with earth. I requested that clean hay be laid on the concrete floor of two adjoining compartments and that the elephants be taken out during the day to exercise in the yard, at all times accompanied by an attendant.

I soon realized that if there were to be any chance of success, a great deal of hands-on supervision would be needed, especially for the night feeds. Baby elephants are difficult feeders when newborn, and in this respect there were still lessons I had to learn about this particular aspect of their upbringing. At the beginning the rangers, or myself, plus the bottles and their milk, were often sent flying, and endless patience was needed just to get the right quantity of milk down for them to be able to thrive. Hence, every three hours throughout the day and night, I drove the twelve and a half miles to the orphanage to supervise the feeding and be on hand to inspect the fallout at the other end. Baby elephants are extremely fragile, prone to diarrhoea and stomach disorders. They can be fine one day, and dead the next, so these calves needed very careful monitoring and the benefit of experience. As days passed into weeks, and then months, both thrived.

Juma was outgoing and brave and enjoyed teasing the lion in the cage opposite, which watched every movement with blazing yellow eyes. Juma would rush up to the cage with his ears out and head up, enjoying the inevitable reaction. The lion would crouch as though preparing to spring, and when it launched itself at the wire with a loud growl, Juma would hurriedly reverse and tear off in the opposite direction, trailed by Bibi, who was not quite as bold, more easily daunted by their noisy neighbour. In time the attendants began to respond to their charges, who were, of course, enchantingly endearing, and this meant that I could trust them with some of the daytime feeds. However, I did not dare risk the nights, and so for an entire year I made the journey at three-hourly intervals throughout the night to supervise the feeding. Sometimes, rather than drive back home, I would just set my alarm clock and doze in my parked car until it was time for the next feed. It was an exhausting, twilight sort of existence.

I knew that if these two baby elephants were to live, I would have to try to get them to Eleanor in Tsavo. Juma and Bibi were proving an enormous attraction at the orphanage, people flocking in on a daily basis to watch them at play, but once they had celebrated their first birthday, I felt the time was ripe for me to press for them to be sent to Tsavo into Eleanor's custody. Still in a state of semi-captivity, these two little calves would be a welcome diversion for her as she equipped them with the skills needed for a life in the wild. As I feared, this entailed a great deal of persuasion before the authorities capitulated, but in the end they gave their permission. It transpired that before leaving both elephants needed surgical attention – Juma because he had become a bit too bold teasing the lion and had had his trunk bitten, and Bibi because her front foot kept swelling and an X-ray revealed that a splinter of bone was the problem.

Juma managed to unravel all the stitches from the tip of his trunk by using his foot to dislodge them, and little Bibi could not be brought out of anaesthesia, despite the desperate attempts of five of the best vets in Nairobi who were in attendance during the operation. No one had ever anaesthetized a baby elephant before, and had yet to understand just how fragile they are, requiring just a fraction of the dose normally given according to weight – another lesson that could not have been learned any other way. I had been an anxious spectator during what should have been a simple operation on Bibi's foot, but left totally unravelled all over again. Nor did it end there. Eleanor lavished all the love in her great elephant heart on Juma as soon as he arrived in Tsavo, but I hadn't foreseen the enthusiasm of the incumbent warden who, believing Juma to be constipated, decided to give him an enema using a hosepipe and ruptured his gut. Two weeks passed before I was even informed of his death. I loved those little elephants and was barely able to contain my sadness at Juma's demise. He had been perfectly healthy and his constipation was nothing that a little brown sugar would not have sorted out.

These were dark days indeed, for the poaching of wild elephants was still going on unabated throughout the country. In Tsavo, entire herds were still being mown down by the automatic gunfire of Somali intruders, falling victim to Wakamba poisoned arrows, or even killed for their tusks by corrupt elements within the Wildlife Department that had embarked on a get-rich-quick crusade. There appeared to be no end to the carnage, and I often felt that perhaps it was a blessing David never lived to see what was taking place in the Park he had established with such sweat and toil and passion. But then, I would think, were he still here, he would have moved heaven and earth to get something done about it.

A heartening development came with the reappointment of Perez Olindo, who had been the National Parks Director during David's latter years and who was returned to take charge of the corrupt Wildlife Conservation and Management Department. It was not long before another request came my way – to help with a rescued baby elephant retrieved from a deep erosion gully and now at the Maralal Safari Lodge. I agreed, but asked Perez whether I could have the elephant at my home, since I simply could not face another year of three-hourly nocturnal drives to the main gate orphanage. In due course the orphan arrived, coinciding with the arrival of David Read, who happened to turn up as promised in order to 'cheer me up'. He suggested that the little bull elephant be named Olmeg – the Masai word for 'an outsider' – since he had originated from tribal lands occupied by the Samburu people, who, although close cousins of the Masai, sharing a very similar language, were considered by the true Masai as 'outsiders'.

Baby Olmeg was not in good shape, having been fed by the well-meaning manager at Maralal Lodge on cow's milk and grated carrot, neither of which had done his tummy any good. He also had a seriously infected umbilicus, which Jill – now returned from France – and I did our best to clean out with hydrogen peroxide. We fed him what remained of Juma and Bibi's powdered Similac, and set about trying to source more. We urgently needed a place to accommodate our new orphan. All we had was the little stone chicken house that Jill and I had thrown together out of rough rock for the Baron, the *Flame Trees of Thika* bare-necked rooster, who now had several wives. There was nothing for it but to relegate the Baron and his wives to a box in the kitchen so that Olmeg could occupy the chicken house. This was a disaster – he bellowed constantly, clearly feeling claustrophobic, until we could stand it no longer and had to let him out. We tried exercising him around the car park for half an hour or so at a time in order to tire him out, but this didn't work either, for whenever we put him back the bellowing began all over again, added to which he clearly enjoyed the nocturnal outings. In the end, Jill suggested he share her bedroom, despite the fact that he was still producing extremely smelly watery stools. We replaced the carpet on her bedroom floor with a bed of hay and here the little elephant eventually settled down to sleep, after several attempts to climb on to Jill's bed.

The three-hourly feeding schedule eventually took its toll on Jill and me, leaving us so exhausted that we could barely function during the daytime. I asked the Wildlife Director to second us a ranger to help with the daytime feeding so that Jill and I could catch up on some sleep. Unfortunately this didn't work out too well, for the ranger had no empathy for elephants and, sensing this, Olmeg simply refused feeds from him.

Looking after Olmeg was a turning point that made us realize with startling clarity that if we were to continue to help rear elephant orphans at my Nairobi National Park home, we would need to be better equipped in terms of elephant accommodation, milk supplies and keepers whom we could train. Jill and I racked our brains about how to raise the wherewithal to achieve all this, but just as Granny Webb had predicted, a door miraculously opened in the person of Dr Bill Jordan, who happened to be visiting Kenya and came to see Olmeg. He volunteered to fund the building of two elephant stables as well as accommodation for the keepers we wanted to employ. He also suggested that his organization, Care for the Wild International, could continue to help us financially through organizing a fostering programme, whereby in exchange for a modest sum in support of the orphans people would be given a video of the elephants and updates on their progress as well as various gift items. For our part, he asked that Care for the Wild be given access to film the orphans. We accepted Bill's generous offer with alacrity and enormous gratitude.

Fortune favoured us in another extraordinary way. It so happened that Don Barrett was now in charge of Wyeth Laboratories, the manufacturers of the SMA baby milk formula, similar to the Similac I had used for Shmetty, Juma and Bibi. During the Mau Mau emergency he had served as a District Officer at Maralal, where Olmeg had been rescued, and offered to donate milk that was not suitable for human consumption free of charge. In addition to this, various sympathetic local sculptors and artists parted with some of the proceeds from their various exhibitions, and pretty soon we found ourselves on a much sounder footing, especially after having recruited and trained several elephant keepers.

It wasn't long before another little bull elephant calf that David Read named Ol Jori ('the friend') joined Olmeg. And shortly after this we learned of yet another orphan down in Tsavo that had been handed over to Eleanor but was far too young to survive without milk. I wondered how it would be possible to remove the calf from Eleanor's care, but fortunately the Park personnel managed to do so by getting a rope and hauling him out from beneath the bars of Eleanor's stockade, having first diverted her attention with a handout of fruit. We named this orphan Taru after the place of his origin, Tsavo at one time having been known as the Taru Desert. Eleanor had been extremely upset to lose him, and I made a silent promise that as soon as Ol Jori was stable, being older than either Olmeg or Taru, I would send him down to her as a replacement and arrange to complete his milk-dependent period in Tsavo.

It was with the arrival of Taru that we recruited Mischak Nzimbi, a former night-watchman who would evolve into the one keeper all our orphaned elephants loved best. He was endowed with a magical and mysterious empathy that all our elephants detected instantly. Mischak could persuade an elephant that had given up the ghost and simply wanted to die, to make the effort to live. Quite simply, he had the right heart and a quiet and confident demeanour to which they responded with a love that was profound and enduring, right from that day to this.

With what looked like becoming a continuous succession of orphaned elephants and rhinos coming into our care, the African Wildlife Foundation decided that, once the funds donated in memory of David had been allocated, the David Sheldrick Memorial Appeal, which hitherto they had handled as one of their projects, should become an independent entity. So in 1987 it metamorphosed into the David Sheldrick Wildlife Trust, a legal entity in its own right, overseen by a dedicated Board of six Trustees among whom were Jill, Bill and Peter. The previous advisory committee, comprising David's friends, remained as a 'think tank' to guide the Trustees, and it was unanimously decided that I should be the Chairperson of the new Trust. We worked for a long time to forge the right words for our mission statement, and these words seemed to us to embody David's essence and vision, enshrining his legacy, which would continue to live on through the work of the Trust set up in his name:

The David Sheldrick Wildlife Trust embraces all measures that complement the conservation, preservation and protection of wildlife. These include anti-poaching, safeguarding the natural environment, enhancing community awareness, addressing animal welfare issues and providing veterinary assistance to animals in need, as well as rescuing and hand-rearing elephant and rhino orphans along with other species that can ultimately enjoy a quality of life in wild terms.

15. Growth

'Anyone intelligent can make things more complex.
It takes a touch of genius and a lot of courage to move
in the opposite direction.'

– Albert Einstein

Many more orphans came in over the next few years – elephants, rhinos and numerous antelopes, all of whom kept us extremely busy. For us, the rearing of the antelope orphans was straightforward; we had handled so many of different species during the Tsavo days, using a formula based on powdered cow's milk. Whereas elephants were very difficult to rear but easy to rehabilitate, the rhinos were the opposite – easy to rear but extremely difficult to reintegrate back into the wild system, as had been demonstrated by our early Tsavo orphans, Rufus and Reudi. Being an ancient, complex and fiercely territorial species, the rhino orphans usually gave us a good dose of anxiety and heartache, so it was not without trepidation that, at the request of the Wildlife Director of the time, I took on Sam, a three-month-old calf who had been mauled by lions in the Masai Mara Reserve. Even though he was only knee-high and injured, we knew that we would be met with aggression, a rhino's means of defence being attack. So, with nerves of steel, cricket pads strapped to our legs, a stout cushion to absorb his onslaughts, plus a bottle of formula milk, Jill and I took it in turns to set about taming this very injured baby. Being such sensuous animals, rhinos are easy to calm, unable to resist the delicious feel of a good tummy rub, and that, combined with the milk for which Sam was desperate, soon had the desired effect.

Nevertheless, his wounds were severe and needed constant attention, and because he cried piteously every time that Jill or I left him, we decided he needed a stable companion until he was up to joining the orphaned elephants. This came in the form of Boozie, a fat-tailed sheep purchased from a passing herdsman. Sam liked the feel of Boozie's woolly coat, and Boozie found her new role as rhino-sitter to her liking, since it involved a life of luxury seldom meted out to her peers. The two quickly settled in together, and unlike the popular belief that sheep cannot think for themselves, this particular one had plenty of personality. She was no pushover, matching Sam's initial head-butts with retaliatory ones of her own.

In time the two joined the elephant orphans, who were escorted out into the Park forest every morning by their keepers, Boozie's fat tail wobbling temptingly ahead of Sam, who enjoyed burying his nose in it. To begin with the elephants regarded the new pair with deep suspicion, their ears outspread as they rushed around trumpeting and downing small shrubs, while Sam huffed and puffed in return and Boozie merely went about her business, ignoring them completely. This was a wise strategy, because curiosity soon got the better of the elephants and they plucked up the courage to investigate more closely. Soon Sam and Boozie were part of the herd, pausing at the wild rhino middens they encountered on the way so that Sam could leave his own contribution, with Boozie waiting patiently for him to do so before both ran off to catch up with the elephants again. This was, of course, the necessary prerequisite to becoming accepted by the established wild rhino community of the Park.

Before long Boozie and Sam were joined by six-month-old Amboseli, who in fact turned out to be the last living Amboseli rhino, her mother and all others having either been poached for their horns, or become victims of ritual spearing by Masai warriors bent on proving courage and manhood. Amboseli was a National Reserve where wildlife was protected, but shared the land with the local pastoral people, who had always lived alongside the natural world. Lions, the traditional target, had been steadily decimated in Amboseli either for ritual purposes or in retribution for killing livestock.

Having bravely protected the body of her dead mother against hordes of predators and vultures, Amboseli came in much feistier than Sam and was more difficult to tame, but with perseverance she ended up inseparable from him and Boozie, and, like them, part of the orphaned nursery herd. Rhinos develop twice as fast as an elephant and live half as long, so once Sam and Amboseli sensed that they had become members of the wild community they became increasingly independent of the keepers and much more adventurous. So much so that one day they trundled out through the nearby Nairobi Park Service entrance and on to the main road, where Sam held up the startled motorists as he deposited a huge pile of dung right in the middle of the road, after which Amboseli felt compelled to do the same. They then moved off to some kiosks near the post office which sold bananas and green maize and began helping themselves to the kiosk contents. Needless to say, all pedestrians took to their heels, since most urbanites had never even seen a rhino before.

The first we knew about it was when a breathless ranger came panting up to the back door urging us to do something about it. All hands were hurriedly dispatched to round up the two miscreants, tempting them back home with more fruity handouts and locking them back in their night stockades, both having long outgrown their original nursery stables. Like the elephants, rhinos have long memories, and both had now acquired a liking for fruit, or for that matter any tasty morsel, so it came as a shock when I returned home from town one day to find Amboseli firmly ensconced in my tiny kitchen, having just managed to squeeze her huge bulk through the frame of the back door. Never far behind, Sam was standing behind nudging her bottom with his horn, frustrated at not being able to join her as she munched her way through a large bunch of bananas that Sheila had brought me from her garden. There was no chance of Amboseli being able to turn round in the kitchen even had she wanted to, for she filled it entirely, and I knew that if I startled her, she would crash through the adjoining lounge as well as the plate glass door leading on to the verandah, demolishing a large part of my house in the process. Thinking fast, I knew that the first priority was to coerce Sam from the doorway, which was easy to do by sacrificing my edible shopping. I attached a bunch of bananas I had just bought to the end of a broomstick and then, passing the broomstick over Amboseli's back, dangled the bananas just above her prehensile lip. Gradually she reversed inch by inch, and although there was an anxious moment when she got wedged in the back door frame, which groaned and creaked ominously, eventually she popped out backwards. Now I had to act rapidly, so, leaving her tucking into the broomstick bananas, I sprinted round the side of the house to access the kitchen from the front and slam the back door shut before she could get back in. Somewhat shaken, I was mightily relieved that my house was still intact, though it was not for long because a few days later the yard man, in my absence, decided to have a go at driving my Datsun 120Y, reversed up the hill, lost the brakes and ended up slap through the wood panelling at the end, not doing either the garage or my car any good at all. Needless to say he became history.

These were challenging times. Jill and I were unaccustomed to dealing with staff issues and the public, and all the paperwork and accounting demanded of a charitable trust, not to mention negotiating endless Government protocol in a diplomatic manner. Meanwhile Angela, studying graphic art at the University of Cape Town, was earning much-needed pocket money through some part-time modelling work. I will always be eternally indebted to Marti and Illie Anderson, neighbours on Galana Ranch during our Tsavo days, who so generously helped me shoulder the cost of Angela's education, not to mention her tickets back home for the holidays. South Africa was still under the Apartheid regime at the time and as such strictly out of bounds for Kenya residents, so getting her to and from school and university was never straightforward.

During one of her trips back home, Angela worked in the wardrobe department of the epic film *Out of Africa*, after which she decided to embark on a course in make-up artistry and prosthetics. She was – and still is – artistically talented, having inherited this from my mother. From David she had a love of design and from his mother a love of clothes, always taking pride in her appearance. She found it just as easy to paint and change faces as to create an image on canvas. Thankfully, once Nelson Mandela became President of South Africa, the stigma of Apartheid disappeared overnight, and having completed her training she found herself much in demand, attached to photo shoots for magazine editorials and commercials and travelling to stunning locations all over the world, which satisfied her sense of adventure. But, for me, it was always very special when she chose to come back to be with Jill and me.

In time Jill's French boyfriend, Jean-François – known to all simply as JF – decided to move to Kenya on a permanent basis, take on Kenyan citizenship and become an indispensable ingredient of our small and somewhat makeshift team. In between filming assignments, he enlarged and improved Jill's rustic rondavel and gave us much-needed practical help in building additional accommodation for Olmeg and Taru, who were rapidly outgrowing their original stables. As a sideline he set up a safari company called Bullfrog Safaris, in conjunction with an African partner, and managed to snag a few unsuspecting overseas acquaintances who were treated to a somewhat unconventional, but nevertheless exciting, basic safari experience. His was a one-man show, never short of amusing escapades – not least having to repossess the roast from a thieving baboon who took it up a tree, luckily when his clients happened to be occupied elsewhere. They were none the wiser, while they were enjoying their lunch, that a baboon had been there before them. As a Frenchman, JF was proud of his cooking skills, and soon also took overall charge of Jill's outdoor kitchen.

Before his arrival JF had gifted the Trust his bright red Renault 4, affectionately known as the Red Peril, and had had it shipped to Kenya for the use of Jill and the Trust. This proved an enormous help, since previously the only vehicle at our disposal had been my personal car. After arrival in the country, he acquired a second-hand Landcruiser which he turned into his safari workhorse and, as a deterrent to potential carjackers, preferred to leave unwashed. He was a lively character who was never dull and whose presence in the family certainly livened things up a great deal. Being practical, he undertook the maintenance and repair of all the Trust's mechanical equipment, making himself and his vehicle available to the Trust whenever he was not working on a film shoot.

Meanwhile, David Read had become more than just a friend. I was not unsusceptible to the advances of a handsome man in the absence of the one I had lost, although David Read could never come close to replacing my David. He filled an important void in my life just when I needed it most, and also introduced a great deal of laughter and fun. He had many admirable traits, but others that I found questionable, not least discovering that I was just one of his many 'lady friends', some past but others still current. Having grown up with the Masai, David was in many ways one of them, and saw nothing wrong with safety in numbers, but he wined and dined me and invited me to accompany him on his rounds to 'flog tractors' for the President's firm, Lima Ltd, introducing me to places in Kenya that I had never visited before. During such excursions David took great delight in offering to barter me to passing Masai herdsmen for livestock, speaking in flawless Maa, which always floored the herdsmen. It amused him that the most he could get was only three cows and one Boozie, since I was beyond breeding age.

After a period flogging tractors, David was asked to manage Kapsitwet, the President's beautiful ex-settler farm at Kitale in western Kenya not far from the border with Uganda, so from time to time I was invited to enjoy farm life again, which reminded me of my childhood at Cedar Park. I was extremely fortunate that Jill and JF were willing and able to hold the fort back home while I was away. Assuming they could arrange for an elephant sitter, they were able to join us, often bringing Angela along too if she happened to be around. From the first Jill encouraged the warming of my relationship with David – or 'the Old M' (shortened from 'Old Masai'), as we called him – relieved, I think, to see me enjoying the lighter side of life again, but on a visit home from South Africa Angela was not quite so accommodating and was distinctly frosty, obviously viewing my new romance as a betrayal of her adored father. However, one couldn't help but like the Old M, for he was good company and always hosted us in great style. Like JF he was particularly territorial in his kitchen, where he brooked no interference whatsoever and where he enjoyed tossing pancakes and omelettes in the air like the professionals. Needless to say, more ended up stuck to the ceiling than on a plate. I will never forget Angela's expression when she noticed pig's teeth and feet bubbling around with the head-meat in a pot of brawn the Old M was brewing up for lunch. However, both my children were exceedingly sceptical about his kamikaze style of driving, whether in a vehicle or on the motorbike he used for his farm rounds. He would crash headlong over obstacles as though they did not exist, and on one occasion, when I was riding pillion on the back of the motorbike, clean through a barbed wire fence. Needless to say, we both ended up in the ditch.

It was in the Red Peril that Jill had to make an emergency dash down to Tsavo in 1988 to rescue a three-month-old elephant named Dika, before Eleanor could commandeer him. It was necessary to do this because he needed milk, which Eleanor was unable to provide. Dika came in punctured by hundreds of long acacia thorns, obviously having fled through a dense acacia thorn thicket from the killers who took the life of his mother. In those days we had no lorries or planes, so with the help of a friend, Jill had to wrestle Dika on to the back seat of the Renault, where he was held all the way back to Nairobi. It took us days to extract all the thorns, and weeks to heal the sepsis of his puncture wounds. But it was the grieving of this baby elephant for his lost family that worried us most. For weeks on end he stood dejectedly beside the little tent we still used to feed newcomers, tears oozing from his eyes and his trunk hanging limply to the ground. He took his milk only very reluctantly and slowly, standing alone as though comatose, showing no interest whatsoever in his surroundings, which left us wondering whether he could be brain-damaged. It was only the arrival and subsequent collapse three months later of another orphan, Edo, that made this sad little elephant come back to life.

Edo was six months old when his mother perished in Amboseli National Reserve, having raided a lodge rubbish tip and eaten plastic bags, bottle tops and even an ash tray in among discarded fruit and vegetables. He was the calf of a famous Amboseli matriarch and an integral part of the researchers' Amboseli elephant monitoring programme, kept under surveillance from the day he was born, so he was unafraid of all humans other than a Masai in a red blanket; red being the traditional colour worn by men of the tribe. However, the sight of Boozie freaked him out, since he associated sheep with the Masai. The Amboseli elephants were often in conflict with the Masai in competition for water and pasture, and over the years many had been speared. More recently others had been killed for cultural purposes, marking the passage from boyhood to manhood in place of the usual target of a lion, lions having become scarce in the area.

Edo collapsed upon arrival in the nursery, and as he lay there barely conscious, while Jill and I contemplated what to do about him, to our surprise Dika left the comfort of his little tent and walked straight up to him, rumbling and reaching down his trunk to touch Edo's face and mouth. Edo opened one eye, just a little at first, then, as reality dawned, wider and wider, struggling to get to his feet, which, with a little help from all the bystanders, he managed. He wobbled unsteadily, watching Dika take milk from a hand-held bottle, then surprised us all by following suit. Much to our joy, after that he never looked back, although he always remained extremely wary of Boozie and went to great lengths to keep all the other nursery elephants between himself and her.

A few months later, in April 1989, we were confronted with Ndume and Malaika, who came in together as three-month-olds from the Imenti forest, a small patch of remnant forest in northern Kenya that was now almost entirely encircled by human settlement and agriculture. Isolated within it there remained a dwindling population of elephants who were in trouble every time they stepped out, their ancient migratory route to the Mount Kenya forests now completely overrun with settlement. The local agricultural community viewed all elephants as the enemy, and when at dawn one morning a herd was found in the middle of a maize field, the locals went berserk. Armed with machetes, spears and axes, banging on tins and sounding whistles, every able-bodied person descended on the terrified elephants, who in the ensuing mêlée did not know which way to turn. One elephant was so traumatized that she aborted a full-term calf, which was instantly hacked to death, and as the adults broke through the wall of humanity to freedom, Ndume and Malaika found themselves two of three calves left behind. By the time rangers arrived to control the frenzied crowd, one calf had already been killed, Ndume had been dealt a savage blow to the head and Malaika's back legs had been slashed by machetes.

This was an emergency, so we chartered a plane with a vet on board to bring the two surviving babies to the nursery. There Ndume fell unconscious, so the vet hurriedly inserted a saline and dextrose drip into his ear vein before rushing to attend to Malaika, suspecting that Ndume was unlikely to come round, so huge was the bump on his head. All attention now focused on Malaika, cleaning the deep gashes on her legs and doing what we could to soothe her, since she was so traumatized that her entire body was trembling violently. Olmeg, Taru, Dika and Edo were brought round to help comfort her and they touched her face and back gently with their trunks, rumbled to her and showed her how to take milk from a bottle, reassuring her that the people who surrounded her now were very different to those who had been so violent. It came as a huge surprise when Ndume began to stir next door and, having got back on to his feet, began trying to scale the stable door, bellowing piteously. Obviously unable to remember what had taken place, he was so disturbed that we felt it better to let him out so that he could see for himself that his mother was not around, but hopefully might recognize Malaika. Running to and fro, bellowing frantically, he scoured the nearby croton thickets for her with a keeper trying to keep sight of him until he collapsed with exhaustion. Only then could we carry him back to his stable. This same pattern was repeated for the next two days, until he finally had to accept that he would never find his mother again and sank into deep depression, standing dejectedly glued to Malaika's side. To begin with we were pleasantly surprised because she seemed unusually upbeat for a newcomer, obviously relieved to find herself being treated with kindness and compassion rather than brutalized. Sadly, this did not last long, and soon she also sank into a long, quiet and seemingly lifeless period of intense grieving as reality dawned on her. Both calves had witnessed unspeakable horror and, like Dika, they mourned their lost elephant family for weeks. Fortunately, though, they took their milk throughout the grieving process and both eventually turned the corner and began to thrive.

Another surprise came when President Moi installed Dr Richard

Leakey as Director of Wildlife, charged with trying to revamp the corrupt Wildlife Conservation and Management Department which had failed the country so miserably, Leakey's brief being to bring the rampant poaching back under some semblance of control. Poaching and bad press were impacting negatively on the country's lucrative tourism industry, with Tsavo, Meru and other wildlife destinations rapidly becoming no-go areas due to security concerns. Dr Leakey was also given special powers – with his rangers empowered to shoot armed poachers on sight if found within the National Parks. Somali poacher/insurgents known as Shifta were on the rampage after David's departure, several wildlife rangers having lost their lives in running battles with the Shifta poachers. Wakamba poachers armed with equally lethal poisoned arrows also posed an ongoing threat, many colluding with corrupt elements within the previous Wildlife Department who allegedly were enjoying high-level protection. In Tsavo elephants had been mown down en masse and black rhinos all but exterminated.

So it was that Dr Leakey created the Kenya Wildlife Service, known as KWS, to replace the previous Wildlife Conservation and Management Department of Government, and reinstated a token Board of Trustees to encourage the flow of incoming donations again, which had all but dried up. He also persuaded President Moi to torch Kenya's huge stockpile of confiscated ivory and rhino horn at an official ceremony in the Nairobi National Park, in order to send out a powerful message that the new Kenya Wildlife Service was determined to conserve the country's elephants and rhinos, an event viewed on television screens throughout the world. A beautiful bronze sculpture depicting a dying elephant being supported by its grieving comrades was erected alongside the large pile of ivory ash left by the bonfire, as a lasting and emotive memorial to the suffering of elephants due to the demand for ivory in the Far East.

With World Bank money, a huge and impressive Headquarters complex sprang up on two levels, surrounded by manicured gardens and even fountains. Many conservationists were sceptical about the wisdom of this, fearful that the demands of a bloated bureaucracy at the Headquarters level could divert funding from the field where it was needed most. Dr Leakey was not allowed the autonomy he would have liked for the new Wildlife Service, which still remained under the overall authority of the Ministry for Tourism and Wildlife, and as such was subject to political meddling. Nevertheless, better field management did begin to bring the poaching back under control, assisted by a blanket ban on the sale of all ivory and rhino horn, agreed at the 1989 International Convention for Trade in Endangered Species (CITES), Kenya having lobbied furiously for this against strong opposition from the southern African states bent on selling their ivory stockpiles. By 1989, within the Tsavo ecosystem – an area of 16,000 square miles, twice the size of the Park itself – the population of elephants had fallen from the original 45,000 to just 6,000. The elephant population within Kenya as a whole was estimated in 1973 to be 167,000. By 1989 it had fallen to just 16,000, the social fabric of elephant society literally having been torn asunder. Only in Amboseli were some elephant families still intact, because there the presence of the Masai inhibited intrusion by poaching gangs.

I attended the next CITES gathering, held in Kyoto, Japan, where the ivory issue again proved a hot topic. Thankfully, after a great deal of heated discussion, the ban held, but I left dismayed at the internal politics inside this important forum and at the elephant supporters, vociferous beyond the hall, who remained strangely silent within, seemingly with a foot in both camps.

The southern African states would get their way at the next CITES gathering two years hence, despite the fact that there had not been sufficient time for even one generation of elephants to be born to replace the massive losses sustained by most elephant range states north of the Zambezi. The stockpile sales that resulted were supposedly to be subject to strict control, but everyone knew that illegal ivory would again be laundered into the legal system, that poaching would escalate, and that as long as there was a legal trade in ivory, elephants would continue to be killed for their ivory teeth. That such highly intelligent animals – who mirror us humans in terms of emotion, who have the same sense of family and of death, and who are meant to tread the earth for three score years and ten – should die so that their teeth could be turned into trinkets seemed sheer madness. It had been a very turbulent and trying few months for us, so it came as both a shock and a pleasant surprise to learn that I had been awarded the MBE in the 1989 Queen's Birthday Honours List. David had been similarly decorated exactly thirty years earlier, and later on so had Bill and my brother Peter. I was humbled to have also been found deserving of such an honour – that my work had been recognized alongside other notable achievers chosen from the people of Great Britain and the Commonwealth countries. David had opted for his presentation to be undertaken locally, but being an ardent royalist I wanted the pageantry of the Palace and the chance to meet the Queen in person, so I travelled to London for the investiture, and was not disappointed. It came as an even greater surprise when, in the Queen's 1996 New Year's Honours List, I was made a Dame Commander of the Most Excellent Order of the British Empire, hitherto to be known as Dame Daphne. I was humbled to hear that it was the first honour of its kind since Kenya had become independent in 1963, which left me dumbfounded but nevertheless extremely proud. My friends and family were amused when the keepers wondered why people were suddenly being disrespectful by calling me 'Damn Daphne'. It was difficult to explain to them the significance of being a Dame Commander of the British Empire, especially as the British Empire as such had long ceased to exist.

When the Kenya Wildlife Service decided to move surplus rhinos from the Solio Ranch in northern Kenya to Tsavo East, in an attempt to restock what had once been the bastion of the species and home to 8,000 of Kenya's previous population of 20,000 black rhinos, it was decided that Sam and Amboseli should be the front runners. Reudi was now the dominant breeding bull of Solio, and Stroppie and Pushmi still lived in their enclosed fifty-acre paddock abutting the main sanctuary, but Sam and Amboseli had taken to invading gardens and fruit stalls beyond the Nairobi Park boundary, near the sprawling suburb of Ongata Rongai. Sadly Boozie was no longer around, having become a glutton and hoovered up a plastic bag containing the leftover lunch of a visiting film crew. She was always eager to sample anything and everything, but on this occasion she blew up like a balloon and died before the vet could come and attend to her. It was a very sad day when we had to bury Boozie in the Park forest behind my house, near the stockades that Sam and Amboseli had once occupied, but there was comfort in knowing that she had enjoyed a better life as a rhino companion than would otherwise have been the case. Sam and Amboseli certainly felt her absence, but strangely enough not nearly as much as the little elephants, who lost their appetites and became unusually subdued, searching the compound and abutting forest for her, in the process affording a reprieve for the Ever Hopefuls, whom they enjoyed chasing. The Ever Hopefuls had proliferated, having benefited from the protection of the elephants and their keepers. They had excavated burrows under all the Trust buildings, begged for handouts at the staff canteen and enjoyed the use of the orphans' mud bath. In fact, one could be forgiven for believing that they were also hand-reared orphans.

It was with mixed feelings that I saw Sam and Amboseli sedated and ushered into two large trucks for the journey to Tsavo, where others from Solio would soon join them. All would be held in mobile holding pens for a time, their dung meanwhile scattered around to anchor them once they were released, as well as to introduce them through scent to the others. Everything went like clockwork until, tragically, Sam was fatally wounded by a large bull elephant after refusing to vacate a mud wallow he had found in a sandy riverbed and which the elephant also now wanted. He was unceremoniously heaved out and in the process a tusk penetrated his side.

Although in great pain, he managed to drag himself back to the holding pens, and as soon as Jill and I were told, we rushed down to Tsavo with the vet to try to patch him up, taking with us a huge basket of fruit as a special treat. But as soon as we reached him we knew the prognosis, for already there was the fetid smell of death. Peritonitis had taken hold, so there was no hope of a recovery. Tearfully we fed him the fruit we had brought him before the vet administered the lethal injection that would end his life and his agony. Thankfully, though, the news of Amboseli was far happier. She went on to have several wild-born calves, having established a territory for herself near Aruba, though not before spending several months searching for any evidence of Sam, during which time she was constantly on the move and wandered far and wide. I was learning that even rhinos, despite their complicated social structure and ancient origin, also made friends for life.

Unhappily, there would be many other rhino tragedies in the future, not least Makosa, who, having killed a keeper, had to be shot. Then Scud, who returned pregnant by a wild bull and with a seriously damaged foreleg in which the radial nerve had been severed. We nursed her until the birth of her calf, Magnum, but the leg withered, rendering her a cripple and unable to keep up with her baby, so she had to be put down and her calf reared as an orphan. He grew up to be a rare rhino success story, as far as we know still living as a wild rhino in Nairobi National Park. Not so the rhino companion who was reared along with him, called Magnet, another Nairobi Park orphan who was mysteriously shot and clandestinely buried by the authorities under suspicious circumstances, which we were cautioned not to investigate too seriously. Then there was the tiny, premature and very precious Maalim, aborted by his mother in the Ngulia sanctuary, so small that he could have fitted into a shoebox; amazingly he lived until he was two, but then ingested some milk into his lungs which his premature cilia were unable to expel. Pneumonia took him from us. Orphan Shida was, we believed, like Magnum, another rhino success until he became unpredictable around the compound, bent on keeping an eye on blind Maxwell, who could never be set free. He was translocated to Tsavo and, unbeknownst to us, tipped out into the Ngulia rhino sanctuary where he was promptly killed by another rhino as an intruder, the necessary lengthy introductory process bypassed. As soon as we heard that he had been introduced into the Ngulia sanctuary we knew he was as good as dead, and rushed to erect a holding enclosure for him, but sadly it was not completed in time.

Following the tragedy of Sam, there was further grim news from Tsavo concerning our elephant orphan Ol Jori, who was apparently suffering a creeping paralysis. Of course Eleanor would not leave his side for a moment, so her wellbeing was also now being compromised. Jill and I therefore decided to bring Ol Jori back to the nursery, even though I knew that removing him from Eleanor would not go down well. It so happened that both Olmeg and Taru were now two years old and could be transferred to Tsavo to replace Ol Jori in Eleanor's affections. And so, as Eleanor lost Ol Jori, she gained two for the price of one and was over the moon.

It transpired that Ol Jori had climbed a large boulder near the stockades, missed his footing, and tumbled off the boulder on to his back. Sadly, he died a few days after coming to us, and a subsequent post mortem revealed that the scar tissue from the accident had constricted the spinal column and was the cause of his paralysis. And so another little grave had to be dug in the forest behind my home, amid more tears, but also anger that the keepers had kept the accident from us, which meant that Ol Jori had suffered longer than necessary.

There have been so many such painful and emotional moments over the years that I have wished at times I had chosen an easier path. Animals weave their way into one's heart so completely that each death is a painful bereavement. But whenever I am embroiled in an emotional meltdown, I force myself to dwell on the plight of the wild elephant matriarchs, who so stoically face the adversity that dogs every step of their long and difficult lives. They grieve just as deeply for each loved one, yet they find the courage to turn the page and concentrate on the living. Life is for the living, not the dead, who belong to the past and are at peace and beyond all further pain and suffering 'somewhere in the great somewhere', as my Granny Webb would say. I liked to think that they would find David at the other side to be there for them. Elephant matriarchs sometimes even have to steel themselves to abandon a living weakling to its fate, walking away with its cries ringing in their ears, since failure to do so would jeopardize the survival of the others in the family and herd. To give up would be a cruel and cowardly course to take, depriving others that might need help, so it was, quite simply, never an option.

I especially needed to draw on the example of the elephants after the death of my parents – first that of my father on 20 April 1987, who, like Grandpa Webb, died peacefully in his sleep, and then on 31 January 1994 my beloved mother, who was happy to join him after the blissfully happy sixty years she had spent by his side. I wept buckets of tears each time and missed them both acutely. My mother was such a gentle, understanding, warm and hospitable lady and my father a role model – his honesty and integrity an inspiration to my siblings and me. Following each death, Peter travelled to South Africa to bring our parents' ashes back and scattered them at the site of the biltong Musandari camp near Narok, a place they both loved and which teemed with wildlife. Had circumstances been different, Cedar Park, our beautiful childhood home, would have been the first choice, but sadly it now bore no resemblance to what we had known, the beautiful cedar panelling turned into charcoal, and the house itself a place for the new owners' livestock.

Time passed, and down in Tsavo Eleanor adored Olmeg and Taru, mothering them as her own. She had also acquired several other orphans who were old enough to bypass the nursery stage – among them a young bull named Chuma, the word for 'iron' in Swahili, who was proving a lively sparring partner for Olmeg and Taru. Young bull elephants, like young human boys, spend a lot of time wrestling together in a test of strength, identity and rank, and during such bouts Olmeg usually came off second best to Taru, who was younger. Olmeg then befriended a young wild bull of similar age whom, although he was wild, the keepers named Thomas, since he was such a frequent visitor to the orphan group. It was Thomas who decided to back up Olmeg in his sparring bouts with both Taru and Chuma, and together they got topsides of both, which boosted Olmeg's hitherto dented confidence no end. I was glad of this, because confidence in a boy is important, and since Olmeg was our first nursery success, I had a particularly soft spot for him.

The year 1990 also saw the arrival of one-week-old Ajok, whose name means 'hello' in the Turkana dialect. He was the youngest elephant orphan we had received in our nursery, rescued from far-off Lake Turkana, the product of strong genes honed by natural selection. He was from a small population of elephants who managed to survive against all the odds in that arid lava desert. For a time he had the nursery mud bath audience all to himself, thoroughly enjoying being the centre of attention and playing to the gallery with a variety of 'party tricks'. He could 'shiver' his trunk repeatedly right from the very top to the very tip, making everyone laugh, wrap it around people's necks and gradually exert pressure to get a reaction, sit down like a circus elephant and even lie with all four legs in the air. However, having been alone in the nursery since he was just one week old, it was important to get him down to Tsavo to join the other orphans sooner than usual to learn the social skills he would need as a wild elephant. He went to join Eleanor's group as soon as he was two.

With the passing of time, Eleanor and the older members of her adopted family took to spending extended periods away with the wild herds. Having been a confident loner for so long, Ajok never entirely fitted into Eleanor's unit. Being subservient to so many older bulls was not to his liking, so he took himself off to seek out some with whom he could spar competitively, spending time away. Mischievous by nature, he also took to going on to Simon Trevor's verandah at night and heaving a camp chair over the low wall with a satisfying clatter. Suspicion fell on one of our ex-orphans, so JF lay in ambush to determine the identity of the culprit and sure enough, it was Ajok who was caught red-handed as JF burst out of the door with a blaringly loud Portoblast. Ajok fled in bellowing disarray, getting tangled up in an electric wire in the process, which persuaded him to sever his human ties completely and become a truly wild Tsavo elephant. We never saw him again, and Simon's camp chair has remained undisturbed on the verandah ever since.

The arrival of Jill's first daughter – my first grandchild – was a moment of immense joy. Emily Laura was born on 22 February 1992. Jill and JF were not officially married, so JF had difficulty convincing the matron that he was, in fact, the father even though he was unable to produce the required marriage certificate. I couldn't help wondering what my very traditional parents and grandparents would have had to say about Jill having a baby out of wedlock. Following the breakdown of her first marriage, she was adamant that a piece of paper and a hollow promise to be with someone for life was unrealistic, and I certainly was not in a position to argue about that. The 'Laura' part of Emily's name honoured Bill's mother, Laura Woodley.

A few months later a one-month-old elephant from Tsavo came into our lives, named Emily in my absence by the keepers in honour of my granddaughter. It was out of character for us to name an elephant thus, for we usually chose place or tribal names that would identify that particular animal's origin and circumstances in our minds. However, the keepers were adamant, so Emily she was.

Emily had been extracted from a disused pit latrine near the Manyani prison camp as her herd crossed from Tsavo West into Tsavo East. Staff from the prison hauled her out covered in human waste, and when her mother returned to claim her, hearing her bellows, she failed to recognize the foul-smelling apparition that confronted her and tossed the baby into the air before fleeing herself. It took time for Emily to recover after being orphaned in such an unsavoury manner, which left her with stomach problems, but in the end she made it and would grow up to become a very important player in the future, the first of our nursery-reared elephants to present us with a wild-born calf. Furthermore, having experienced the nursery, she understood how the orphans came to be with us, and after the birth of her own first calf was sufficiently confident to share the baby with her human family and the keepers who had reared her.

As time went by our ex-orphans in Tsavo grew in number, with regular additions from the Nairobi nursery. Reunions in Tsavo among those who had known one another in the nursery were always extremely touching, for recognition was instant and the welcome always exuberant. Eleanor was always overjoyed to welcome additions to her adopted unit, all the orphans regarding themselves as 'family'. Unfortunately, though, the eating habits Eleanor had acquired during the bad old roadside days remained in evidence, so in order to prevent her from corrupting the new intake of nursery-reared elephants, we had to electrically fence the KWS Voi Headquarters compound. Hand-feeding the orphans was strictly forbidden at the nursery and now also at Voi, being the sure recipe for a bullet should corrupted elephants become a threat in human habitation while they were seeking handouts. The keepers had instructions that whenever the orphans crossed a tourist road, the men had to hide so that tourists would not be able to differentiate between the orphaned herd and a wild one.

There had been a succession of other Wildlife Directors to head the Kenya Wildlife Service, following a terrible plane accident in which Dr Leakey lost both his feet. Radical changes would take place within the structure of the service which would compartmentalize all aspects of field management, depriving the field wardens of direct control and instead disseminating it to a host of officers senior to them, based mainly back at the Nairobi Headquarters. As predicted, funds for the field were compromised due to the financial burden of such an unwieldy bureaucracy at the Headquarters level. As a result, we at the Trust found the need to play a key role in support of the field in Tsavo, through regular donations of fuel to keep the anti-poaching forces mobile, to fund additional de-snaring patrols, assist with the repair of vehicles, drill boreholes and install windmills – in fact generally to bridge the financial gaps whenever possible and meet contingencies that cropped up unexpectedly. Poaching was a problem all over again, with illegal hauls of ivory intercepted en route to the Far East. Another serious problem was the bush meat business. Whereas previously this business had been mainly for subsistent purposes, now it had turned commercial, viewed as a delicacy in West Africa, where animals had been almost eaten to extinction. It was now exported there from Kenya as well as to the Middle East, where it was also on the increase, and even to the capitals of Europe, which were now home to a large number of West African immigrants.

In January 1994 we were presented with another real challenge which would be a first for the Trust, for this little elephant arrived still covered in foetal material. His mother had been shot in the process of giving birth to him near the Imenti forest, home of both Ndume and Malaika, and because it was obvious that he had never been able to benefit from her first colostrum milk, we knew that his immune system would be defective, leaving him vulnerable to disease, and that it would be just a question of time before another little grave had to be dug in the Park forest. We named this orphan Imenti and he was heartbreakingly perfect, with soft, shiny, supple skin and petal pink ears, and so trusting and unafraid that he snuggled up to whichever pair of legs happened to be nearest. Eventually the vet suggested a radical solution: to take the blood from a healthy elephant, separate the plasma and infuse this into the ear vein of the calf, hoping that this might replace the role of colostrum and trigger the immune process. The only other elephant in the nursery at the time was Emily, the survivor of the pit latrine, who was still too fragile to be a possible blood donor, so we arranged for the vet to fly to Tsavo and sedate Malaika, who by now had evolved into the matriarch overseeing the keeper-dependent group whenever Eleanor and the older elephants were taking a wild walkabout, which they were now doing more frequently. And so, within forty-eight hours, Imenti received the plasma from Malaika's blood and, miraculously, after a shaky start, it had the desired effect. It was not beyond the realms of possibility that perhaps he and Malaika shared the same gene pool, since very few elephants remained in the Imenti forest. The lessons learned with Imenti would enable us to save other such candidates in the future, one being yet another Imenti forest orphan called Wendi, whose name means 'hope' and who, like Emily and Imenti, would grow up to become an important player in the Trust's orphans' project of the future. Imenti would also turn out to be the catalyst that would enable us to establish a second rehabilitation centre at Ithumba, in northern Tsavo.

It was also around this time that Eleanor's unit acquired Mary, a ten-year-old female elephant who had been at the Mount Kenya Safari Club in Nanyuki since the age of two, her eventual destiny a zoo in America. Thankfully, Mary's owner, Don Hunt, decided instead to send her down to join Eleanor and the other orphans in Tsavo, initially sceptical about how she would be received and be able to cope. He need not have worried, because she was embraced with the usual outpouring of joy from all the resident orphans, including Eleanor, and went on to give birth to a baby bull fathered by a wild suitor. We named her calf Donald, in honour of the man who had granted her freedom. It surprised us that Eleanor, who was older than Mary and who had enjoyed much more wild contact, had not also fallen pregnant and given birth by now. Researchers suggested that it could be because she had not been mated in her teens, as was the norm, and as a result might be sterile.

It was now, with the birth of Mary's baby, that we witnessed at first hand the abduction tendencies of female elephants from a disrupted social background. Essentially maternal by nature, female elephants from disrupted families are desperate to try to recruit other babies to build a replacement family of their own, behaviour that has frequently been reported among our ex-orphans and recorded in the present-day keepers' diaries. In this case, Eleanor immediately set about attempting to take possession of Mary's calf, steering him beneath her body and urging him to suckle her dry breasts, denying Mary access. When no milk was forthcoming, the baby bellowed loudly, becoming increasingly frustrated and hungry. Mary was beside herself with anguish but there was little she could do to reclaim her calf, for Eleanor was older and as such higher-ranking as well as a lot bigger in body. The hierarchy among the females is equally as binding as that of the bulls and is also related to age. It was Taru and Chuma who eventually ganged up to free the calf from Eleanor and steer him back to his rightful mother. Mary then took her calf and left Eleanor's unit entirely, attaching herself instead to another wild herd that had a more structured wild family of its own, including some newborns. From then on the keepers would come across Mary from time to time out in the bush, and although she greeted them briefly, she clearly had no desire to renew her acquaintance with either humans, Eleanor, or the nearby orphans' stockades, which so obviously reminded her of her many years of captivity at Nanyuki.

Eleanor came to befriend a wild cow with a family of her own, who was so often seen in Eleanor's company and had become so accepting of the keepers that, although they never usually named wild elephants, they gave her the name Catherine. On that ill-fated visit to Tsavo, in search of Eleanor, it was Catherine who tossed me into the air, leaving me with a smashed leg that took fifteen months to rebuild. Eager to find Eleanor to show her off to one of the Trust's visitors, I made a mistake that I should really never have made. I was so convinced that no wild Tsavo elephant would ever walk up to strange humans that when Catherine did respond to my call – even though instinctively I was troubled by the build and eye colour of this elephant – I convinced myself in those split seconds that she was indeed Eleanor. After all, why else would she approach us so trustingly? She allowed us to touch her face and trunk and to feel the coolness of her tusks, but when I extended my arm to the hind side of her ear – something I always did with Eleanor – I felt her flinch and the next thing I knew, I was being hurled through the air, landing with such force against a pile of boulders that my right leg shattered on impact. I lay in a pool of blood in which I could see chips of my own bone, a curious crunching sensation enveloping my body.

Every time I reflect back on this terrifying incident, I remind myself how lucky I am to still be alive. And I have come to understand that on that day I was given a valuable lesson, in which I experienced the sophistication and complexity of inter-elephant communication. For, having thrown me into the air, Catherine towered menacingly above me and could easily have snuffed out my life. After the cruelty inflicted on her species by humans, I am astounded that she chose not to. Instead, having been 'told' by Eleanor that I was, in fact, a friend, she behaved differently, inserting her tusks beneath my broken body to try to lift me back on to my feet.

Catherine's handiwork entailed emergency blood transfusions and surgery the moment the Flying Doctors delivered me to the casualty department of the hospital in Nairobi. After a nine-hour operation I woke to find my leg in plaster from hip to toe, with a great deal of hardware implanted along my smashed femur and broken knee, plus massive blood blisters left by the tourniquet that had encircled my thigh to limit the bleeding. These blisters turned out to be almost as problematic as the leg, and rendered me out of action for some time. Fortunately, Jill and JF took over all the responsibilities of the nursery, JF having to combine his film work with running around delivering wages, maintaining vehicles and buildings and collecting supplies for the orphans, for Jill was heavily pregnant with her second daughter, who was born on 22 October while I was still in Nairobi hospital. She was named Zoe Emma Marjorie, and I was overjoyed to see her the moment that I came home on crutches, although the joy of her arrival was tempered by sad news as well, because Bill's wife, Ruth, had lost her long battle against cancer. Ruth had been a close friend to me and a kind and loving stepmother to Jill, so we were devastated by her untimely death, as, of course, were Jill, Bill himself and Ruth's three sons, Jill's half-brothers.

Bedridden, for the next six months I watched enviously through my bedroom window as the birds soared high in the sky and the little house martins swooped down to nest as usual in the rafters of my verandah. However, I was able to work and my bed became my office, my portable typewriter perched on my lap and the telephone at my side. A steady stream of friends and well-wishers kept my spirits up, as did periodic visits from the Old M whenever he happened to hit town. However, five months later I was still in excruciating agony, and an X-ray confirmed that an immediate bone graft was necessary, the femur having failed to knit.

Fortunately Angela happened to arrive home just in time to persuade me to travel to South Africa, rather than risk a bone graft in Nairobi. She contacted a university colleague who was now an orthopaedic surgeon and he urged that I travel immediately to South Africa, since bone grafting was a complicated procedure and not one to be taken lightly. He referred me to Dr Paul Firer, who was considered the best in the business and who was always known as 'Ponky' – apparently meaning 'wild dog' – which seemed somewhat disconcerting.

And so, occupying three seats of one entire row of the aircraft, with my leg rigid and encased in plaster, I flew to South Africa. During another gruelling ten-hour operation, everything that had been done in Nairobi had to be undone and I woke up with one hip on fire as well as the leg, since stem cells had now been taken from the hip for insertion into the broken leg. As my leg had been so infected, Ponky had not been able to do the bone graft, and instead his colleague, Dr Jeff Sochen, had inserted bone irrigation pipes while I was still under. 'You're a good conservationist given the ten different bacteria in your leg,' joked Ponky when I came round. 'Thanks a lot,' I replied, 'Get them out!'

Getting them out entailed another six weeks on my back undergoing bone irrigation. I didn't need to stay in hospital for this, and my niece Sally offered to accommodate me – and all the required paraphernalia – in her Johannesburg home. Betty flew up from Durban to nurse me, while I was anchored to a bed, lying on an eggshell mattress and sheepskins, with a thirty-pound weight attached to my foot to keep the length of my leg intact. Sally set up a small television and video at the end of my bed and together Betty and I watched every episode of *Dad's Army*, in between reminiscing about our childhood days. My sister and her daughter were angels who made my bone irrigation ordeal pleasurable. Those weeks spent in Sally's home were the turning point that saved my leg, precious time that I felt grateful to have had, for four years separated Betty and me, a large gap during our childhood years.

I had to wait another month for all the irrigation holes to heal entirely, this time in Betty's Durban home, before returning to Johannesburg for another ten-hour operation and, on this occasion, a successful bone graft with cell material taken from the other hip. Ponky also now designed a pin for the break in my knee, having been able to assess the actual damage first-hand during the first graft attempt. However, this time the agony on waking up was so acute that I was on morphine for a few days, before enduring the misery of the 'bending machine' and physiotherapy to try to get flexibility back into a knee that looked as though it would never move again. I was told in no uncertain terms that only when I could walk the length of the ward on crutches without fainting would I be released from hospital. I was so feeble that at first I thought I would never do it, collapsing frequently in the chair that a nurse constantly moved up behind me. Ponky monitored my progress daily, doubtful that I would ever get more than a forty-degree bend back in the damaged knee, and gently prepared me for the prospect of having to live with the extensive hardware he had inserted, since at my age my bones were too fragile to risk its removal.

Unbeknownst to me, many friends and sympathetic elephant supporters, along with Jin Tatsamura's *Gaia Symphony* fans, had donated money to Jill to cover the cost of my treatment, with others pledging further help if necessary. I was immeasurably touched by this, and the fact that I now have a working leg is entirely thanks to those kind folk, the expertise of Ponky, and Dr Jeff Sochen, one of the few specialists worldwide at that particular time in the relatively new field of bone irrigation. To all those incredibly kind and generous people I shall always be eternally grateful.

Jin and his Japanese supporters treated Angela and me like royalty when we went to Japan, showering us with gifts and donations in support of the elephants. At each major city we visited, Jin organized a lecture hall which was always filled to capacity so that I could pass on the message about elephants and ivory. Every day I was treated by a top acupuncturist, a herbal specialist and a masseuse, who worked wonders on my leg. I was particularly taken with one 'alternative' remedy that involved immersing myself in the hot springs, known to have curative healing powers, which bubbled from an active volcano in the mountains. There was a succession of spas ranging from very hot, to much cooler further down. Entry to the spa was a bit of an ordeal for me! You had to leave your shoes outside the door, strip naked, place your clothes in a small locker, and, along with all the others taking the waters, get in. For me, no lightweight as were most trim Japanese ladies, this appeared daunting, but my acupuncturist was adamant that it had to be, so I sent Angela along during the lunch hour to assess the number of shoes outside each door before deciding which spa to select. She returned with the news that only the very hot one seemed vacant. Hurriedly I went off and got in, but to my dismay and embarrassment, several Japanese ladies turned up to share the spa with me. I was determined not to expose myself and was becoming redder and redder, literally being boiled like a lobster as I waited for them to leave, Angela all the while castigating me for being such a 'wimp'.

As promised, upon my return to Nairobi, Dr Ponky Firer visited me, having initially appeared somewhat sceptical about whether the alternative remedies would, in fact, make a difference. He was pleasantly surprised to find me with a fully functional knee, conceding that my Japanese trip had done wonders for the 'elephant leg'. And all these years on I walk with no problems, only occasionally returning to crutches when a certain sideways twist of the body makes the old knee remind me to treat it more gently.

Jill kept me in touch with events at home while I was away. Upon my return, the first phone call I received was from her father. Bill and

I had a long chat, catching up on each other's news, so it came as a terrible shock to learn the next day that he had suffered a massive stroke that plunged him into a coma from which he would never emerge. Jill and her half-brothers insisted that he be transferred to Nanyuki Cottage Hospital to be near his friends and the Mountain National Parks which he so loved. When he died, his ashes were scattered on the Aberdares and Mount Kenya along with those of Ruth. Bill had been my first love, my first husband, Jill's devoted father and my life-long friend as well as an essential element in the spirit and workings of the Trust. We also shared a thirty-five-year love of Eleanor.

Meanwhile, Angela's life was changing. She had fallen in love with Robert Carr-Hartley and he with her. I was astounded that she had not known him before, because the Carr-Hartley family were old friends of our family; Robert and his two siblings had grown up on their grandfather's farm at Rumuruti, not far from our Cedar Park, the progeny of an old Kenya settler family who had been neighbours to many of our Aggett relatives in the early days. Like Angela, Robert had ridden a rhino long before a horse, was passionate about wildlife and the bush, but was also proficient in a city, fulfilling two of the requirements Angela was seeking in a partner. His family had been professional game trappers in the early days, capturing animals rodeo style for sale to zoos long before the days of immobilizing drugs. In fact, Robert's father, Roy, often came to help Jill and me move our nursery elephants to the rehabilitation centre in Tsavo.

On 7 December 1996 they were married in the Karen church where the funeral service for David had taken place. Angela looked stunning in a gown of pale champagne-coloured silk, with five little bridesmaids in attendance, Robert's three angelic blonde nieces – his sister's children – and my two granddaughters, Emily and Zoe, both of whom let the side down by firmly refusing to follow the bridal entourage into the church. Angela entered the church on the arm of her half-brother Kenneth, David's son by Diana. I had wanted Angela to have a traditional Kenya settler wedding, so friends and family came from afar, many from South Africa and England, turning it into a wonderful social gathering. It was a grand occasion, and I knew that David would have wanted me to do her proud.

After a honeymoon at the coast, the newly-weds settled down at the Borana Lodge near Nanyuki, Robert having recently acquired the management lease from the landowners. Together, he and Angela transformed the lodge into one of the most prestigious safari venues in Kenya. I knew that David would have approved of Angela's choice of husband, as did I, delighted that she had returned home rather than settle in southern Africa, and proud of the daughter who was so like him in many ways. At Borana she was in charge of stocking and managing a beautiful up-market shop, as well as overseeing all the menus and catering arrangements. With her innate flair for all the special details that make a lodge stay memorable, she and Robert turned Borana into one of the most sought-after safari destinations. Every guest enjoyed personalized attention, assured of everything they could possibly want, so for Jill, JF and I, who were used to a simple life in Nairobi, a few days in Borana with Angela and Robert made a luxurious and very enjoyable break.

Meanwhile, the David Sheldrick Wildlife Trust had grown and become a lot more efficient. Our fledgling orphanage was becoming well known, and we were welcoming visitors each afternoon to enjoy our growing herd of orphaned elephants. People from all parts of the world were eager to mingle with the orphans, including grow-ing numbers of the local African schoolchildren, which was very heartening.

We lived a privileged life, surrounded in our Nairobi Park home by our animals – the warthogs, whose lives we had now followed for some fifteen generations; the two wild bushbuck, who fed from an outstretched hand and slept beside the night-watchmen, knowing that there they were safe from predators; the birds and the squirrels, who came for mealworms when called and whose fortunes and mis-fortunes we shared; and the old wild buffalo bulls, whom we named Horatio, Hardnut, Hellier and Helmet, who drank regularly at our waterhole and contributed to our security at night. I had a vested in-terest in these buffalo, who might well have been direct descendants of the sixteen-plus orphans of our Tsavo days who had founded the current established resident buffalo herd of the Nairobi Park.

The Trust invested in some land along the southern bank of the

Athi, an area that before his death David had campaigned to protect
as a National Reserve because it had long provided a launch pad into
the Park for bush meat poachers as well as for the ivory and rhino
horn hunters. Although the new Ngai Ndethya Reserve had been
agreed, it had never been signed into law before David died and had
since been occupied by squatters. A prerequisite to owning land in
Kenya was to establish a presence, so having purchased the land from
the African squatter owner, our Trustees went with us to choose a
site for the building that would ultimately be known as Saa Nane and
serve the interests of the Trust as a venue for important donors, as
well as being a base for our Tsavo field operations. David had often
spoken wistfully of owning a parcel of wilderness and its wild inhabitants, and since he was never likely to have been in a position to do
so, we knew this project would definitely have had his approval. Saa
Nane (called by David's African nickname) was designed by Angela
and Robert and constructed on the south bank of the Athi River by
Robert's cousin, overlooking the smoky Yatta Plateau where David's
presence lingers still. Saa Nane generates money for the Trust by
hosting up-market Trust donors who pay for the privilege of enjoying it, as do the clientele of mobile safari operators in between camp
moves. It also serves as our Tsavo home when duty calls there. Huge
basement rock slabs bejewelled with garnets, which formed part of
the original kopje, or outcrop, are incorporated into the building, as
are some of the original trees – a candelabra euphorbia and a boscia
both protruding through the concrete of the verandah overlooking
the river, while ridges within the strata of the rock reflect the geography of Tsavo's terrain. My only input was to insist that Saa Nane
must have a flat roof on which we could sleep and enjoy the stars on
clear Tsavo nights, something that always reminded me of my
mother, who made a point each night of stepping outside to gaze in
wonderment at the stars in the universe above.

   Later, the Trust would purchase Kaluku Farm from Jill and JF. The
two of them had long harboured dreams of a simple lifestyle living off
the land, and when a plot on the Mtito Andei watercourse boundary
to the Park came up for sale, they bought it at the same time that the
Trust bought the land on which Saa Nane stands. Making use of the

original mud dwellings, they added a simple living rondavel, created a tree nursery and initiated the first anti-poaching de-snaring patrols to collect and destroy wire snares set to trap wild game for bush meat. JF, an old hand at saving unfortunate captives, populated the farm with some scruffy chickens rescued from the main Nairobi–Mombasa highway; a cantankerous male duiker and a crocodile from the wild animal 'orphanage' at the Nairobi Park main entrance; and a couple of large tortoises 'freed' from a tiny cage at a roadside lodge. He also built a special house for bats so that they could perch on rails inside without disturbance, and provided hives for the bees, not with the intention of taking their honey but simply to assist them. It was this compassionate side of JF and his passion for an animal's quality of life that Jill so admired and cherished, plus the fact that he could dispatch a suffering victim quickly, cleanly and efficiently should the need arise. The two of them were instrumental in pioneering the Trust's community input by providing sports equipment, textbooks and a mobile cinema to neighbouring schools, work that the Trust has since enlarged to encompass a host of other community schools abutting Tsavo.

Sadly, it was an armed robbery at our Nairobi orphanage, in which Jill was forced at gunpoint to hand over all the staff wages, that proved the catalyst that later made JF decide that his family had to up sticks and move to France. The only son of ageing French parents, he felt they both needed his presence as well as time with their only grandchildren, added to the fact that he wanted his two daughters to be fluent in French as well as in English. When Jill and my granddaughters left for France I thought my heart would break, and later, when I learned that Jill had been so homesick for Kenya that she had wept almost every day during her first year there, I wished so much that it could have been otherwise. But sometimes things are meant to be, and unfold for the best. Today Jill is happy to have a base in France, as well as a home in Kenya, which the families can share. She is still very much involved, and she and the children spend time with us in Kenya whenever they can, but JF says that to return to the transformed Kaluku establishment would prove too painful for him and he prefers to devote his time to his elderly father, now a widower who needs him more.

I can only think that someone in the 'great somewhere' was still looking out for me after Jill and JF left, for their departure coincided with the return of Robert and Angela, whose Borana Lodge lease had been unexpectedly terminated when the landlord's son wanted to take over management of the lodge. In fact, this turned out to be a blessing in disguise, because the next few years suffered a tourism decline due to the global economic downturn and this would have made things very difficult for Angela and Robert, who had to shoulder the running costs as well as the lease fee. I have to smile – to one side of my modest Timsales prefab home, which remains unchanged, is the very basic rondavel that Jill left behind, now serving as a guest house, with my own spare room now a strong room following the armed robbery. On the other side is Angela's beautiful new house, which she and Robert funded and designed, having obtained authority from KWS. These two establishments accurately reflect the very different characters of my two very different daughters: one who shuns the elaborate trappings of modern living and consumerism, preferring simplicity and the old ways; another who loves beautiful things and a beautiful home, with all the latest gadgets. Angela has David's flair and love of construction. She loves nothing better than upgrading the Trust's existing buildings to smarten up the establishment, designing and overseeing the construction of any new ones, and, of course, being in overall charge of any interior decorating.

In May 1998 Angela's first son and my first grandson was born, named Taru David Roy – Taru because the Taru Desert is, in effect, now the Tsavo National Park, David after his maternal grandfather – my David – and Roy in honour of Robert's father. Two years later, in July 2000 – millennium year – Angela's second son, Roan Alexander William, arrived, according to ancient Chinese mythology a very auspicious time to be born, making him a 'Golden Dragon'. And so I have been blessed with two beautiful granddaughters and two wonderful grandsons, all of whom are equally passionate about wildlife.

Angela took over as my right arm where Jill had left off, and some of her loyal workers from the Borana Lodge followed her and Robert to work for the Trust as accountants, mechanics, cooks and elephant-keepers. Before their arrival the David Sheldrick Wildlife Trust did have a basic website, courtesy of a kind donor, but it was rudimentary at best, since neither Jill nor I were truly computer literate. In contrast, both Robert and Angela are tech-savvy, adept at embracing the latest innovations. Angela designed and created the Trust's highly successful digital fostering programme, enabling people all over the world to foster an elephant in return for regular educational updates, instilling an interest in the orphaned elephants and our work throughout the world, thanks to the internet age. She has taken the Trust to a new level, as Jill happily acknowledges. Sadly, the escalation of poaching, fuelled by a newly rich China combined with a mounting human population, is depriving elephants of their ancient migration routes and space; this, added to more frequent drought conditions due to global warming, has left mounting numbers of baby elephants orphaned. Additional stables and stockades have been built and existing ones upgraded. Robert, who along with his brother William operates his own high-end mobile safari company, has taken over the supervision of the Trust's growing fleet of vehicles, water bowsers, generators and other equipment, and has installed tracking devices on all the de-snaring team vehicles so that their movements can be followed. JF's Kaluku Farm has been transformed into the Trust's working and efficient field base in Tsavo, Angela having designed a new and more comfortable rondavel home for the field manager/pilot. There are now workshops, offices, staff quarters, a beautiful orchard and vegetable garden that serves the community's needs and a hangar at the nearby Trust airstrip for the Trust's new Top Cub aircraft, modelled on the hangar that David built at the Park's Voi airstrip. The Kaluku Field Headquarters is now fully solar-powered, with wireless coverage over the entire Park to keep in close touch with the de-snaring patrols as well as internet access. My younger daughter and her husband, and their two sons Taru and Roan, have injected a magical energy into the Trust and I am continually surprised by their commitment and dedication. The Trust's footprint in Tsavo has made a huge difference, and continues to do so.

Sitting under the stars, I often reflect on how fortunate I am to still be here and remain inextricably entwined with this magical place. I miss Jill and my parents, along with the other special people who have been an integral and important part of my life, and the ache of losing David has never really left me, but I am contented and fulfilled in my twilight years. As I contemplate my grandsons, I know that the continuity of the Trust, along with David's legacy and vision, has been ensured, and I am eternally deeply humbled by the global support that the Trust's work has enjoyed from people in faraway places.

Over the years, I have often wondered what prompted Eleanor to sever her human ties for so long and leave her orphan charges to Catherine. I think I now have the answer. Once pregnant, and never having been through the Nairobi nursery herself, Eleanor thought I might take her calf from her, puzzled as to how I acquired the many elephants I had handed into her care over the years. Thinking as an elephant, she suspected that I had hijacked them from their rightful mothers, just as she had once tried to take Mary's newborn herself.

16. Achievement

'And how shall we find the Kingdom of Heaven?' the disciples asked.
'Follow the birds and the beasts,' came the reply.
'They will show you the way.'

– St Thomas, Apocryphal Gospels

The David Sheldrick Wildlife Trust has now become internationally known, thanks to the internet and the international film crews who come to document the elephants and rhinos in our care. Thousands of people all over the world now foster our orphans and follow their progress through the worldwide web. The Trust has a presence in the UK and the USA, where dedicated teams busily submit proposals for projects, organize fund-raising initiatives and generate public awareness of wildlife issues. David would be astonished to know how far his legacy has extended and that his name is now synonymous with the conservation, preservation and protection of wildlife the whole world over.

The Elephant Diaries, made by the BBC in 2005 and shown globally, did much to raise our profile. Filmed over a year, it was rated one of the most popular programmes of the time, attracting millions of viewers each night in the UK alone and later an even wider audience on the Animal Planet. This generated a marked increase in the number of overseas visitors to the nursery, people keen to see the elephants' daily mud bath and watch them being fed by their keepers. Many of these visitors go on to explore other parts of Kenya, enjoying safaris, experiencing the thrill of the flamingoes at Lake Nakuru, the migrating wildebeest in the Mara, the spectacular landscape of the arid north, and, of course, Tsavo. It is wonderful that our elephants have been able to contribute so positively to the Kenyan tourist industry. Our profile was further boosted when the prestigious American CBS *60 Minutes* team came to film, raising awareness of our work across the whole of the United States, being featured in the September 2011 issue of the *National Geographic Magazine* and mentioned in *The Oprah Winfrey Show*. We continue to welcome numerous film crews from Europe and the Far East, and recently Warner Brothers made a 3D film of our orphans that ran across the world in IMAX screens and continues in science museums. *Born to be Wild* featured some of our keeper-dependent orphans as well as those now living wild, and their wild-born babies. This film has enabled even more people to understand the very human nature of elephants – how those now independent and living in the wild still care deeply about others who remain in the care of their surrogate human family. Known as the ex-orphans, they return regularly to escort newcomers out into the wild, introducing them to their new friends. In glorious 3D, the awesome majesty of one of the few huge tuskers left in the world, tusks reaching to the ground, appears life-size, almost within reach. The film also captures the rescue of an orphan and its journey from a terrified wild baby into a loving and trusting elephant.

Even against the backdrop of this particularly turbulent century, the Trust has continued to provide funding for environmental, educational and social initiatives and has been able to support the Kenya Wildlife Service in its task of protecting Kenya's wildlife heritage. We continue to provide assistance in many ways. We manage and fund additional mobile anti-poaching de-snaring teams who patrol alongside the Kenya Wildlife Service rangers to keep the Park boundaries free of the wicked wire snares set to trap wildlife. We provide fully equipped mobile veterinary units, staffed by vets seconded from the Kenya Wildlife Service, which patrol and deal with sick or wounded animals promptly, proficiently and unobtrusively, just as David would have wanted. We have drilled boreholes, installed windmills in Tsavo, helped maintain the roads in remote corners of the Park; expanded the Park's radio network and been able to assist with crucial aerial monitoring and surveillance using the Trust's Top Cub aircraft. We have also worked tirelessly to secure and protect as much wild land as possible beyond established National Parks.

All this David would recognize as a continuation and growth of the initiatives he pioneered, but when I see the work of our community outreach programmes, I know that he would be both surprised and delighted. The Trust continues to provide textbooks, desks, sports equipment and additional teaching aids now to twenty-eight schools a year that border the boundaries of Tsavo. In our donated bus, we organize field trips for disadvantaged schoolchildren who would otherwise never have the opportunity to even see the wildlife of their country and experience the orphans in Tsavo, and we have mobile field cinema units that travel around showing films to engender an appreciation of wildlife in the local children. I am also proud that we have been able to supply every National Park in Kenya and many beyond with a copy of *The Wilderness Guardian*, a comprehensive field manual compiled from David's field notes and records, as well as those of other experienced field wardens, by Tim Corfield (whose grandmother was a sister of my Granny Chart), so that vital knowledge and first-hand field experience are not lost in the mists of time.

My little Timsales house has remained unchanged over the years, apart from the huge thorn trees that now tower over it, having been planted as tiny seedlings thirty-five years ago, and the groves around it, also transformed by colourful garden flowers that thankfully the wild community do not favour as part of their diet. The elephant nursery remains an extension of my home, but has grown in both capacity and levels of expertise and has now been responsible for rescuing close on 200 elephant orphans, over 100 of whom are now living wild, none of whom would otherwise be alive today.

The general regime is that after spending their first two years of life in our Nairobi nursery our orphans move on to one of the two rehabilitation centres run by the Trust, one just behind what used to be our Tsavo home in Voi, in the same stockades that David constructed all those years ago to house Samson, Fatuma and Eleanor and which have since been extended and upgraded. The other rehabilitation centre is in the northern area of Tsavo at Ithumba, just below the impressive Ithumba massif. For David, the northern area was the jewel in Tsavo's crown, an area he loved deeply, and whenever I return I recall the many happy hours we spent watching herds of elephants tunnelling into the dry Tiva riverbed for water, and those determined rhinos who braved the elephants to drink from their waterholes. The tragedy was that after we left Tsavo, rampant and uncontrolled poaching in the north drove all elephants out for three decades, with none then to be found in its vast 3,000 square miles of wilderness. The catalyst that brought the wild elephants back to the north was our northern orphan rehabilitation facility at Ithumba. For several years, only the bulls – the scouts of elephant society – visited the orphans in their night stockades, under cover of darkness, communicating with them in low rumbles, until they were convinced that it was safe for the cow herds to return. Wild elephants now come to drink at the stockade trough there in growing numbers and fraternize with our orphans on a daily basis, even tolerating the presence of the keepers.

Today we have over fifty dedicated elephant-keepers proficient at raising a newborn elephant without my supervision, even though, in my twilight years now, I am still very much involved. Angela now runs the Trust and has become my right hand, ably abetted by her husband, Robert. I know that David would take great pride in his Pip and her two sons – our grandsons – who will take up the mantle when the time comes. Jill is still also very much part of the team whenever she returns from France, and my granddaughters have inherited their mother's passion for her homeland, its wildlife and wilderness.

Thirty-five long years have passed since David died, but I still feel him close to me on a daily basis and in my thoughts share with him all I have since learned about animals. My fifty-plus years of hands-on experience with animals, coupled with the privilege of rearing their orphaned young, have allowed me unique access through which to observe and understand their inside story. The orphanage's methods of care and rehabilitation have drawn on this cumulative knowledge, yet it is just the foundation upon which we will continue to build. But, like me, David would be very conscious that nothing is achieved alone in this field of work and that any progress is a hugely collaborative effort, with countless people working tirelessly and passionately to provide the best environment possible for the animals that come into our care. Perhaps one of the most rewarding aspects for me has been watching empathy for the elephants dawn and flourish within our keepers and, by extension, in local people.

For the success of our orphans' project is largely due to our internationally recognized keepers – whose green jackets and brown dustcoats have become synonymous with our work. David would delight in talking to all our keepers, and particularly to Mischak Nzimbi, the original keeper who came with Taru all those years ago and who has since been the favourite of all the elephants that have passed through our hands, irrespective of their origins or age. Many of our other keepers now possess the magic that was once unique to him, and have been responsible for miraculous recoveries in orphans whom we at first considered hopeless cases. Our keepers pass on their knowledge through radio broadcasts in their own tribal languages to their tribesmen in distant corners of Kenya, who at one time would either not have bothered to rescue a baby elephant, or might even have killed it, but now go to great lengths to save an orphan. There is no one better qualified to educate communities about the elephants than the elephants' human family, who speak from the heart.

Our keepers are recruited from Kenya's many different tribes – men who need employment and can work away from home. I am often asked why our keepers are all men. Some years ago we did have a mix of men and women, but elephants are keeper-dependent for up to ten years before making a full transition into the wild, and we found that women were unable to commit for this period of time, because they saw their main duty as being to their own children.

Once recruited, the keepers are taught how to measure and mix the elephants' milk, how to cover elephant stools instantly with soil and remove them hurriedly before there is a build-up of flies, burying those that are loose in pits dug in strategic places or, if firm, simply shovelling them into the bush for the dung-beetles to roll into balls and bury. The orphans have an uncanny knack of being able to read your heart, so it is in a new recruit's interest to work towards earning the love and respect of his charges, interacting and talking gently to them, touching and caressing them, playing with them,

picking suitable leaves and, most importantly, exuding a genuine
affection. And because elephants never forget, it is essential that they
be treated only with love and kindness. None of our keepers carries
even a twig, but instead they control their charges by tone of voice,
the waggling of a finger and, only if absolutely necessary, a sharp
disapproving shove to demonstrate displeasure over bad behaviour.
The orphans grow to love their human family and derive pleasure
from pleasing them, but just like human children, they can be deliberately mischievous and have disagreements with each other, grudges
they want to settle. While the keepers will move in to separate antag-
onists, keeping order within the unit is the role of the older females,
who rapidly come to the rescue of any elephant who bellows for
help, driving the trouble-makers off to spend time out – the elephant
way of punishing wrong-doers, for it deprives them of the feeling of
security within the main group.

During the orphans' nursery period, the keepers are in physical
contact with the babies twenty-four hours a day, sufficient in number
to represent the orphans' lost family herd. Each night, when the
orphans return to their stable, a different keeper will sleep in with a
different elephant, rotating from one charge to another to avoid any
deep attachments, as these can prove counter-productive, as it did for
me all those years ago with Shmetty. The keeper sleeps on a raised
platform within reach of the elephant's trunk, and milk is freshly
mixed every three hours throughout the night, as well as by day. Cut
greens are hung in each stable as a browsing incentive during the
nursery stage, but even though browse is eaten by an elephant from
the age of about four months onwards, elephant calves are milk-
dependent for the first three years of life and cannot survive without it.

Young elephants have a rapid metabolism. A newborn will suckle
its mother about once every ten minutes, ingesting little and often, so
in the nursery, newborns are fed on demand, encouraged gradually
into a three-hourly routine. We add cooked oatmeal porridge to for-
tify the milk after the age of four months, and once the calves are
three, we wean them off milk. By this time their intake of natural
vegetation will have increased but they will still need supplementary

assistance in the form of coconut, which contains the kind of fat an elephant can assimilate. The condition of an elephant is reflected in the face, not the stomach, which becomes bloated when malnourished. The cheekbones beneath the eye sockets should not be visible, for baby elephants, like their human counterparts, should have chubby cheeks.

Every keeper will know the history of each orphan in our care, their particular story being key to the understanding of any strange behaviour patterns when they first come to us. It is important to ensure that the orphans are kept as happy as possible during their nursery time, so that they heal psychologically and behave normally by the time they are re-exposed to the natural world. Over the years we have learned a lot about the disturbed psychological state of traumatized orphaned elephant young. Their behaviour often mirrors the post-traumatic stress syndrome of humans. Healing the psychological effects of such stress is imperative, for if an elephant is not psychologically stable, it will risk rejection from the wild herds.

Thanks to modern technology, we record our orphans' rescues on film and chronicle their daily progress in the keepers' diaries, sharing this through the Trust's website. Every orphan has a harrowing story, most orphaned as a result of human activity of some sort: a mother killed by poachers for her ivory tusks; mothers and babies falling down wells dug in dry sandy riverbeds by pastoral people for their livestock; more frequent drought conditions due to global warming; calves dying from milk deprivation because their mother's milk is compromised through drought. Some arrive savagely mutilated by brutal people bent on retribution for elephants having destroyed crops. More recently, domestic livestock have illegally invaded the National Parks, introducing stomach parasites and diseases that contribute to the demise of elephants and other wild inhabitants. Furthermore, the general proliferation of the human population is creating mounting competition for both water resources and grazing, and, of course, the loser is always the wildlife.

Our elephant-keepers rotate between the Nairobi nursery and the two Tsavo rehabilitation facilities at Voi and Ithumba, so that all the elephants know all the keepers, and all the keepers know all the orphans. In this way the elephants understand that separation from a human loved one is just a temporary measure, and that they have not permanently lost another loved one as they did their elephant mother and family. Once psychologically stable and physically healed, usually after a couple of years in the Nairobi nursery, we transfer our orphans to one of our two rehabilitation centres in Tsavo, transporting them in a specially designed 'elephant mover', which can comfortably accommodate three nursery elephants at a time. Resting on the substantial chassis, the truck's body, designed by Robert, has three separate spacious compartments, accessed through a side panel that folds flat against the loading, or unloading, bays so that the animals can walk in, and out. Surrounding these compartments is a corridor, so that the keepers who accompany the elephants can move easily around them to comfort and feed them during the journey.

Mysteriously, at the other end the ex-orphans who are now living wild anticipate ahead of time the arrival of new nursery elephants. How they know this defies human interpretation, but it happens far too often to be chance. Mobile phone signals are poor in Tsavo's remote north, and there have been occasions when even the Ithumba keepers have been unaware that the new elephants are on their way, yet the independent ex-orphans are the 'giveaway', turning up unexpectedly to wait at the stockade compound for the new arrivals. We can only assume that telepathy is at work, and, even more astoundingly, that such telepathy can only be between the ex-orphans and the Nairobi keepers, since there have been instances when new transferees are not known by those now living wild.

The reunions that take place are always joyful, involving trumpeting, the intertwining of trunks, urinating and rumbling, with the newcomers always welcomed with a great outpouring of love. During the rehabilitation stage the orphans walk in the bush with their keepers to browse on natural vegetation and enjoy a noon mud bath; they continue browsing through the afternoon and return to the safety of their spacious night stockades in the evening, where cut browse awaits them. Now the keepers no longer actually sleep in with the orphans, but are within earshot should the need arise to investigate any disturbance and calm fearful youngsters. The elephants are housed together in the stockades at the rehabilitation facilities, and instead of being fed three-hourly, receive just three milk feeds each day – morning, noon and evening – with cut vegetation that they can eat during the night.

To begin with the orphans follow their human keepers when taken out to browse in the bush, but during the rehabilitation stage a change takes place. The orphans now begin to decide themselves where they want to browse each day and make their own plans, through low frequency infrasound, to meet up with the ex-orphans, whom they regard as part of their extended elephant family. It is now that they begin to socialize with their wild kin, introduced by those that have already accomplished the transition. While fraternizing with wild elephants, the keepers simply sit under a tree at a safe distance until such time as the orphans are ready to move on and come and seek them out again.

The call of the wild is strong. Each orphan answers that call in its own time, dependent upon how well the elephant can remember being part of a wild family. Those orphaned in very early infancy will be too young to recall their previous wild life and tend therefore to remain with the human family longer, but in the fullness of time, every elephant that passes through our nursery ends up leading a perfectly normal wild elephant life among the wild elephant community of the Tsavo National Park. More importantly, at 8,000 square miles, Tsavo is sufficiently large to afford elephants the space they need for a good quality of life in wild terms, for they cover enormous distances – sometimes hundreds and even thousands of miles – in their long-range wanderings to meet up with family and friends and seek out fresh pastures. It is also remarkable that when walking with their keepers out in the bush, our orphans will protect their human family when confronted by a threat. Tsavo's wilderness remains a hostile environment for an unarmed human on foot, inhabited as it is by fearsome lions with man-eating tendencies, by grumpy old buffalo bulls holed up in thickets, and by aggressive elephants that have no reason to trust or love humans, having been harassed and poached for decades. Yet the keepers know they can rely on the orphans to detect a threat and protect them, crowding around while the more senior orphans chase off any suspected danger. Although elephants are essentially peaceful animals, living in harmony with all other members of the animal kingdom, they are the strongest mammal on earth, and if turned aggressive due to cruelty and harassment, they can be a formidable foe, especially since they, like us humans, can reason, plan and think.

Older orphans instruct newcomers with gentle patience, teaching them not to touch electric fencing, escorting newcomers out to browse, joining them at their noon mud bath, introducing them to known friendly wild elephant herds they happen to meet in their daily wanderings. It is usual for senior ex-orphan females to select a smaller baby as their 'chosen' one. This is a much sought-after privilege, when leader elephants will allow smaller calves to head a column on the way out of the stockades in the morning or to and from the noon mud bath and back again in the evening. Although elephants are born with a genetic memory programmed with elements important to survival, this memory has to be honed by gradual exposure to a wild situation. Our elephants are never just tipped out into a wild situation but are rather just introduced gradually, through access and exposure that can span ten years to enable such natural instincts to become honed. As all the orphans who have grown up together regard themselves as family, those that have accomplished the transition to 'wild' status like to keep in touch with others that remain keeper-dependent, returning from time to time to keep contact with whoever is still in the stockades, understanding that others like themselves can benefit from elephant reassurance and guidance.

Frequently stockade-based juniors are selected by a senior to accompany them for a trial 'night out' in the wild, but should the novice feel insecure without the protection of their human family, that is understood as well. He or she is escorted back to the stockades and handed over to the keepers again. The fact that elephants never forget has been proved to us time and time again, once by Eleanor in her forties, when she returned to the stockades after many years of wild living and a man who was a stranger to the incumbent keepers happened to be approaching from a distance. Up went Eleanor's trunk, her ears stood out, and much to everyone's alarm, she ran at speed towards the stranger, enveloping him with her trunk and treating him to a highly charged elephant greeting. It turned out that he had been her keeper when she was five years old, and even though thirty-seven years had passed since she had seen him last, her recognition was instant.

Time has also taught us that the ex-orphans now living wild know where to come for help should they ever need it. A number have come back to the stockades over the years with wire snares around a leg, or with arrow and spear wounds inflicted by hostile people, and even to give birth within reach of the human family. Emily and Edie, who were nursery-reared from early infancy, and are now the mothers of wild-born babies, managed to get their babies back when their milk failed during the 2009 drought. In Emily's case, her calf was so weak that it could barely walk more than a few paces at a time when the keepers happened upon them during the course of one of their routine surveillance patrols. They sent for keeper Mischak, who helped Emily get her calf back to the Voi stockades where we fed her nutritious dairy cubes and other supplements to get her milk flowing again. Edie's calf was younger but stronger, and she managed to get it back unaided; once the milk flowed again as normal, both calves were saved. Similarly, an orphan named Solango, accompanied by his ex-orphan friend Burra, returned with a seriously damaged back leg, unable to even put it to the ground. Laboriously he managed to get back to the Voi stockades, and for the next four months we treated him with homeopathic healing aids, during which time his friends came to visit him regularly, just as we do an ailing relative in hospital. Elephants are, indeed, just like us, and in many ways, better. It is indeed comforting for those of us who love them to know this in the ele-unfriendly world of today, but knowing elephants so intimately, I also know without any shadow of doubt that not one of them would exchange their wild existence, despite all its hazards, for a safer life incarcerated in captivity.

Here in Nairobi, the nursery is a hub of activity from dawn to dusk. I am up at first light every morning to inspect each elephant's nightly feeding record, and from those notes I get early warning of whether or not all is well. Over the years I have learned that any loss of appetite, change in stools or sleep pattern is an early warning of trouble, and that with elephant babies things can go very wrong very rapidly and unexpectedly. I deal with any problems that have arisen overnight, talk to the keepers, seek the help of a vet should I feel it necessary, and make sure we are prepared for the day's programme. Just before eleven, I hear the wheelbarrows approaching as the keepers bring loads of large bottles of milk through my front yard and carefully place them at separated intervals on the ground. At the same time other keepers erect a cordon around poles in order to segregate the orphans' mud bath from the line of tourists, locals and schoolchildren, who have already started queuing in order to share the one hour when we are open every day and watch the elephants take their noon milk feed and, weather permitting, a cooling mud bath. As soon as the keepers bring the milk, a palpable sense of excitement sets the crowd talking, the children chattering happily as they wait expectantly for the elephants to appear from the nearby forest. Their patience is rewarded as the nursery elephants come running from forest cover closely followed by their keepers, who always have a hard time keeping up with them.

Each elephant homes in on its particular spot, knowing exactly which bottle is his or hers. Some hold the bottle themselves, curling their trunk around it and tipping it up until it is drained, downing the contents greedily before waiting for the keeper to hand them another. The visitors are spellbound, because elephants have their own magic attraction for most humans – perhaps because they are so like us. The click and whirr of cameras and videos hangs in the air until another burst of delight erupts as the smallest of the orphans, unable to run as fast as their older peers, are gently steered towards hung blankets so that they can rest the tip of their trunk against something that feels a little like a mother's body. Standing behind the blanket, a keeper lifts the lower end up to insert the large rubber teat into the little elephant's mouth once its trunk has found a suitable spot on the blanket. These very young newborns require endless patience in order to get them to take the quantity of milk essential to ensure survival – at least twenty-four pints in twenty-four hours. Anything less means that the elephant will rapidly lose condition and become skeletal within days.

Once the milk has been consumed, the orphans themselves decide whether or not the day is warm enough to merit a cooling mud bath. If it is, they get down to play in the mud, rolling around, climbing on each other, tossing their trunks in the air, and then running around to play football with the keepers. Baby elephants clearly enjoy an audience, never failing to respond to the buzz in the crowd, kicking the ball with front and back feet and running after it with outspread ears. Often the warthog descendants of the Ever Hopefuls turn up, also hoping for a mud bath, and their appearance always triggers amusing entertainment for the visitors as the little elephants begin to chase them, but only as long as they oblige by running away. Should a mother pig stand her ground, confusion reigns and the elephants back off, terrified. The orphans are scared even of something as small as a dikdik or a dung beetle – indeed one of our orphans trembled all day after a chameleon fell on her back from a tree on which she was browsing.

If the weather is cool, each of the nursery elephants will need a blanket over its back for warmth, tied beneath the belly by soft, pliable, discarded panty-hose stockings, but as soon as the weather warms up, these blankets are removed. Elephants have no sweat glands, so cannot perspire to adjust body temperature. When it is hot, they seek the shelter of shade, fan their ears, or cool themselves down by means of water. In extreme circumstances, as David discovered all those years ago much to the scientists' disbelief, with their trunk they can draw on reserves of stomach water to spray behind their ears and over their body. Newborns are also vulnerable to sunburn – in the wild they would shelter from the sun underneath the body of their mother, or conversely be protected from the wind and the rain by being always surrounded by a close-knit family. Visitors are amused to see the keepers rubbing sunblock over delicate and vulnerable baby ears, laughing as they put up umbrellas to shade the newborns from direct sunlight, but both are very necessary to counteract the harmful effects of sunburn.

But it isn't just the elephants: over the years we have also been able to share our expertise with others rearing rhino orphans on Kenya's private ranches, and in this way we have been responsible for saving many rhino calves that would otherwise have been lost. Our visitors are fascinated by the rhinos at the orphanage, especially Maxwell, a fully grown rhino who, although blind from birth, gallops around his stockade at great speed expertly avoiding every obstacle. He lives for the remote contact he enjoys with Solio, an orphan from the ranch that has sheltered Pushmi and Stroppie all these years, and where Reudi grew up to be the breeding bull who sired many of Kenya's current living rhinos.

I smile when I think back to the safari on which David and I discussed the prospect of retirement. It wasn't really an option then, and it certainly isn't an option now, even though I am well past the normal retirement age. I will simply have to drop on the job, and I wouldn't want it any other way without David by my side. I have lived each day since his death with David in my heart, and when I look at the orphanage and all the work we have managed to do in his name, I know that he would be happy.

David taught me to respect, love and understand animals, and for me, the words of Henry Beston, an American First World War veteran who sought solace in nature and wrote about his experiences in *The Outermost House*, best capture David's essential beliefs: 'We need another wiser and perhaps more mystical concept of animals. In a world older and more complete than ours, they move finished and complete, gifted with extensions of the senses we have lost or never attained, living by voices we shall never hear. They are not brethren, they are not underlings, they are other Nations, caught with ourselves in the net of life and time, fellow prisoners of the splendour and travail of earth.'

And while I still have much to learn, this much I know: animals are indeed more ancient, more complex and in many ways more sophisticated than us. They are more perfect because they remain within Nature's fearful symmetry just as Nature intended. They should be respected and revered, but perhaps none more so than the elephant, the world's most emotionally human land mammal.

Epilogue: David

'With the death of an Elder, an entire Encyclopedia goes with him.'

– Anon

The love songs of the fifties and sixties, for me, are exceedingly emotive. I close my eyes and am transported back thirty-five years, enveloped in David's arms during a Saturday night dance at the Voi Hotel, and my memory allows me to feel and live the enchantment all over again.

Seldom a night passes that David does not appear in my dreams, and the sense of loss on waking still leaves a void in my heart. When David died on 13 June 1977, aged fifty-seven, I can honestly say that I was more deeply in love with him than ever. We were married for seventeen enchanting years, and for all that time I experienced a pervading sense of loving warmth and security coupled with deep admiration and respect. David was always there for me, always right; there to make decisive difficult decisions, to take control, to sort out problems, to create, inspire or fix anything. He was an exciting man to live with; knowledgeable, passionate, considerate, compassionate and kind. He loved and protected me in the truest sense.

Life with David was a continuous adventure of seeing and understanding. When we worked together it was as though a magic wand made everything intriguing and interesting. The brilliance of his enquiring mind and the imprint of his deep respect and love of Nature continue to inspire me and the work of the Trust established in his memory every single day. He would be especially proud of our success in raising the orphaned elephants and other wild animals so that they can return to the natural wild life that is their birthright.

I have turned many pages since David's death, but he is never far from my thoughts. I loved him with all my heart and soul, and I miss him sometimes so much that it hurts. And yet, if David had lived to grow old with me, he would be in his nineties now, something I cannot envisage, for he remains forever timeless in my heart and mind, magnetic, strong and handsome. I know that he would be immeasurably proud of Angela and all his grandchildren, of their love of Nature and wildlife. He remains a role model for Angela's two boys, who mirror him in many ways. He would be proud of the work of the Trust that seeks to perpetuate his ethics and his contribution to the natural world, for which he cared so passionately. I would like to think that this book is a fitting tribute to him, but also to other early Park Wardens like him who battled against all the odds to ensure that the current generation of Kenyans retain their irreplaceable indigenous wildlife to enjoy for themselves and share with the rest of the world. It is a priceless resource that enriches them and their country immeasurably.

Acknowledgements

I owe my love of animals to my wonderful parents, who right from the word go instilled in me empathy for all life. My late husband, David, reinforced that and further enriched my understanding of animals. As a naturalist he was a veritable encyclopedia of knowledge, way ahead of his time, recognizing the inter-relatedness of every form of life as vital to the health of the whole. His humility, professionalism, unwavering courage and impeccable integrity have been the guiding lights in my own conservation career. My gratitude to him for everything that he was, for the magical years that we shared, and for what the Trust, established in his memory, has been able to achieve is infinite.

I am deeply indebted to my family as a whole, but especially to my two sisters, Sheila and Betty, who have always been there for me during the dark days of life, and to David Read for injecting fun and laughter back into my life. My daughters have been a source of pride and strength, by my side throughout, and have given me the gift and endless joy of grandchildren. Jill has been my companion, shouldering the early hard graft with me when the David Sheldrick Wildlife Trust was in its infancy. Together we pounded the streets and did the rounds with cap in hand to raise funding for the wildlife cause. She shared her bedroom with the first orphaned elephant before we even had a stable, and more recently has been my travelling companion, sympathetic to my phobia of being lost. Her father, and my first husband, Bill Woodley, was my friend throughout, a truly enlightened man.

Angela, my talented, beautiful and artistic daughter by David, is so like him, excelling at all she undertakes. She was only thirteen years old when David died and I will always be deeply indebted to Marti and Illie Anderson, Galana Ranch neighbours during our Tsavo time, who sponsored her Cape Town University course and enabled her to travel home for the holidays so that we could be together. In adulthood Angela has taken the David Sheldrick Wildlife Trust to new heights in a way that I could never have achieved. Her sharp business acumen, perception and wisdom have steered the Trust proficiently, true to David's conservation principles. I am similarly deeply indebted to the husbands of my two girls, whose help I have always been able to count upon, and who have unselfishly shared my daughters with me. It was Jean-François Chavrier, Jill's French husband, who gave the David Sheldrick Wildlife Trust its first vehicle, his own little Renault 4 shipped to us from France, and who with Jill helped establish the Trust's first anti-poaching de-snaring patrols to rid Tsavo's boundaries of the infamous wire snares that have caused so much animal suffering to this day. Angela's husband, Robert Carr-Hartley, has been the steadfast and stable 'rock' on whom we can always rely to calm troubled waters, and is unstintingly there for us whenever needed. Robert's passion for wilderness and all that it encompasses, his perceptive vision, his quiet determination and endurance to achieve his conservation dreams, are a rare gift that has richly rewarded the Trust and benefited the greater conservation cause as well.

My thanks are due to Simon Trevor, who, in the Trust's infancy, allowed us access to the documentary films he made alongside David while working in Tsavo. I thank him also for introducing us to what is now the Trust land abutting Tsavo's Athi River boundary that serves as the base for all the Trust's field operations.

The David Sheldrick Wildlife Trust owes its inception to the vision of the late John Sutton, and my brother Peter (now also deceased), who obtained permission for me to reside in the Nairobi National Park. I am deeply indebted to the compassion and kindness of the Kenyan authorities for granting me this privilege and to those Wildlife Directors with whom I have been able to work closely since David's passing. But it was the late Bob Poole, Head of the Kenya Office of the US-based African Wildlife Foundation, who nurtured the fledgling David Sheldrick Wildlife Trust and gave it wings to fly independently in the fullness of time. I am likewise deeply grateful to the Trustees and Advisory Committee of the Trust, who have guided its conservation contribution, faithful always to the mission statement, of which David would have approved.

Never a day passes that I do not silently give a prayer of thanks to the skills of the South African surgeons who saved my leg after I had been felled by a wild elephant I mistook for Eleanor, leaving me on crutches for fifteen long months. Dr Ponky Firer expertly repaired seriously shattered bones, restoring to me a working limb that has given me little trouble since, and Dr Jeff Sochen saved it through bone irrigation, ridding it of the bacteria that had invaded the compound fracture. My younger sister, Betty, selflessly and diligently nursed me throughout this ordeal, and I will always be most deeply grateful for her patience and companionship and to my niece, Sally, for taking me in. I am deeply indebted to all who contributed financially towards the repair of my leg; to Jin Tatsumura, with whom I did the elephant slot for the prestigious *Gaia Symphony* and who treated me to specialized alternative medicine in Japan. That I now have a fully functional right leg is due in no small measure to him and the amazing hospitality afforded us in Japan.

This book would probably never have made the shelves had it not been for my agent, Patrick Walsh of Conville & Walsh, who travelled to Kenya and forced me to sit down and write the outline needed to attract publishers. I am also deeply indebted to Gillian Stern, my editor, who so willingly and proficiently undertook the daunting task of compressing over 1,000 pages of original material into the current manageable memoir. Thank you, Gillian, for doing an unenviable and remarkable job. I also thank Eleo Gordon, my Viking publisher, for her guidance and understanding throughout this process.

I sincerely thank the many people around the world who have generously and consistently supported the Trust's efforts, and thank our US Friends' Board and local Trustees who have given of their time free to empower the Trust further. I personally owe a huge debt of gratitude to the US Friends' Founding President, Stephen Smith, for help over personal legal issues relating to filming contracts. Thank you so much, Stephen.

And last, but by no means least, my life has been enriched every day, beyond measure, by the many animal orphans that have passed through our hands over the years – even though rearing wild orphans is invariably a cocktail of joy tempered with a good dose of tears. It has been the elephants themselves, who by example have demonstrated how to cope with adversity – to mourn and grieve, as one must, but then to turn the page and focus on giving to the living. They, who have suffered so much at the hands of humans, never lose the ability to forgive, even though, being elephants, they will never be able to forget.

Index